# Guidebook for Explore Theatre:
# A Backstage Pass

Michael Mullen O'Hara
and
Judith A. Sebesta

**Allyn & Bacon**

Boston  Columbus  Indianapolis  New York  San Francisco  Upper Saddle River  Amsterdam
Cape Town  Dubai  London  Madrid  Milan  Munich  Paris  Montréal  Toronto  Delhi
Mexico City  São Paulo  Sydney  Hong Kong  Seoul  Singapore  Taipei  Tokyo

3 4 5 6 7 8 9 10—V036—14 13

**Allyn & Bacon**
is an imprint of

www.pearsonhighered.com

ISBN-10:     0-205-11582-9
ISBN-13: 978-0-205-11582-2

# BRIEF CONTENTS

# CONTENTS

# PREFACE AND ACKNOWLEDGMENTS

The ephemerality of the electronic mirrors, in some ways, the ephemerality of theatre. As printed text goes digital, we lose some things even as we gain new possibilities. The authors have tried to create a digital textbook in which more is gained than lost. We hope it is a space where we can successfully introduce digital natives and digital "tourists" alike to the ancient art of theatre. Among the many benefits this digital text affords are access to the Internet, a lower cost to students, and the opportunity to see and hear the artists of theatre speak for themselves.

This textbook is unique in many ways. First and foremost, this text was not developed first as a printed text and then ported over into a digital layout. The authors have tried to incorporate the strengths and opportunities provided by a digital format into all areas. Another innovation is that we attempt to show the nourishment of many forms of contemporary storytelling by the deep roots of live theatre, and to demonstrate that the people who create such stories are but branches on a larger family tree. By this, we hope to help students become more thoughtful and informed viewers of any form of dramatic storytelling. We also hope that digitally native students might come to know the special powers of live performance and will use that new appreciation to demand better of the mediated forms they view, particularly those readily available on the Internet.

While any textbook is a Sisyphean task, a digital textbook required the contributions, support, and generous gifts of countless people. Nearly everyone who meaningfully contributed to this work is given credit within; however, there are several individuals and institutions that deserve special thanks. The Institute for Digital Entertainment and Education of Ball State University, under the direction of Dr. Rodger Smith, initially saw the possibilities of a digital text for theatre and offered the first, and most important, support we received. Without Dr. Smith's friendship, leadership, and support, this "book" would not have been possible. The faculty and students of Ball State University were essential to this work, and the authors cannot thank them enough for the time, resources, and passion they shared. The Universities of Arizona and Missouri also contributed in immeasurable ways, and to each of these institutions the authors are enormously grateful. Finally, Algonquin Productions, Brooklyn Writers Space, Electronic Theatre Controls, Mid-America Sound, ZFX Flying Effects, Klispch Audio, and Apollo Design Technology each offered us unprecedented access, and we are very grateful for their generous help and expertise.

Among the many individuals who were essential to the work required for this digital text, a few deserve special thanks here. Our thanks to Chris White, the author of *Two Character Play*, for sharing her joy and passion for live theatre and for generously allowing Maggie Kubley to adapt her script into a screenplay. Thanks to JD Ostergard, who filmed, edited, and re-edited much of the material for *Two Character Play*, as well as many other sequences throughout the book. The authors owe an immeasurable debt of gratitude to Annette Reynolds, who filmed, edited, and re-edited all the material for *Finale*, the filmed sequence within *Two Character Play*, and *The Pedlar*. Our thanks as well to Travis Hatfield, who not only filmed and edited many sequences within the book but also coached and assisted both students and authors alike.

There are personal thanks that must be offered as well. Michael O'Hara would like to thank his wife, Dr. Laura O'Hara, who has supported both the process and the person, and without whom this work—and its author—would be poorer. Thanks to my very large family, but especially my parents, Pete and Pat O'Hara, who took me to my first live theatre when I was but five years old. Thanks too to Patti Gillespie, who remains the most influential teacher I have known. Thank you to the many students who have helped with research, office work, and the occasional editing, but chief among them are Danielle Ireland, Teresa Sabatine, and Samantha Cains. Finally, I would like to thank my co-author. Her partnership on this long, strange journey—seven years in the making—continues to be one of the best things gained in going digital.

Judith Sebesta would like to thank her family, including her parents, Fred and Jean Sebesta; her brother Stephen Sebesta and his wife, Amy; and her sister Julie Gurecky and her family, for all of their support during this process. I also owe a great debt to my mentor, the late Oscar G. Brockett, and words cannot express the depth of my appreciation to my co-author; my collaboration with him has not only made me a better author but a better person as well.

# INTRODUCTION

For thousands of years, theatre artists have transformed words on a page into wonders on a stage, entertaining and enlightening audiences across the generations. As the ancient art of storytelling moves into the digital age, actors, writers, directors, designers, and other theatrical artists have incorporated many digital tools into their live and recorded performances. *Explore Theatre: A Backstage Pass* not only seeks to have theatre artists tell their own stories with their own voices, but also hopes to engender a richer understanding of the people and processes that comprise contemporary theatrical practice. This digital textbook invites readers to both read and hear from artists, scholars, and critics while they learn about both the rich history of theatre and its continuing relevance today. We start with our own voices in the video on the home page of www.exploretheatre.com.

# What Is Performance?

## Chapter Outline

*To view the figures in this chapter, log on to www.pearsonexploretheatre.com.*

## INTRODUCTION

We are surrounded by performance. We watch film, television, theatre, and sports, to name but a few examples. Many scholars agree that today's audiences watch more performance more often than any other audience in history. By the time the average 18-year-old has reached college, he or she has watched tens of thousands of hours of television, hundreds of films, and countless sporting events, both live and on television. In fact, according to the 126th edition of the *Statistical Abstract of the United States* (2006), adults in America watch an average of 1,661 hours of television a year, or nearly 4.5 hours every day. While most 18-year-olds have seen at least one live theatrical performance, most do not attend live theatre regularly. Only 15 percent of all 18- to 24-year-olds are likely to have attended a musical play in any year, and only 11 percent are likely to have attended a nonmusical play. On the other hand, 83 percent of young adults have been to a film in the past year, and 46 percent attended a live sporting event.

**FIGURE 1.1**

So, while contemporary audiences have significant experience in viewing many types of performances, they tend to have little experience with live theatre in particular, and they have little knowledge of the history and practice of performance in general. This first chapter, then, is designed to aid the reader in identifying and analyzing performances, placing them in both historical and contemporary contexts. The ability to do so is crucial in a modern, democratic society in which freedom of expression and freedom of attendance demand that the viewing audience share responsibility for what they and their children watch.

After reading Chapter 1, you should be able to:

⬚ Recognize the basic characteristics that all performances share and use these characteristics to differentiate various types of performances.

⬚ Discuss the theatrical paradigm and describe how it is used to understand both theatrical and nontheatrical activities.

⬚ Determine how a performance functions as a ritual, a work of art, and/or a cultural artifact.

⬚ Discuss the differences and similarities between live and mediated performances and suggest how these factors influence both artists and audiences.

## CHARACTERISTICS ALL PERFORMANCES SHARE

What are the characteristics shared by multiple modes, or types, of performance? An ancient Greek play, a classic Hollywood movie, a contemporary television sitcom, a football game, and a role-playing video game all share some basic characteristics. The five basic characteristics are:

- Actor (a person who does something)
- Action (a thing done)
- Audience (witnesses to the thing done)
- Arena (place where the thing is done)
- Arrangement (how the thing itself is spatially and temporally arranged)

Although in later chapters we will go into more detail for each term, some further clarification here is necessary. **Actors** are people who perform actions such as enact a script, perform a ritual, run with a ball, or aim a virtual bow and arrow. **Actions** are the things actors do, such as tell a story, make a touchdown, or look for treasure. **Audiences** are the people who watch those things being done, and sometimes audiences participate as actors in those performances. **Arenas** are the places in which those people gather to perform or watch or both. **Arrangement** refers to the ways in which the action itself is organized in real and symbolic space and time, such as how places, times, beginnings, middles, and ends are made clear to actors and audiences.

**FIGURES 1.2, 1.3, AND 1.4**

We can use these five characteristics to describe and classify a wide range of human activities. We could compare a football game to a theatrical performance, for example. Actors (the football players or the theatre actors) follow a script (a game plan/playbook or a dramatic play script) to perform an action (the game or the story) in front of an audience (football fans or a theatre audience) in an arena created for that purpose (stadium or a theatre) in a specific arrangement of those elements (the rules, time outs, first downs, quarters, etc.; or a curtain rise, intermission, and final bows). We could perform similar exercises for a street fight, people flirting at a dance club, television shows, movies, and many other human activities.

**FIGURE 1.5**

## PARADIGM OF PERFORMANCE

Indeed, the idea of theatrical performance as a **paradigm** for studying human activity has recently developed into its own field of study: **performance studies**. Paradigms are models made up of theories that help explain or predict phenomena. Scholarly paradigms are generated by theories and can also be understood as "world views" that help scholars predict and understand how performance, or other phenomena, work.

For example, early attempts to explain and predict electricity started with a paradigm of electricity as attractive forces, such as rubbing a balloon on your scalp to produce static electricity. That view was eventually replaced by a paradigm of fluid, as seen in Benjamin Franklin's experiment with the kite and key, and controlling electricity via conduits and valves. The paradigm of fluids was so powerful and productive that many electrical terms are also terms related to water, such as *capacitor, saturation,* and *flow*. Today, the scientific community has more complex paradigms for explaining electricity, far different from the early paradigms of attraction or fluid. Each early paradigm was useful in explaining and exploring some aspects of the phenomenon of electricity, and each paradigm changed as the phenomenon was better understood.

**FIGURE 1.6**

Performance studies use theatrical paradigms to explain the significance of performances that range from the personal performance of your own identity before your friends or family to the large and public performances of national identity in culture or politics. We cannot hope to cover the breadth and depth of contemporary performance studies, so we must limit what we mean by *performance*. Narrowing our definition does not, however, also narrow our potential to understand and analyze the performances we will exclude—quite the opposite. Because the same characteristics of actors, actions, audiences, arena, and arrangement are present in all types of performances, the intellectual tools and skills you develop here will be useful in a variety of inquiries.

## PURPOSE OF PERFORMANCE

We can begin to narrow our definition by focusing on traits that distinguish one type of performance from another. Important ways in which performances differ include a performance's

- Objectives (what both the actors and audiences expect, the reasons performances occur)
- Organization (how actors, audiences, actions, arenas, and internal arrangements of those elements are organized in relationship to one another)
- Consciousness (the degree to which actors and audiences are conscious of each other and their objectives

To return to our football game example, the objectives of football players differ from those of theatrical actors. The players seek to win a game whose outcome is unknown. The actors, on the other hand, know the outcome of the performance, the ending, even if they are acting the role of a football player in a game, such as Burt Reynolds in *The Longest Yard* or Adam Sandler in the remake.

**FIGURE 1.7**

The *organization* of the elements of performance in each example is different. Audiences at football games help determine the outcome by how loudly they cheer, but audiences at theatrical events do not help determine the outcome of the plot, which was predetermined by the playwright. Theatrical audiences do, however, help determine the quality of the experience for both themselves and the actors by how well they respond to the play.

Finally, football fans usually are highly conscious of their possible effects on the players' morale and strive to make their presence known, especially when the opposing team has the ball. Cheerleaders sometimes lead football fans, directing them to cheer or boo when advantageous to their own team. Theatrical audiences are less conscious of their effects on the actors' morale and sometimes do not know how or when to respond to shows, although live television shows do have something similar to cheerleaders—signs that light up to direct the studio audience to laugh, applaud, or even cheer at specific cues. Movies and live theatre do not have cheerleaders to help audiences know when or how to react. Although football games, movies, television, and live theatre share many characteristics, their objectives, organization, and consciousness are different, sometimes greatly different and other times less so.

## HOW PERFORMANCES DIFFER

Our first narrowing of focus will exclude those performances that do not share theatrical objectives, organization, and consciousness. **Film, television, new media**, and **live theatre** share the common qualities of actors, scripts, and audiences. Each is organized slightly differently, but their similarities far outweigh any differences, especially when we compare these theatrical performances to non-theatrical ones. For example, a film, a television sit-com, a Flash animated short film on the Internet, and a live play share more in common with one another than any one of them shares with a football game.

For our purposes, theatrical performances are ones that enact stories about human beings before other human beings. Theatrical performances organize actors, authors—or their scripts—and audiences into specific relationships, all of whom share a consciousness about their activities: They are knowingly engaged in creating or watching a theatrical performance.

Our primary focus is on live theatre because it is the precursor to both film and television and because it is likely the least familiar performance mode for contemporary audiences. We believe that a systematic understanding of the people and processes that create the ancient art of live theatre will help you become a more informed and more intelligent audience for, or participant in, film, television, new media, and live theatre.

The objectives of film and television are to make money, for the most part, and to exploit the camera's gaze as an integral part of storytelling. Most live theatre, excluding Broadway, is not-for-profit, and therefore rarely counts "to make money" among its primary objectives, though it must raise enough funds to pay for itself. Moreover, live theatre cannot completely control the audience's view of the stage, as there is always residual light that illuminates other parts of the stage, other actors, or even the audience.

The various elements in film, television, and new media are organized around the camera, and the camera dictates how the other elements—actors, actions, arenas—will be seen. The camera is difficult to fool—for example, with respect to age. Very expensive makeup and lots of special effects are required to make young actors appear old, or vice versa, and even then the effort is not always successful.

The stage can be more flexible than film or television because the imagination of the live audience is more important in the absence of a camera, which mediates viewing. Actors in live theatre can enact a wider range of characters and ages than they might in a film or television show. Audiences are organized differently for each as well. Film and live theatre gather their audiences to specific arenas at specific times, but television can be in any arena at any time. Multiple audiences at remote locations can watch the same film or television show at the same time—such as the Super Bowl or the latest blockbuster movie—but only the audience present in one theatre can watch a live theatre performance. Multiple audiences can also watch the same film or television show over time, but because live theatre is **ephemeral**, existing for only a moment in time before it is gone, no two audiences will ever see exactly the same show. In addition, the actors in film and some television are completely separated from their audience, who thus can have no immediate effects upon their performance because the audience is remote from the actual creation of the performance. Actors in live theatre are intimately conscious of their audiences, who collaborate with the actors to create each evening's or afternoon's performance.

Finally, if we limit our exploration to just live theatre, we can see that different types of live theatre are also distinguishable from one another by variations in their objectives, organization, and consciousness. A big, Broadway musical must satisfy objectives far different than a small, experimental theatre performance by a single artist. The musical must attempt to make money to pay back the investors, entertain thousands of audience members equally well, and sustain interest for many years among both native New Yorkers and tourists from around the world. The experimental performance might hope to appeal to a select audience, perhaps only women, and the artist might be seeking to empower her audience rather than simply to entertain them. The musical is organized around music, dance, and some dialogue and features show-stopping special effects and lavish production values. The experimental performance usually has none of those features, but instead offers its much smaller audiences a rare intimacy in performance. The Broadway actors and audiences usually are highly conscious of their status as Broadway theatre participants, whereas the experimental theatre participants are equally aware of their marginalized status—we even call such theatres "Off-Off-Broadway" to signify their relationship to mainstream, Broadway theatres.

## PERFORMANCE AS RITUAL

We can see that all performances share some basic characteristics, and that performances can be classified by how they differ from each other in their **objectives, organization**, and **consciousness**. No one of these different modes of performance is better than another, just as no two songs are alike and one is not inherently better than the other. So, too, although film is different from theatre, which is different from television, there is remarkable stability in that which is similar to all three. However, theatrical performance is both a contemporary human phenomenon and an important cultural repository of past human knowledge and experience. Theatrical performances, understood as stories enacted by humans for other humans, have appeared in every known culture in the world, from prehistory to the present.

**FIGURE 1.8**

Most theatrical performances in ancient cultures appear to have had a relationship to ritual, either by evolving or by borrowing from religious and social rituals. Some scholars and critics have spent their entire lives attempting to identify and describe these early theatrical performances, but there is little agreement on how or why these forms emerged. Nevertheless, a closer examination of ritual can reveal some of the forces at work in both ancient and contemporary theatrical performances. Indeed, a ritual itself can be understood as a kind of theatrical performance, usually having some sort of **text**, either oral or written, that dictates how the actors behave and what is to be expected from its participants and audiences. Rituals often incorporate theatrical elements such as masks, costumes, dance, and music, with the aid of which the actors impersonate or are possessed by legendary ancestors, gods, ghosts, or spirits.

Indeed, rituals share common characteristics with other performances. Rituals have actors, who enact either characters or a change in status for themselves or their community. The actions of rituals range from weddings to funerals to worship to brushing one's teeth. Audiences for rituals often participate directly in the performance, chanting, singing, or dancing. Rituals sometimes happen in special arenas set aside for those activities, such as churches or temples, and other times happen in arenas temporarily converted to that purpose, such as a parade down a street. Rituals arrange time symbolically, occur on special and, usually, regular occurrences, and involve a high level of consciousness shared among participants and audiences. Rituals usually perform some cultural work—to heal, to mourn, to marry, to honor—and usually mark some significant occasion—coming of age, peace treaty, death, birth—for that community. Finally, rituals usually serve to reinforce the community bonds among its participants.

We can see that rituals seem to share theatrical objectives and organization with theatrical performances. Rituals, like theatrical performances, hope to affect the participants, to move them to greater unity or an elevated status of consciousness as a community. Both rituals and theatre cannot ensure that the expected outcome will be achieved; for example, a rain dance does not guarantee rain, and slipping on a banana peel does not guarantee laughter. Rituals and theatre occur at special times, with actors, audiences, and actions.

Theatre is primarily distinguishable from ritual because theatre is also an art, in that theatre self-consciously attempts to be theatre. A bride is probably conscious of her costume that signifies her changed status and her position as the center of everyone's spectatorship, and she and the groom may have memorized their vows, but neither the blushing bride nor the nervous groom is consciously trying to be a work of art for the consumption of their audience. The audience to the wedding, although they may have bought a gift for the couple, did not buy a ticket to watch the wedding. The same ceremony in a play or a film, however, would be art, and the actors who played the bride and groom would not really be getting married.

## PERFORMANCE AS ART

There are many kinds of art, such as painting, music, literature, sculpture, dance, and theatre. Distinguishing one kind of art from another follows many of the same procedures that we use to distinguish one type of performance from another, and the differences that we discover will help us decide what we will agree to actually label as art. First, we must identify the several characteristics that all forms of art share.

**FIGURE 1.9**

- All art is a self-conscious creation of a person.
  The terms *artifice, artificial*, and *artifact* all share the same root, and all describe something that a human did. Art does not exist in nature; humans make it, even when it is made to closely resemble nature or natural objects. Artists make **art**. In this sense, we also exclude things created by accident, by nature, by people who do not intend to create art, or by animals. Without the conscious intent of the artist, we will not call it art, though we may call it decoration. A road sign may be beautiful in some way, but its creator probably did not intend to create a work of art.
- All art seeks to produce an **aesthetic response**.
  Critics, scholars, and even artists themselves are not united on what an aesthetic response actually is, but most would agree that the response is usually centered around an appreciation of the work that goes beyond merely understanding what it is or being entertained by it. Aesthetic responses are usually characterized by a positive response to the art's form and the quality of its execution.

**FIGURE 1.10**

- All art has both **social and aesthetic values**.
  Art is recognizable by the value that people place on it, and while some art serves a practical purpose, like a vase, most art exists for its own sake. Some art is valued for its rarity, such as a painting by a now-deceased artist, and other art is prized

purely for its aesthetic qualities, such as a piano sonata. Because society changes over time, the value that we place on art changes, too.

All art is not the same, of course, and we can also distinguish one art from another by how they vary in their objectives, organization, and consciousness. Artists have historically divided themselves into the **visual arts** and the **performing arts**. The visual arts include painting, drawing, sculpture, literature, and poetry—the latter two sometimes separated out as literary arts. The performing arts include dance, music, singing, and theatre.

**FIGURE 1.11**

- Art forms have different **objectives**.
  The visual arts, for example, generally expect a solitary audience, whereas the performing arts usually expect more than one person in attendance. The visual arts tend to want a spectator who appreciates the art's form, the material result of the artist's activities, whereas the performing arts expect audience members to appreciate the art's execution by the actors, dancers, or musicians as it is being created. Excellent performances often continue to be done long after the original composer or playwright has died, though some, like the works of Shakespeare and Mozart, are famous regardless of who performs them. Indeed, they are known by a single name, like modern pop stars.
- Art forms have different rules of organization.
  Some art forms unfold through time, such as novels and plays, while others exist in space, such as paintings or sculpture. The medium on which it is organized or arranged also characterizes each art. Paintings exist on canvas, paper, or wood; literature exists on pages, either virtual or paper; and theatre, opera, and dance exist on stages and in performers.

**FIGURE 1.12**

Theatrical performances have a very complex relationship with all of the other arts. Theatre begins with a text, which is sometimes studied and valued as literature. Costumes and scenery use techniques from sculpture and painting, and some costumes and sets have become works of art themselves, collected for their beauty or historical importance. Dances from plays and operas often come from both social dance and artistic dance, and vice versa. Music appears so often in theatre that we now separate "musical theatre" and "dance theatre" as subfields for study. Opera companies perform some musical plays, such as *Sweeney Todd, Porgy and Bess*, or *Die Fledermaus*, as often as do non-opera theatre companies. Popular music groups or musicians are the subject matter for, or creators of, Broadway musicals, like ABBA's *Mamma Mia!* or Frankie Valli and the Four Seasons' *Jersey Boys*.

Sometimes, the same story is told in multiple art forms. Shakespeare's *A Midsummer Night's Dream*, for example, is a play, a ballet, and several different films. It inspired famous Swedish filmmaker Ingmar Bergman to create *Smiles of a Summer Night*, which in turn inspired a Broadway musical by Stephen Sondheim, *A Little Night Music*. Each use of Shakespeare's play focused on different parts of the original story that each medium could successfully exploit. In other words, the artists selected specific ideas or forms that were best suited to how their particular art form is organized. The play and the films focused on the poetic language of Shakespeare, following the words that the actors spoke and their actions as they related to the text. Ballet focuses on movement, and would not be concerned much with the dialogue, but it would still attempt poetic sensibility through dancing. Opera exploits those moments best suited to song and sometimes includes features from ballet as well.

**FIGURE 1.13**

Each art form, by exploiting those organizational rules that each follows, focuses our attention on a different aspect of human existence. For example, when Timberlake Wertenbaker adapted Thomas Kenneally's historical novel *The Playmaker* for the stage, the mostly true story of that moment in history was unchanged: The first fleet of the British navy arrives in Australia with its cargo of convicts from England. The Royal Marines, who served as jailers, resented being ordered to this ignoble duty in such a remote part of the world and often took out their frustrations on the prisoners. One of the officers decided to put on a play for the enjoyment of the entire camp, using the convicts as his cast. No one had any experience in the theatre, and only a few of the convicts could read, but, against all odds, they performed the first European-style play on the Australian continent, teaching themselves and their observers about compassion, cooperation, and creativity.

The novel, a work of historical fiction, focused on the internal conflicts and moral agony of the officer who directed that play, Ralph Clark, who falls in love with one of the female convicts despite having a wife and children back home in England. The novel also focuses on the feelings of isolation that both the guards and the convicts felt in what was then an alien landscape. The play, however, focuses on the power of theatre to transform lives, to empower dehumanized convicts and restrain brutal guards, and to create civilization by practicing it on stage. Novels allow us in an excellent way to peer inside characters' heads and read what they are thinking. Plays allow us to watch characters behave, to see what they are doing and how they overcome their obstacles.

**FIGURES 1.14 AND 1.15**

In summary, theatrical performances—stories enacted by humans—share some characteristics with all types of performance and other characteristics with some types of art. In performances, theatre has *actors, actions, audiences, arenas*, and *arrangements* of the first four in time. As art, theatre is the self-conscious creation of people who seek to produce an aesthetic response. It has both social and aesthetic values assigned to it by both its participants and its audiences. Theatrical performances differ from other types of performances and other types of art in its objectives, organization, and consciousness. Theatrical performances enact stories before audiences, written by authors, using actors and other artists who all share a consciousness of the performance as theatrical. Theatrical art often incorporates many of the other arts into its performances, but regardless of the addition or incorporation of paintings, poetry, or sculpture into a performance, theatre remains a performing art.

## LIVE AND MEDIATED THEATRICAL PERFORMANCES

Now that we have distinguished theatrical performances from other performances and other arts, we can focus on the primary characteristics of theatrical performances.

*Film, television, and live theatre use actors, performers who impersonate people other than themselves*. Those actors are usually under the guidance of a director who coaches them on their performance and determines the overall look and feel of the production. Actors differ from other performers, such as athletes, people flirting at a dance, or politicians speaking at a political rally, because the other performers attempt to be themselves.

*Film, television, and live theatre require audiences to complete the art form*. If a tree falls in the forest, does it make a noise? Perhaps, but theatrical performances exist for the purpose of attracting audiences to watch them, and only live theatre requires the physical presence of both live actors and live audiences. Film and television require neither live actors—you could see a movie for the first time starring an actor who has been dead for years—nor live audiences—you can watch the film or television show years after it was made. In fact, the overwhelming majority of film and television audiences do not watch the performances until much time has passed, months or weeks for many television shows, and years for most films. Because live theatre requires both actors and audiences to be present now, it is both ephemeral and immediate. Live television performances are usually not theatrical; that is, they do not use actors who follow a script, but are more often sporting events or newscasts, which create a similar sense of immediacy with audiences, but are not ephemeral. They can be watched from tape or a digital recorder at a later time, sometimes skipping commercials. Thus, the urgency of television is not the same urgency of live theatre. Films might have a limited run of only a few weeks or a few nights, but you can always see the same show no matter what night you see it, and you can wait until the film is released on DVD and still watch the same movie, with a few added extra features as a bonus.

**FIGURE 1.16**

*Film, television, and live theatre depend on actions written by authors, called screenwriters or playwrights, to organize and bind the theatrical performance.* Teams of authors often write film, television, and many musical theatre scripts, whereas a single author usually constructs scripts for live theatre. The actions (or story) written down by authors for theatrical events are about the things that the characters do in a fictitious world created for those actions. The world and characters created are not real, but they are, nevertheless, representative of the real world. Sometimes, those creations are so powerful, so lifelike, that we feel as if we know those characters better than we know our families or friends. We sometimes even talk about characters and their worlds as though they were real, but they are the collective creation of actors, authors, and other theatre artists. Because a camera mediates film and television, it directs our vision and controls who we see at every moment; the primary focus is on the visual elements of the characters, their stories, and their worlds. Because live theatre is unmediated by a camera, the primary focus is on both the visual and bodily presence of the actors, and the details of their worlds are less important. In all theatrical performances, however, the script is the starting place for all the other artists involved.

 *Film, television, and live theatre's fictitious worlds are more condensed and powerful than the real world.* Theatrical performances are both less than and more than the real world from which they select their stories and characters. Theatrical performances do not show every moment in a character's daily life, but only the parts that are essential to the main action, or story, being enacted. Thus, theatrical performances are less than real life because they select only certain parts of it. On the other hand, romantic mood music, or the just-right lighting for our hair, or the just-in-time-arrival of the cavalry rarely appear in our normal, everyday lives. Thus, theatrical performances are more than real life because they augment the depiction of those lives. The fictitious worlds are more powerful because the artists have selected everything you see—every costume, every setting, every prop. Each thing is more meaningful than those same things in the real world. A kitchen knife on the countertop in real life usually means nothing more than the fact that someone forgot to put it in the dishwasher, but in a theatrical performance it usually signifies something more and creates suspense. Because film and television depict their fictitious worlds through a camera in the real world, such as filming real settings, real props, and real car chases, those elements such as settings, props, and special visual effects are more like those things in the real world. These effects are sometimes, but not always, symbolic. Live theatre must take great pains to put things on stage, and so nearly everything on stage is symbolic, suggesting something important to the audience and helping to create mood or understanding of a character. Great theatrical performances are not ones that merely imitate life, but rather are ones that present selected versions of life that create heightened awareness in their audiences.

**FIGURE 1.17**

*Film, television, and live theatre use real spaces and things, but those spaces and things are artificially arranged.* Theatrical performances must be mounted in a real space, and the construction of that performance must employ some real things, such as props, materials, and clothing. Those real spaces and materials are, nevertheless, artificial, selected and arranged by humans and not simply "natural" backdrops or things in actors' hands. Film and television often use real places (New York City, for example) to depict both real (New York City) and fictitious (Gotham City) places. Whether the places or things are real or fictitious, film and television show creators select the images, only certain real spaces are seen, and sometimes a place other than "real" place is used to construct the setting. For instance, a different location might be used for a backyard scene because the house used for the other shots doesn't have a big enough yard. Live theatre, on the other hand, can only suggest real places, though it may use real doors, real walls, and even real trees. Many real places and things that are easily shown on film or television, such as a car chase, are impossible to literally put on a stage, though such efforts have been part of theatre's past. Film and television can control the experience of both a love scene and a car chase by varying the camera angle and shot. A close-up of the couple's eyes with a tear glistening in the corner of his eye or a helicopter shot of the heroine being chased by hundreds of cars that are crashing into each other behind her can enhance our experience of that moment. Live theatre has no medium shot or close-up, and it has no camera, usually, to show the reverse angle if the actor has his or her back to the audience.

**FIGURE 1.18**

Live theatre, on the other hand, sometimes is more powerful than film or television because the audience becomes actively engaged with the actors and other artists in constructing the places or things being depicted. When they complete the setting of two men trapped on the side of a mountain, such as in Patrick Meyers's play *K2*, they can become greatly moved by the success of the actors and designers who help them really believe that the Styrofoam platform is an ice ledge thousands of feet above sea level. In the past, many audiences would happily go see a bad play that had an impressive visual effect, and impressive visual effects can add to an already good play. Although a beautiful camera shot is very moving, when a similar effect is achieved in live theatre, audiences seem to appreciate the extraordinary effort and artistry demanded to produce such an illusion.

**FIGURE 1.19**

*Film, television, and live theatre are organized, arranged, and enacted in both symbolic and real time.* The time experienced by characters is usually far different from the actual time experienced by the actors and the audiences. The symbolic time in theatrical performances, such as "A long time ago, in a galaxy far, far away," or "Later the next day," is flexible and fluid, shaped to the needs of the fictitious worlds inhabited by the characters. Theatrical performances, however, start at real times, not flexible ones, and if you're late, you may not be allowed into the theatre. Once started, performances move forward through time until complete, and then they cease to exist. In the case of film and television, they cease to exist only temporarily. If you have a VHS or digital recorder, you can pause television programs that you record and then start them up again, or rewind and watch the whole thing again. However, if you see a film in a cinema, or watch broadcast television, or see a play in live theatre, you cannot pause the experience and rewind it. Such experiences proceed regardless of the state of individual audience members. Additionally, because live theatre is ephemeral, it cannot be recovered at a later date for you to finish your viewing experience. Live theatre thus demands more of its audience than most film or television, because you have one chance at watching, one chance at hearing what the actors say, that one night only. Even in the case of a long Broadway run, where you could see the show a second or even a third time, no two nights will be exactly alike.

*Film, television, and live theatre are created collaboratively through the unique contributions of many artists and technicians.* Authors, actors, makeup artists, set designers, set decorators, set builders, stage or production managers, directors, producers, lighting designers, lighting technicians, costume designers, costume makers, and countless others are involved in the creation and presentation of theatrical performances. Each of these people contributes to the whole, and if you change any one of these, you change the final product. In the case of film and television, we end up with a finished **artifact**, a thing that we can hold in our hands (the DVD or tape). By "finished" we mean that the film or television episode will remain unchanged regardless of how many times or under what circumstances it is viewed again. The audience might change (e.g., you alone, you with a date, you with your family, or your friend to whom you loaned the DVD), which could change your experience of it, but the artifact itself does not change. Only changes made while the film or television episode is being shot, such as in the cast or crew, will dramatically affect the final outcome. In live theatre, however, no two shows can ever be exactly alike because each night is constructed again from whole cloth. Live theatre is not an artifact, then; it isn't a thing that you can hold in your hands. It is a process, a **system**, of constantly changing relationships that produce the ephemeral event.

**FIGURE 1.20**

The power of the camera to shape film and television experiences in ways that are different from live theatre should not be underestimated. Throughout this text, we will continue to explore ways in which those differences affect film, television, and live theatre. For the moment, we will simply note that the camera causes film and television to be experienced differently, but not so differently that some skill in analyzing one form cannot contribute to your success in analyzing the others.

Film, television, and live theatre are play. The characters in theatrical performances have no life outside of the performance except in the memories of their audiences. Actors who portray presidents do not necessarily become presidents, nor do movie villains become criminals in the real world. We do not mean to suggest, of course, that film, television, and live theatre have no effects in the real world because they are merely play. Quite the contrary, as scientists in cognitive psychology have documented the importance of play in both the development of children and in the mental health of adults. Indeed, one of the important ideas in this text is the importance of such "play," the work of film, television, and live theatre, in our lives, our culture, and our nation. Combined, the "play" of American film, television, cable, and live theatre generated the very real and impressive sum of over $117 trillion in 2001. Put another way, the actions of people who are not doing anything "real" in the world generate about 2 percent of the total gross national product for the United States of America. When we say "not real," we mean that the quality of the work done in theatrical performances is different from that same work (mowing a lawn, fixing a bike, baking a pie) in the real world.

Although we play in the real world, and some of us even play in theatrical performances in amateur productions, the play within theatrical performances is itself not real. It rarely has consequences for its participants outside of the performance. Harrison Ford was not really frozen in carbon when he played Han Solo in *The Empire Strikes Back*, and he did not suffer frostbite. Some performances attempt to affect the real world: An anti-war play might seek to motivate its audiences to protest against a war, or a movie about a gay man with AIDS may seek to create empathy and tolerance for homosexuals in society by depicting him as a human being, but these plays or movies do not actually make wars stop or people more tolerant. They do have some effects—indeed, we argue that all theatrical performances have *some* effect in the real world—but those effects depend on complex factors that include not only the quality in the theatrical performance but also political, social, and religious factors both in the culture and in individual audience members.

**FIGURE 1.21**

Many "not real" theatrical performances often seem so lifelike, even when they are very fantastical, that they become metaphors for life itself. Many historical examples exist: Shakespeare's "All the world's a stage/and all the men and women merely players," Horace Walpole's "Life is a comedy for those who think...and a tragedy for those who feel," and Oscar Wilde's "I regard the theatre as the greatest of all art forms, the most immediate way in which a human being can share with another the sense of what it is to be a human being." Indeed, at various times in history, people believed that theatrical performance and life were linked in very powerful ways. In ancient Greece, for example, actors did not impersonate death or bodily mutilation on stage, but rather dressed the characters who had been killed or maimed off stage and then brought them into audience view on a wagon called an eccyclema. In the Middle Ages, great pains were taken to reenact the miracles that saints performed and the suffering of martyrs in order to move the audience to greater piety.

## PERFORMANCE OF SELF, CULTURE, HISTORY

We have identified theatrical performances as those which employ an actor enacting a script authored specifically for that purpose and are watched by audiences who are conscious of their status as auditors to something that is not really happening to those actors. However, there are multiple ways in which we enact scripts, consciously or unconsciously, for each other, for strangers, and for our fellow citizens. As you progress through this text, you will gain vocabulary and critical thinking tools that you can apply to multiple contexts in order to develop your own conclusions about the nature and power of "performance" in your life.

Many scholars have noted the power of theatre to help explain or examine a wide variety of cultural and social processes and artifacts, in part because the boundary between so-called real actions (e.g., kissing your lover) and theatrical ones (e.g., kissing another actor on stage) is not always easy to discern. For example, some lovers kiss "for show," not really wanting to let possible observers see that they are actually having an argument. Some actors perform a stage kiss, but discover that they really mean it, and a relationship flowers between them despite efforts to stop such feelings. Because theatre artists enact the very same behaviors that we all enact in real life, albeit in heightened or extraordinary circumstances, many scholars use a theatrical paradigm to expose underlying themes or forces in real life.

**FIGURES 1.22 AND 1.23**

This blurring of the boundaries between real life and deliberately performed acts within life prompts some thinkers to question the very notion of "real actions." If, for example, you alter your voice and body posture when talking to a small child or a puppy, are you "performing"? If you practice a conversation that you want to have with your lover or your employer, and then later you have that conversation, were you "acting" a certain way, or were you simply "being yourself"? Such questions are not always useful or answerable, but sometimes they can open up new understandings of how we interact with others, how our culture sends messages to us, and how we respond to those messages.

By focusing on deliberately theatrical performances, the authors of this text hope to prompt your own reflective learning on how both deliberately theatrical performances and accidental performances shape and affect your life.

## For Further Information

Elam, Keir. *The Semiotics of Theatre and Drama*. 1980.

Goffman, Erving. *The Presentation of Self in Everyday Life*. 1959.

Huizinga, Johan. *Homo Ludens: A Study of the Play Element in Culture*. 1950.

McBride, Kecia Driver. *Visual Media and the Humanities: A Pedagogy of Representation*. 2004.

Pavis, Patrice. *Analyzing Performance: Theater, Dance, and Film*. 2003.

Rozik, Eli. *The Roots of Theatre: Rethinking Ritual and Other Theories of Origin*. 2002.

Schechner, Richard. *The Future of Ritual*. 1993.

Scheie, Timothy. *Performance Degree Zero: Roland Barthes and Theatre*. 2006.

Turner, Victor. *From Ritual to Theatre: The Human Seriousness of Play*. 1982.

Worthen, W. B. *Modern Drama and the Rhetoric of Theater*. 1992.

## Suggested Films

*Crimes and Misdemeanors* (1989): Woody Allen is a documentary filmmaker who inadvertently mixes film, art, and real life.

*Moon over Parador* (1988): A comedy in which a little-known actor is working on location in Parador when its dictator dies. The dictator's right-hand man hires the actor to play the dictator, fooling the masses, but not close friends or employees of the dictator.

*Protagonist* (2007): A documentary that explores the relationship between human life and Euripidean dramatic structure by examining the stories of four men: a German terrorist, a bank robber, an "ex-gay" evangelist, and a martial arts student.

*The Truman Show* (1998): The film chronicles the life of a man who discovers that he is living in a constructed reality soap opera, televised 24/7 to billions across the globe.

*Wrestling with Angels: Playwright Tony Kushner* (2006): A documentary on the personal, professional, and political life of Pulitzer Prize-winning playwright Tony Kushner.

## Glossary

**allusion**   A reference to another work of literature, art, historical event, or person outside a play.

**actions**   The things actors do, such as tell a story, make a touchdown, or look for treasure.

**actors**   People who perform actions such as enact a script, perform a ritual, run with a ball, or aim a virtual bow and arrow.

**aesthetic response**   An audience's positive response to an art's form and the quality of its execution.

**arenas**   The places in which audiences and actors gather to perform or watch or both.

**arrangement**   The ways in which the dramatic action itself is arranged in real and symbolic space and time, such as how places, times, beginnings, middles, and ends are made clear to actors and audiences.

**art**   A thing made by a self-conscious human artist that has social and aesthetic values.

**artifact**   A thing made by the conscious effort of a human being.

**audiences**   The people who watch the actions. Sometimes, audiences also participate as actors in those performances.

**consciousness**   The degree to which actors and audiences are conscious of each other and their objectives in a performance.

**criticism**   An informed, orderly, and reasoned judgment, analysis, or interpretation that seeks to clarify or illuminate a work of art rather than to dictate what it ought to be.

**ephemeral**   From the Greek ephemeros, literally, "lasting only one day"; refers to things that are transitory, existing only briefly. Because live theatre is not usually recorded, it can exist only ephemerally in the moments that it is performed.

**film**   A recorded performance of actors that a live audience watches asynchronously (not at the same time as the actors' performance) in a specific place designated for that performance.

**live theatre**   The live performance of actors shared with a live audience in a specific place designated for that performance.

**new media**   A live or recorded performance of actors digitally broadcast via the Internet which audiences watch synchronously or asynchronously in any place that an Internet device is found.

**objectives**   Those things that both the actors and audiences expect in a performance. Objectives are usually the reasons that performances occur.

**organization**   The way actors, audiences, actions, arenas, and internal arrangements of those elements are organized in relationship to one another during a performance.

**paradigm**   From the Greek paradeigma, a composite word that means roughly "to show as example" and refers to any thought pattern (or world view) in a scientific discipline or other epistemological context.

**performance studies**   A relatively recent area of intellectual inquiry that combines several older disciplines, such as anthropology, theatre, rhetoric, philosophy, and ethnography, to explain the significance of "performance behavior" in multiple aspects of human experience, not just aesthetic experiences.

**performing arts**   Refers to those artistic activities which typically produce an event that is carried out by an artist, such as dance, music, singing, and theatre.

**social and aesthetic values**   The value that an audience places on art, which may be based on its rarity or aesthetic qualities and can shift as society's values change over time.

**system**   A set of interacting or interdependent processes—such as acting, design, direction—that form an integrated whole—such as theatre.

**television**   A live or recorded performance of actors broadcast via public airwaves that audiences can watch synchronously or asynchronously in any place in which a working television exists, such as their own homes or bars and restaurants.

**text**   Refers to any script or scenario that guides a performance. Performance texts can be made up of words (scripts), visual images (mime), or behaviors (dance) that communicate meaning to an audience.

**theory**   An intellectual construct created to explain or predict a phenomenon; also called a hypothesis.

**visual arts**   Those artistic activities that typically produce an artifact which is distinct from the artist himself or herself, such as painting, drawing, sculpture, literature, and poetry.

## Key Concepts

- Because performances surround and penetrate modern culture, having some knowledge of how performances work is important.
- Performances of all kinds share basic characteristics, but they are distinguished by their objectives/purposes, organization, and self-awareness/consciousness.
- Performances have been part of human culture since the beginning of human history, and modern performances share some similarities with ancient practices.
- Performance is both a behavior and an art.
- Understanding the history and nature of performance can help us understand our lives.

# The Text

**Chapter Outline**

*To view the figures in this chapter, log on to www.pearsonexploretheatre.com.*

## INTRODUCTION

When we think of a text, we tend to think of something that comprises the printed word, such as a book, a poem, or a play. Although this chapter will focus primarily on plays, it is important to understand that the term "text" has a much broader meaning. A **text** is anything that can be read and analyzed, interpreted, and critiqued. Texts can be books, stories, poems, plays, screenplays, or television scripts, but they can also be websites, visual art, video games, films, TV shows, or performances of plays. Even the body can be read as a text. A text is not fully meaningful in and of itself; the meaning lies not just in the text, but also in the reader and viewer of the text—for example, how he or she interprets it.

**FIGURE 2.1**

For the purposes of this chapter, we will examine plays as texts, although it will be useful to make some comparisons between play texts and the related—but always created for **mediatization**—screenplay and television scripts. A **play** is a plan, blueprint, or outline (two-dimensional) for a production, consisting of stage directions, dialogue, and dramatic action (the question, problem, or theme that forms the central focus of the play). However, the two-dimensional play, or dramatic text, is always incomplete, for plays are written to be performed as theatre, which is a three-dimensional text. The same holds true for screenplays and television scripts, both of which are incomplete until they are mediated by the lens of a camera. A play—or screenplay or television script—is only one part, albeit an important one, of the more complete experience of production.

**LEARNING OBJECTIVES**

**After reading Chapter 2, students should be able to:**

- Read a play analytically.
- Define Aristotle's six elements—plot, character, thought (or theme), diction (or language), music, and spectacle—and understand how these are used in a play.
- Define genre, as well as the types of genres, in theatre—tragedy, comedy, melodrama, and musical theatre.
- Explain the characteristics and historical development of the different genres in theatre.

## READING AND ANALYZING A PLAY

Seeing and reading a play are different experiences. Analyzing each requires a separate approach. Chapter 3 will focus on the act of seeing a play; this chapter focuses on the act of reading a play. Thinking of reading a play as an action is crucial to an understanding of the text, as it is when examining any text. It requires a very active process of critical thinking, a way of thinking that can be learned and becomes easier the more plays you read. This chapter will provide you with the tools to be able to closely analyze, interpret, and understand a play; the next chapter will provide you with the tools for a better understanding of the complete theatrical event.

Only in the past 500 years since the invention of the printing press have we read plays. Before, drama was an entirely theatrical, not literary, form. Shakespeare's plays were not printed and disseminated until late in his life, in spite of the great popularity of productions of those plays, and the survival of his work can only be credited to a collection of his plays published after his death. Even Shakespeare's actors (called "players" during the English Renaissance, when Shakespeare wrote) did not have copies of the entire play, but only "**sides**," or pages that included only their lines.

**FIGURE 2.2**

As more printed texts became available, theatre historians and theorists—especially in the nineteenth and twentieth centuries—tended to privilege the study of periods and cultures in which the play text was available. Their reasons were pragmatic: The play is a tangible artifact, albeit two-dimensional, from an ephemeral, intangible event. When other evidence was scarce, these historians were able to rely on at least the play to try to understand theatre. However, the danger became relying too much on the written play and not viewing it as just one part of a whole. It is fortunate that this emphasis on the play as text over the performance as text is shifting.

Closely analyzing the play text is still an important part of understanding theatre. Here are some useful steps that may help you analyze the text more effectively:

1. When you sit down to read a play, consider reading it in one sitting, taking short breaks between the acts.
2. Notice the title: It can contain important clues as to the meanings in the play, as can recurring images, words, and objects.

3. Carefully read the cast of characters and any information that is given about them.
4. Be sure to read all stage directions, which can help you imagine what the play might look like on the stage.
5. Think of the play as constructed of actions, not words, and visualize those actions.
6. Finally, remember that plays are not fully meaningful in and of themselves.

All readings and productions are interpretations, and a play can have many different interpretations. The experiences and points of view that you bring to the text, and use to construct meaning from the text, are important. However, there can be *wrong* interpretations. For example, if one stated that Sophocles's *Oedipus Rex* was about a girl who goes to Hollywood to become a star, this statement would be extremely difficult to support.

## ARISTOTLE'S SIX ELEMENTS

**FIGURE 2.3**

To fully analyze the play, you should read it once superficially, as an overview, then read it again more slowly in order to fully consider all of the elements that a playwright uses to communicate. All plays can be broken down, roughly, into six basic elements. These elements were first articulated over 2,000 years ago by the Greek philosopher Aristotle. His description of drama, which he called "an imitation of an action," still holds true today. Therefore, we will organize this section according to his six elements: plot, character, thought, diction, music, and spectacle.

Aristotle describes all six in his *Poetics*, written around 33 BCE. Writing after the height of Greek theatre, which was during the fifth century, Aristotle was trained as a biologist, but wrote about a variety of fields, including theatre. *Poetics* continues to be one of the most influential works on theatre, particularly tragedy (discussed later). Historians believe that we have only part of the text of *Poetics*, because although it promises to discuss comedy and tragedy, it covers only the latter at length. Note that the six elements are interrelated parts of a whole. A change in any one element will inevitably change the others. Which of these six elements are most important can depend on the play and the theatrical conventions of the culture in which it is created. It is interesting to note that Aristotle, in his *Poetics*, lists them hierarchically, considering plot most significant and spectacle least. Today, many would argue that his hierarchy has been reversed, particularly as many works of theatre attempt to compete with the spectacle of many films.

### Aristotle's Six Elements: Plot

The **plot** is both the story told in the play, or the collected events that occur in the play, and the meaningful arrangement, or structure, of those events. The plot most often consists of actions and conflicts between and among opposing forces; these conflicts occur when the opposing forces are fighting for their goals. The most common structure is often referred to as the "climactic," or cause-to-effect, structure, and it is as old as drama itself, having been utilized in some form by the great Greek dramatists such as Aeschylus, Sophocles, and Euripides. This structure is also one of the most common for narrative film and television. It can be broken down into the following:

1. *Exposition*: Information about events that occurred before the start of the play, about the identity and relationship of the characters, and about the present situation is called **exposition**. Exposition can happen throughout the play, but often

much of it is conveyed at the beginning of the play. The point of attack determines the amount of exposition required.

2. *Point of attack*: The moment at which the action of the play starts in relation to the larger story is called the **point of attack**. Plays with a climactic structure usually have a late point of attack and, thus, a lot of exposition.

3. *Inciting incident*: An **inciting incident** is an occurrence that sets the dramatic action of the play into motion. The incident usually leads to the primary dramatic question or issue around which the play revolves.

4. *Complication*: Any new element that alters the direction of the action, usually introduced by discoveries or reversals.

5. *Discoveries*: Revelations of new information, opposition to a plan, identity of a character, and so on.

6. *Reversals*: The point at which the action suddenly turns in a completely different direction (i.e., "does a 180"). The series of discoveries, complications, and reversals, in what is termed rising action, leads logically to the **climax**.

7. *Climax*: The moment of crisis when the original question(s) of the play must be answered. When it is, there is a release of tension leading to the **dénouement**.

8. *Dénouement, resolution, or falling action*: Loose ends are tied up, any unanswered questions are answered, and tension caused by the action is released.

**FIGURE 2.4**

Shakespeare's plays generally follow this model, although they tend to have an early point of attack. Instead of using a great deal of exposition, Shakespeare chose to dramatize most of the action. During the nineteenth century, this form was codified to an extreme, in what is termed the "well-made play" format, first by Eugene Scribe in France. Eventually, it was perfected by the Norwegian playwright Henrik Ibsen in plays such as *A Doll's House, Hedda Gabler,* and *Ghosts*. Although the term was meant as a compliment at first, it eventually became an insult, as this structure—taken to extremes in the late nineteenth-century style known as *naturalism*—became mechanical and contrived. Still, the climactic structure is the most common structure seen in Western non-musical theatre today.

Alternatives to the linear cause-to-effect structure do exist. In **episodic play** structures, instead of a linear cause-to-effect arrangement, the incidents are ordered into episodes by the exploration of a theme. These plays often have an early point of attack and tend to explore a condition rather than to tell a story. Each episode into which the play is divided can, ideally, stand alone. A good example is such work of twentieth-century German playwright Bertolt Brecht as *Mother Courage and Her Children, The Caucasian Chalk Circle*, or *The Good Person of Setzuan* (also known as *The Good Woman of Setzuan*).

**FIGURE 2.5**

Sanskrit drama provides another alternative. The goal of classical Indian Sanskrit drama is not to reach a climax, but to induce the appropriate rasa, which can be translated as tone, mood, or flavor. Like episodic plays, these plays tend to explore a condition. *Sakuntala*, by Kalidasa, is one example.

And under the somewhat ambiguous umbrella of **postmodern plays** fall works that abandon a linear narrative altogether for **pastiche** (hodgepodge or juxtaposition of seemingly disparate things, such as different historical periods) and fragmented language. These plays avoid closure of meaning in favor of open-ended interpretations and often embrace nostalgia, parody, and technology. Samuel Beckett's plays, such as *Waiting for Godot*, are precursors to postmodern drama, such as Heiner Muller's *Hamletmachine*.

**Aristotle's Six Elements: Character**

The characters are the fictional people who perform the actions in the play and are the primary element out of which plots are created. Playwrights give four main types of character information:

1. *Physical or biological*: External appearance, such as species, sex, age, color, weight, hair and eye color, or height.
2. *Social*: The character's place in his or her environment, such as economic status, profession, family, relationships, and so on.
3. *Psychological*: The inner workings of the mind that precede the action. This element is probably the most important, as most drama arises from conflicting desires, goals, and objectives.
4. *Moral/ethical* (mostly implicit): Moral choices and decisions; values; what characters are willing to do to get what they want.

This information is conveyed in four primary ways:

1. Description (e.g., stage directions)
2. What the character says
3. What others say about the character
4. What the character does (often the most accurate)

When assessing a character, do not simply list traits; instead, ask how the character functions in the action. You can do this by determining the character's **objectives** (what does the character want in each scene?) and super objectives (what does the character most desire overall?). You should also examine the conflicts between or among characters, which most often result from conflicting objectives, especially between the **protagonist** (the central character, who is also often the character who changes most) and the **antagonist** (the chief adversary who opposes the protagonist). Other types of characters include the confidante, in whom the protagonist confides; **raisonneur**, who speaks for the author; the narrator or chorus, who speaks directly to the audience and may serve as the raisonneur; and the **foil**, who sets off another character by contrast.

Characters can be sympathetic or unsympathetic, complex (usually, the leading characters with a capacity for awareness, adaptability, and change) or more stereotyped (usually, the secondary characters). Also note that characters may not always be people (e.g., the cart in *Mother Courage*).

**FIGURE 2.6**

**Aristotle's Six Elements: Thought, or Theme**

By "thought," Aristotle means theme, or the intellectual issues expressed by the play—the questions, topics, and meanings raised. The best plays offer many themes, although there may be one central one. Themes are present in all plays (and musicals), even the most light-hearted. They are expressed directly or indirectly through:

1. The title of the play: Although the title may provide few clues, as in a title that reflects the main character (Antigone, Hamlet), it may provide an immediate window into the theme through such things as metaphor, as in *A Doll's House*.
2. Dialogue: **Dialogue**, the actual words spoken between and among the characters, provides some of the clearest expressions of theme.
3. Epigram: A brief, quotable saying that compresses human experience into a verbal generality is called an **epigram** (e.g., from Hamlet: "Frailty, thy name is woman").
4. Allusion: A reference to another work of literature, art, historical event, or person outside the play is an **allusion**. Those who catch it get additional insight into the play.

5. Monologues: Often important ideas are expressed in these one-person speeches (e.g., Hamlet: "To be or not to be").
6. Imagery: Repeated words that have a larger meaning (e.g., decay in *Hamlet*).
7. Prologue or epilogue.
8. Character: Certain characters—particularly the narrator, chorus, raisonneur, or confidant—should be listened to carefully to understand theme.
9. Climax: The most concrete illustration of the main theme usually can be found in the climax.

Some themes are less obvious than others, as in *Waiting for Godot*; the meanings suggested by the two characters waiting seemingly endlessly for the mysterious figure Godot are myriad. But keep in mind that even in plays which seem to express theme most explicitly, there may be many possible interpretations of the meanings that a play conveys. There are wrong interpretations; statements of theme should be supported by evidence from the text. But meaning can lie outside of what one believes that the author intended.

**FIGURE 2.7**

## Aristotle's Six Elements: Diction, or Language

"Diction" refers to language, or the words in the play—monologues, soliloquies, dialogue, narration, choral odes—and the arrangement of those words. Language conveys character, plot, and theme and is the playwright's primary tool. It serves many purposes: to give basic information about plot, to characterize, to reveal themes, to establish mood or tone, and to set the rhythm of the play. The language of a play is more carefully constructed than ordinary conversation, even in the most realistic plays. Most often, the language is heightened, and playwrights carefully choose punctuation to affect the rhythm of the language. A character's lack of words can say as much as any speech (as in *Anton Chekhov* or *Harold Pinter's* works). The best language is a mixture of the familiar (for clarity) and the strange (for variety).

When one character speaks for an extended time, it is called a *monologue*. If the character is alone on stage or speaks as if the others cannot hear him or her, it is a *soliloquy*. A brief remark to be heard by the audience, but not the other characters, is an aside.

Words can have a variety of qualities: abstract (words that name qualities concepts, ideas) or concrete (words that describe things that can be seen or touched), formal or informal, jargon (professional's or a discipline's specialized vocabulary) or slang (nonstandard, everyday speech), poetry or prose. For much of the history of dramatic literature, most serious plays were written in verse or a combination of verse and prose. Authors may write dialects or accents into the language of characters, as in *August Wilson's* plays.

**FIGURE 2.8**

## Aristotle's Six Elements: Music and Spectacle

Music, as we understand it today, and spectacle can only be suggested in the printed text. Aristotle included music in his six elements because of its importance in Greek theatre, although most theorists argue that his discussion of music also referred to the sound, rhythm, and "melody" of the language.

Besides the "musicality" of dialogue and other speech in plays, and the obvious use of music in musical theatre, music can play an important role in realistic theatre, as in Tennessee Williams's *A Streetcar Named Desire*. This play is set in New Orleans, and music from the New Orleans French Quarter underscores much of the action. August Wilson's plays, which chronicle the history of African Americans in the twentieth century, are permeated with music, such as blues, jazz, and gospel.

**Spectacle** refers to the visual elements called for in the play (e.g., scenery, costumes, and lighting). Some playwrights explicitly suggest setting, whereas others imply it, leaving choices up to the production team. Spectacle is the most difficult of these six elements to understand from the text alone. For more information, see Chapters 7 and 8.

**FIGURE 2.9**

## GENRE

A **genre** is a kind or type of something and is used to categorize art, music, film, literature, and plays. Although not everything fits neatly into categories, humans have a need to organize the world around them, and genres help in the study of things, as well as serve to frame audience or reader expectation.

In film, genres include musicals (*Moulin Rouge*), science fiction (*Star Wars* or *Transformers*), horror (*Saw*), and westerns (*Brokeback Mountain*). In television, sitcoms (situation comedy, such as *The Office*), police drama (*Southland*), and reality shows (*The Bachelor*) are just three popular genres. Both media also intermingle genres, as in *Aliens* (science fiction and horror) or the short-lived Steven Bochco 1990 television series *Cop Rock* (police drama and musical).

Historically, genres have been taken to extremes with governments even defining what plays could or could not be considered a part of a certain category. As a result, some critics and authors have rebelled against the idea of genre altogether. For the purposes of this text, it is useful to describe four of the most (historically) predominate genres of plays—tragedy, comedy, melodrama, and musical theatre—with the caveat that, as with film and television, much of dramatic literature might not fit neatly into any one category, and in fact might be a mixture of those genres (e.g., Beckett's *Waiting for Godot*, which he called a "tragicomedy," or Chekhov's plays).

**FIGURES 2.10 AND 2.11**

### Genres: Tragedy

A tragedy is a serious play with an unhappy ending brought about by the actions or decisions of a leading character who is compelled by fate, moral weakness, psychological problems, or social pressures. It is concerned with significant social issues or fundamental moral questions and, historically, has been about the upper classes. Tragedy literally refers to the ancient Greek "song of the goat," which might refer to early rituals centering on the sacrifice of a goat or for which a goat was awarded as a prize. Eventually, these rituals became what we know today as tragedy.

It is useful to return, once again, to Aristotle's *Poetics*, in which he delineates characteristics of a classical tragedy (original Greek terms are in italics):

1. Features a tragic hero or heroine (*protagonist*) who
    a. is sufficiently superior to inspire admiration (classically, being of high birth, such as royalty, was enough to make someone "sufficiently superior"), but
    b. is sufficiently imperfect to be partially responsible for the tragedy. His or her downfall results because he or she
    c. has a tragic flaw (*hamartia*): a serious personal misjudgment in the character that leads to the climax. The most common: *hubris*, or pride. He or she also will
    d. suffer a major reversal of fortune from good to bad (*peripeteia*);
    e. have a psychological realization that he or she is at least partly to blame for the situation (*anagnorisis*); or
    f. inspire pity and fear: The audience will have sympathy for the plight of the tragic hero or heroine.

2. Includes *catharsis*: The audience will experience a release of tensions and purging of the pity and fear as a result of the climax. Tragedy allows us to experience, in a way, actions and emotions that we would likely never experience in real life. We can live vicariously through tragedy.
3. Sometimes includes comic relief.
4. Usually has a late point of attack, and thus a lot of exposition.
5. Utilizes a unity of place: The tragedy often occurs in one location.

In ancient Greece, tragedies (and comedies) were originally performed in Athens at an annual festival, titled the City Dionysia, honoring, as the name suggests, Dionysus, the god of all things fun—fertility, wine, and revelry. Dramas were performed as a part of contests in which prizes were awarded to the playwright judged best by a group of citizen judges. The oldest surviving Greek plays are by Aeschylus (c. 523–456 BCE), who began competing about 499 BCE and won 13 times at the City Dionysia. Although 80 titles of his plays are known, only six actual plays have survived (e.g., *Oresteia* and *Prometheus Bound*). Aeschylus introduced the second actor (before this point, plays were performed with just one actor and a chorus), and his plays often call for amazing spectacle.

**FIGURE 2.12**

Although Aeschylus's plays are rarely produced today, Sophocles (496–406 BCE) wrote plays that still capture the contemporary imagination, such as *Oedipus Rex* (which Aristotle deemed the most perfect tragedy) and *Antigone*. He wrote more than 120 plays, although only seven have survived, and won 24 contests, the first by defeating Aeschylus. He introduced the third actor, fixed the Greek chorus at 15, and invented scene painting.

Less popular at the time, perhaps because his plays were ahead of their time in many ways, was Euripides (480–406 BCE), of whose 90 plays 18 have survived, including *The Bacchae* and *Medea*. He won only four contests, perhaps because his often violent, melodramatic, sexual subjects were thought unsuited to the Greek stage, but he was extremely popular in later periods.

Tragedy is certainly not confined to Ancient Greece; it has been a vital, popular genre throughout the history of theatre. Besides having origins in Greece, it is especially associated with Renaissance England and the work of Shakespeare, including such plays as *Hamlet*, *Macbeth*, and his earliest and perhaps bloodiest tragedy, *Titus Andronicus*. Also, although tragedy is not the focus of most classical Asian theatrical forms, elements of it do appear in such forms as Kabuki and Sanskrit drama. Tragedy is less common in theatre after the nineteenth century, partly because, some critics argue, it is difficult for today's "common man" to fulfill one of the first rules of tragedy: that the hero be "sufficiently superior to inspire admiration." In other words, the hero or heroine must be significant enough to make the events truly tragic. But Arthur Miller and other playrights have argued for a tragedy of the "common man," with Miller's *A Death of a Salesman* being perhaps the best example. And the works of such playwrights as Tony Kushner (*Angels in America*) and Martin McDonagh (*The Pillowman*) are infused with tragic elements, bringing the form into the twenty-first century.

### Genres: Comedy

A comedy is a play which deals with ordinary life in a predominantly funny way and then ends happily. It is often based on some deviation from normal behavior in action, thought, character, or speech, taking social norms and making them appear ridiculous. However, the deviation cannot be too serious or threatening, as in a tragedy, for comedy demands distance and objectivity: You cannot laugh if you are too close to the subject.

The genre concentrates largely on social relationships of humans, as opposed to deep moral or spiritual issues. Nevertheless, it may have a serious purpose and can be about relatively serious conflicts. But all conflicts are resolved in the end, with a return—often celebratory—to normal behavior and social order.

Comedy includes a variety of categories and sub-categories:

1. *Comedy of situation* shows the ludicrous results of placing characters in unusual circumstances, as in many of Neil Simon's plays or a TV show like *Cheers* or *30 Rock*. It is related to farce, which includes comedies that rely chiefly on broad physical action, buffoonery, accident, and coincidence, such as *The Importance of Being Earnest*, *Noises Off*, or the *Three Stooges* (slapstick).
2. *Comedy of character* grows out of the eccentricities of the protagonist. It is related to romantic comedy, which usually chronicles the struggles of likable characters, often in love affairs (e.g., *Twelfth Night*).
3. *Comedy of ideas* focuses on a conflict over an idea (e.g., *Lysistrata*). It is related to comedy of manners, which exploits the incongruities that arise from misdirected adherence to an accepted code of behavior (e.g., *The Country Wife*).

Almost all comedies can be placed in one of these categories, but most have elements that relate to more than one type. For example, *Gilligan's Island* is both a comedy of situation (castaways stuck on an island) and a comedy of character (much of the comedy grows out of Gilligan's eccentricities). *Tartuffe* is a comedy of both character and idea.

Comedies were first performed at the City Dionysia in Athens about 487–486 BCE, although the real home of comedy was a winter festival, the Lenaia. Aristotle states that they grew out of phallic rites (phallic symbols are representations of male sex organs, signifying fertility). The only comedies that we have from fifth-century Greece are by Aristophanes (448–380 BCE), who wrote approximately 40 plays, with 11 surviving. His plays, such as *Lysistrata*, *The Birds*, and *The Frogs*, are largely satires that comment on society, politics, and theatre. One focus, for example, was the Peloponnesian War, a war between the Greek city-states of Athens and Sparta that devastated Athens. Organized around a central ruling theme, Aristophanes's plays emphasize eating, drinking, bodily functions, sex, wealth, and leisure, and include some of the funniest, most obscene passages in Greek literature!

**FIGURES 2.13 AND 2.14**

Romans based their comedies on Greek comedy of a later period. During the Italian Renaissance, a popular form called *commedia dell'arte* developed partly from the stock characters of Roman comedy. These stock characters can be divided into three categories: lovers, masters, and servants. The lovers were often the children of the masters, who attempted to block their love affairs. The three primary masters were the Pantalone, an elderly merchant; the Dottore, a lawyer or doctor who liked to show off his (often incorrect) learning; and the Capitano, a braggart soldier who was actually a coward. The most varied commedia types were the servants, or *Zanni*, who often aided the lovers while attempting to get the best of the masters. The most popular was Arlecchino, or Harlequin, a trickster who could be identified by his costume of multi-colored patches.

**FIGURE 2.15**

These stock characters appeared to some degree in Shakespeare's plays, as well as in those of seventeenth-century French playwright Moliére, and they continue to influence comedy today, as do the comic "bits," called *lazzi*, developed out of improvisations by commedia performers.

### Genres: Melodrama

The melodrama genre—the most popular of the nineteenth century in Europe and America—grew out of the nineteenth-century Industrial Revolution. As a result of the increase in factory production, large segments of rural populations moved to the cities, which increased in size. Due to the lack of labor regulation and the overcrowding of the cities, the working class suffered poor working and living conditions. In their entertainments, they looked for ways to escape from these conditions.

**Melodrama** offered an escape and grew in popularity throughout the century. The plays are about the conflict between good and evil, with poetic justice (good triumphing over evil) the rule. Thus, melodramas always end happily. They often involve lightning conversions, in which characters can go instantly from bad to good; suspenseful plots with narrow escapes; variety via novelty, such as exotic locales and special effects; suspenseful plots with common devices such as abductions, hidden documents, and concealed or mistaken identities; strange coincidences; and comic relief by a servant, ally, or companion. The term "melodrama" means "music drama," and musical accompaniment was an important part of heightening the emotions in the early productions.

Although melodrama is related to tragedy through the seriousness of actions portrayed, it also relates to comedy through the requisite happy ending. Few pure melodramas are found in theatre now, although you can see melodramatic characteristics in many plays. Many films, however, display most of the characteristics of the genre (e.g., *Raiders of the Lost Ark*, Star Wars films, *The Mummy*, *X-Men*), as do many television shows.

**FIGURE 2.16**

### Genres: Musical Theatre

**Musical theatre** is, in its most basic form, the combination of music and theatre onstage, although the term in the United States has come to refer to a genre that most often includes actors singing onstage, accompanied by a live orchestra, and dancing. The most popular form of theatre in America today, musical theatre will be discussed at length in Chapter 13.

Although all plays are different, common elements and genres help us to understand many of them better. A careful analysis of the play's text can provide a solid base from which to view or create a production of the play. Professional actors, directors, and producers must read and analyze scripts constantly—each of them searching for the next big hit, the historic play, or the story that resonates with the spirit of the time. Most audience members rarely read the scripts to the movies, TV shows, or plays that they go see. Nevertheless, practicing this skill can help audiences not only better understand performances, but also enjoy them more.

**FIGURE 2.17**

## For Further Information

Andrew, Richard. *Scripts and Scenarios: The Performance of Comedy in Renaissance Italy*. 1993.

Aristotle. *Aristotle's Poetics*. Trans. S. H. Butcher. 1968.

Ball, David. *Backwards and Forwards: A Technical Manual for Reading Plays*. 1990.

Barranger, Milly S. *Understanding Plays*. 2004.

Bordwell, David, and Kristin Thompson. *Film Art: An Introduction*. 6th ed. 2001.

Hayman, Ronald. *How to Read a Play*. 2nd ed. 1999.

Kerr, Walter. *Tragedy and Comedy*. 1985.

Thomas, James. *Script Analysis for Actors, Directors, and Designers*. 1992.

## Suggested Films

*Adaptation* (2002): Writing process, screenplays.

*Finding Neverland* (2004): Writing process, nineteenth-century drama, *Peter Pan*.

*Julia* (1977): Lillian Hellman (playwright), writing; a true story.

*The Name of the Rose* (1986): Aristotle's *Poetics*, genre.

*Rosencrantz and Guildenstern Are Dead* (1990): Shakespeare, writing, understanding *Hamlet*.

*Shakespeare in Love* (1998): Shakespeare, writing, understanding *Romeo and Juliet*.

*Sunset Boulevard* (1950): Screen writing, movie making.

## Glossary

**allusion**   A reference to another work of literature, art, historical event, or person outside a play.

**antagonist**   The chief adversary in a play who opposes the protagonist; it can be a thing or condition, as opposed to a person.

**aside**   A brief remark to be heard by the audience, but not by the other characters.

**characters**   The fictional people who perform the actions in the play and are the primary element out of which plots are created.

**climax**   The moment of crisis when the original question(s) of the play must be answered.

**comedy**   A play which deals with ordinary life in a predominantly funny way that ends happily.

**commedia dell'arte**   A comedic form, influenced by Roman comedy, that developed as popular street performances in Renaissance Italy and later influenced the writing of such playwrights as Moliére.

**confidante**   A character in a play in whom the protagonist confides.

**dénouement**   The resolution, or falling action, of a well-made play.

**dialogue**   Actual words spoken between and among the characters.

**diction**   Aristotle's term for the words in the play, or language, and the arrangement of those words.

**epigram**   A brief, quotable saying that compresses human experience into a verbal generality.

**episodic play**   As an alternative to the well-made play, emphasizes organization around an idea or theme, with various parts—scenes and/or acts—standing on their own instead of relying on cause-to-effect.

**exposition**   Information about events that occurred before the start of the play, about the identity and relationship of the characters, and about the present situation.

**foil**   A character in a play who sets off another character by contrast: brave versus cowardly, foolish versus wise, funny versus stoic.

**genre**   A kind or type of something, used especially in reference to artistic, musical, or literary composition.

**inciting incident**   An occurrence that sets the dramatic action of the play into motion.

**mediatization**   The process of filtering a text through technology, such as the lens of a camera.

**melodrama**   "Music drama" that grew out of the social ills of the Industrial Revolution to become the most popular Western form during the nineteenth century. It is marked by a strict adherence to poetic justice, stock characters, and escapism, as well as accompanying music that underscores the action.

**monologue**   A speech delivered by a single character in a play, or a period in which one character speaks for an extended time.

**musical theatre**   In its most basic form, the combination of music and theatre onstage; often involves actors singing onstage, accompanied by a live orchestra, with dancing.

**objectives**   What a character in a play wants.

**pastiche**   Hodgepodge and/or juxtaposition of seemingly disparate things, such as different historical periods or styles.

**play**   A plan, blueprint, or outline (two-dimensional) for a production, consisting of stage directions, dialogue, and dramatic action (the question, problem, or theme that forms the central focus of the play).

**plot**   Both the story told in the play or the collected events that occur in a play, and the meaningful arrangement, or structure, of those events.

**point of attack**   The moment at which the action of the play starts in relation to the larger story.

**postmodern plays**   Plays that abandon a linear narrative and cause-to-effect events for pastiche and fragmented language; avoid "closure of meaning" for open-ended interpretations; and often embrace nostalgia, parody, and technology.

**protagonist**   The central character of a play, also often the character who changes most or represents the author's point of view.

**raisonneur**   A character in a play who speaks for the author; sometimes, a narrator or a chorus serves as the raisonneur.

**Sanskrit drama**   Plays of classical India (200–600 CE) written in the language of Sanskrit.

**sides**   Pages from a play for an actor that include only his or her lines.

**soliloquy**   A monologue delivered when a character is on stage alone.

**spectacle**   Within the context of Aristotle's *Poetics*, refers to the visual elements called for in the play (e.g., scenery, costumes, and lighting).

**text**   Anything that can be read, analyzed, interpreted, and critiqued.

**theme** The intellectual issues expressed by the play.

**tragedy** A serious play with an unhappy ending brought about by a leading character with a tragic flaw. Although Aristotle provided a definition in his ancient text *Poetics*, the term is nearly indefinable now.

**well-made play** The climactic play structure codified by Eugene Scribe and marked by cause-to-effect action, with heavy reliance on exposition, discoveries, complications, and reversals. The term is now sometimes used derisively.

## Key Concepts

- A text refers not only to the written word, but also to anything that can be read, analyzed, interpreted, and critiqued.
- A play is merely an outline for a more complex production; reading and seeing a play are two very different experiences.
- Close analysis of a play text is an important part of understanding theatre.

- Analysis of a play involves examining plot, character, theme, language, and sometimes music and suggested visual elements.
- Although the most common structure for Western drama has been the climactic, or well-made play structure, other possibilities include episodic and postmodern, among others.
- Plays may be written in a variety of genres, such as tragedy, comedy, or melodrama, or may be a combination of these and others.

## APPENDIX A: Questions for Analyzing Plays

### General

- What are the given circumstances?
- How is that information communicated?

### Plot

- What happens in the play? What are the major conflicts? Are there subplots?
- How is the story organized? What is the structure? If it is a climactic structure:
  - Where is the point of attack?
  - What is the inciting incident?
  - What are the discoveries, complications, and reversals?

### Character

- Who is the protagonist? The antagonist?
- What do you learn about each character's physical, social, psychological, and moral makeup?
- What do the characters want? What are their goals or super objectives?

### Theme

- What is the significance of the title?

- What are the recurring images in the play?
- What are the major themes suggested by the play?

### Language

- What is your general impression of the language? Is it formal or informal?
- Does the author employ special uses of language (e.g., dialects)?

### Music

- Is music utilized? If so, how and why?

### Spectacle

- What production methods or styles does this play imply or suggest (e.g., lighting, costume, set)?

### Other Questions

- What is the overriding tone of the play?
- Under what genre does this play fall?
- When was the play originally produced?
- How did the production circumstances of the time affect the play's creation?

## APPENDIX B: Analyzing Scripts (Film, TV, and Stage)

Many sources on the Internet purport to help actors prepare for roles in film and television. Although each acting teacher or producer has a particular point of view, some shared approaches can be noted.

Regardless of the medium (live stage, film, television, webisodes), most approaches to script analysis cast the actor in the role of "primary storyteller" and stress the importance for all the actors to understand the entire script, no matter how small or how large their respective parts are. All scripts have a story (either sim-

ple, such as a TV commercial, or complex, such as an epic movie), a theme (or idea), and characters. If the actors do not understand how these elements "fit" into the script, then the characters that they create probably won't "fit" on the stage, set, or location.

The first task is to determine the structure of the script. Most contemporary scripts follow a classic three-act structure:

1. Exposition (Boy meets Girl)
2. Conflict (Boy loses Girl, fights to get her back)
3. Resolution (Boy gets Girl)

Another way of naming this structure is to use Aristotle's Wholeness of Action, or "Beginning, Middle, and End." Many approaches to script analysis focus on finding the "wholeness of action" in every part of the script, regardless of length or complexity. In other words, even one line in the text could be understood to have a beginning, middle, and end. Thus, even a script with four, five, or even ten "acts" could share this same overall structure. Most professionals agree that all stories have a beginning, a middle, and an end.

For example, the physical structures of TV scripts are generally rendered as follows:

- Half-hour episodic TV (22 to 25 pages and two acts)
- One-hour episodic TV (50 to 65 pages and four acts)
- Two-hour TV Movie (100 to 110 pages and seven acts)

Television scripts can also further be broken down by use of a teaser and a tag. So a one hour TV script would be structurally analyzed as having six parts:

1. Teaser
2. Act One
3. Act Two
4. Act Three
5. Act Four
6. Tag

Regardless of the number of physical parts to the script (a single act or multiple acts), the story itself will always have a beginning, a middle, and an end.

As professional actors approach scripts, whether for television commercials, movies, or stage plays, they ask themselves many of the following questions:

1. What is the plot? (What is the story about?)
2. What is the theme? (What is the main idea or message?)
3. What is the logic? (How does this story unfold; what mechanisms move it forward?)
4. Where does the story take place (location, time)?
5. What is exposition? (What is the conflict in the story?)
6. What is the complication? (What is the conflict in the story?)
7. What (or who) creates the tension? (What will happen next?)
8. What is the major struggle? (What problem is to be solved or overcome?)
9. What is the primary action? (What event hooks the audience?)
10. What is the cause of the action? (What happens to the main character?)
11. What is the resulting action (the resolution of the major struggle)?
12. What is the conclusion? (How does the story end?)
13. Who is the protagonist (the main character?)
14. Who is the antagonist (could be one or more characters)?
15. Who are the other characters? (What functions do they fulfill in the story?)

Once the story as a whole is understood and charted by the actor, then the real work of analysis begins: scene analysis.

Most systems of contemporary script analysis agree that each scene is (or ought to be) logically connected to the larger story. Thus, scripts are broken down into acts, units (major segments of action), scenes, and beats (the smallest unit of action that retains a "wholeness of action"). Actors will then ask a series of questions about each part of the script, even ones in which their character does not appear, in order to fully understand and artistically contribute to the story that is being told. Some questions are as follows:

1. What is the intent of the scene? (What is the scene used for dramatically?)
2. What are the plot points (points that move the story forward)?
3. What is the climax of each scene? (What is the turning point?)
4. What is the resolution? (How is the theme resolved?)
5. What is the conclusion? (How does the story end?)
6. What are the important lines of dialogue (containing story points)?
7. Which character controls the scene? (Who pushes the story forward?)
8. What are the beats or unit changes? (Where does the story change directions?)

Actors, directors, designers, and technicians try to define other structural elements in their textual analyses. Depending on the type of script (comedy, tragedy, horror, farce, melodrama, etc.), other elements may be more or less important to the actor. These other elements include the following:

- foreshadowing
- recurring motifs
- scene transitions
- counterpoint
- repetition
- contrast
- clarity of information
- action and stunts
- comedy scenes
- special effects (explosions, etc.)
- visual effects (CGI, green screen, live media mixing with recorded media, etc.)
- locations (usually more complex in film and TV than in live theatre)

Script analysis for professional actors is a never-ending, widely variable, very important activity. An actor may read a side for a television commercial in the morning and a script for a major motion picture in the afternoon, and lovingly work on Shakespeare in the evenings. In the case of any one script, with each repeated reading, the actor will learn something new about the story or the characters, and so most actors read scripts many times.

In the case of scripts with living writers, especially in TV and film, the scripts themselves will change from the first reading to the final version. Often, these changes occur because the actor themselves have brought their own ideas to the process of creating a performance. The actors' command of the story itself, and of all the parts of that story allows them to negotiate and adapt to all of the changes and demands that the director, producer, or design team places upon them.

# 3

# Who Decides What Is Good Performance?

**Chapter Outline**

Introduction
Learning Objectives
The Audience
  The Audience as Community
  The Audience in History
    *In Sacred and Religious Theatres*
    *In Professional Theatres*
    *In Democratic Theatres*
    *In Non-Western Theatres*
  Contemporary Audiences
The Critic

The Theorist
The Dramaturg
Theatre as Business
  The Producer
  The Marketing Team
  The Agent
For Further Information
Suggested Films
Glossary
Key Concepts

*To view the figures in this chapter, log on to www.pearsonexploretheatre.com.*

## INTRODUCTION

Aesthetic value judgments—decisions about whether or not some form of art or popular culture is good—are in many ways subjective, but not impossible. Two people can view a Picasso painting at the same time and in the same place, but one can proclaim it bad art while another declares Picasso a genius.

Personal, visceral, and emotional responses certainly have validity. In addition, over time, standards for judging art develop. Although Picasso was less than appreciated by most of the public and art critics during his time, experts in art have since reevaluated the aesthetic value of his paintings, making them more appreciated (and extremely expensive due to that appreciation) today. Still, a contemporary art critic schooled in a form of non-Western art may have an entirely different reaction.

*Les Demoiselles d'Avignon* by Pablo Picasso (Spanish, 1881–1973) marked a revolution in modern art when it was first viewed in 1907.

**FIGURE 3.1**

Suffice it to say that what makes art—whether visual or performative—good or bad is often relative to the period, the place, and the viewer. This is equally true of both live performance and **mediated performance**. Perhaps the primary arbiter of taste in performance is the audience, but between the production and the spectator are often

28

a number of "filters" who attempt to shape the lens through which the audience views the performance. These include the critic, the theorist, and the dramaturg. Additionally, those involved in theatre as business, such as the producers and other funders, the marketing team, and agents, can shape the way that performance is viewed, processed, and judged.

## LEARNING OBJECTIVES

### After reading Chapter 3, you will be able to:

- Explain how the audience serves as a community that shares in and influences the experience of attending a theatrical performance.
- Explain how the behaviors and expectations of audiences have changed throughout history.
- Define the roles and understand the importance of the "filters" between the cast and crew of a play and the audience: critics, theorists, dramaturgs, producers or financial investors, marketing teams, and agents.
- Understand what makes theatre both an art and a business.

## THE AUDIENCE

Audience member is the role that you, the student, will most likely take in the theatrical experience. But do not underestimate the importance of this role. Numerous legendary theatrical figures, from British director Peter Brook to acting teacher and theorist Viola Spolin, have emphasized the necessity of a witness to the act of performance for it to be classified as theatre. As Spolin points out in her book *Improvisation for the Theater*, all of the efforts of the production team—from actor to director to designer—are for the benefit of the audience. Without an audience, the performance would have little point. For it is through the mind of the audience that much of the meaning of theatre is made. In fact, in some performances, such as the Blue Man Group's *Tubes*, the audience makes most of the meaning.

Playwrights, actors, and directors may have intentions for how a play and/or production should be interpreted. However, this does not mean that those who are reading a play or viewing it in production will have the intended interpretation. A play can have as many interpretations as there are audience members (although some may be more grounded in the text and production than others, and thus likely more valid). Therefore, one of the primary goals of the members of the creative team is to shape the audience response in ways considered appropriate and in accordance with their intentions. But audience response can be shaped by a number of other factors, including the audience's function as a community or the period and culture in which it is situated.

### The Audience as Community

Any audience can be viewed as a community of people sharing a performative experience. This sharing can be a dynamic, important part of the event; some audiences watch each other as much as they watch the performance unfolding before them. The audience's reactions to both the performance and themselves affect how they experience the event. And afterward, audiences talk about what they have seen.

This community is affected by a number of factors, including the size, arrangement, and makeup of the audience. An audience of one will have an experience that is completely different from an audience of hundreds. Of course, the experience can be affected by the space. An audience of one in a tiny space will be more comfortable than an audience of 20 in that same space. Conversely, two people sitting in a theatre meant for thousands will likely not enjoy the performance as much as the thousands will.

Also, audience members who can see each other—for example, in **theatre-in-the-round**—might share a more communal experience than audience members in a **proscenium** theatre who see only the backs of the heads of the audience members sitting in front of them, although they will likely hear the responses of those behind them.

Finally, a homogenous audience might feel more like a community than a heterogeneous audience. For example, an audience for a production at a small, Midwestern liberal arts college made up of students with relatively similar backgrounds might feel more togetherness than might an audience made up of people of varying ages, classes, and races.

**FIGURES 3.2 AND 3.3**

Today, members of even the most heterogeneous of audiences tend to behave in similar ways. They are expected to engage in a "**willing suspension of disbelief**"; in other words, they know that the events unfolding in front of them are not real, but for the time that they are in the theatre they react emotionally as if the events are real, laughing, crying, applauding, or, more rarely, booing. These reactions, theorized over 2,000 years ago by Greek philosopher Aristotle in his *Poetics* through such concepts as **catharsis**, allow the audience the opportunity to experience emotions in the relative safety of the theatre, perhaps alleviating the need to experience or express some emotions—particularly those most severe—outside the theatre.

To show approval, audiences engage in the convention of clapping; in cases of exceptional approval, audiences may give a standing ovation, a practice that, much to the chagrin of many in the theatre, has become more and more common, making it less meaningful when it occurs. Silence in the theatre can mean many things, including boredom and disapproval; however, it can also signal that the audience is listening intently or, in the case of the end of the show, that the audience is absorbing the effects of the piece before clapping. Booing is rarely a good thing (except in cases such as melodrama in which the audience is encouraged to "boo" the villain). In rare instances, the audience might leave the performance before the show is over.

Today's audiences are most often expected to sit quietly and attentively at a performance, communicating their responses only at appropriate moments. Such disruptive devices as cell phones and pagers—or less technologically advanced candy wrappers—are verboten.

## The Audience in History

Contemporary expectations of the audience have shifted over time and by location, and it is interesting to note that the ideal audience of today, passive and quiet, is a fairly recent phenomenon. Previously, since the theatre of Ancient Greece (and possibly, before), audiences have been more active, vocal, responsive, and even unruly.

**FIGURE 3.4**

**IN SACRED AND RELIGIOUS THEATRES** Theatre to the Greeks of the fifth century BCE was a special event, part of religious festivals held only occasionally. It is quite possible that these festivals were expressions of the entire community, with men, women, and children in the audience. Scholars who support this idea point to an ancient biography of the playwright Aeschylus, in which the author claims that when, at a performance of the play *The Eumenides*, the playwright "introduced the chorus in wild disorder into the orchestra, he so terrified the crowd that children died and women suffered miscarriage." Possible hyperbole aside, this account suggests that women and children were in the audience. Other evidence suggests that only citizens (meaning men) were allowed either to perform or view the performances.

Greek audiences could be quite large: The Theatre of Dionysus, on the hillside of the Akropolis in Athens, seated as many as 7,000. Performances lasted all day, and as a result, the audience—regardless of whom it comprised—came and went, ate and drank, talked, and felt no qualms about expressing immediate approval or disapproval of the action on stage. However, violence in the theatre was controlled by the threat of capital punishment.

**FIGURE 3.5**

Both Roman and medieval audiences at the theatre consisted of all segments of society, and were equally, if not more, vocal and active as Greek audiences. By the time of the Roman Empire (see Figure 3.8), audiences' thirst for variety, violence, and spectacle, both in text-based theatre and the more sports-like **paratheatricals**, such as chariot racing and gladiator combats, was insatiable. Audiences' attention spans were short, and spectators could be rowdy. In a prologue to a play, the famous comic writer Plautus admonished against behavior that must have been common in the theatre: "Let no worn out prostitutes sit in the front part of the auditorium, nor the guards make any noise with their weapons, nor the ushers move about in front of spectators or show anyone to seats while the actors are onstage…Don't let slaves take up seats for free men…let nursemaids keep little children at home. Let matrons…refrain from gossiping."

**FIGURE 3.6**

Much of medieval performance regained the sacred function that had been lost in ancient Rome. Its function as a teaching tool of the church restored many of its communal functions, and audiences were homogenous in their allegiance to (at least publicly) the pervasive Catholicism of the period in Europe.

Audiences were often even more dynamic bodies than before, due to the mobile nature of much of the religious theatre. In **liturgical dramas**, occurring in the churches or cathedrals, audiences moved around from **mansion** (set piece) to mansion. If a performance was outside the church at **cycle or mystery plays**, audiences stood around **pageant wagons** (similar to modern-day floats), even moving with a favorite wagon as it processed through a city. Although some of the religious dramas were presented statically, in fixed staging with the audience standing or seated in front of platforms, mobile staging seems to have been more common.

**FIGURES 3.7 AND 3.8**

**IN PROFESSIONAL THEATRES** As theatre moved indoors and became professionalized, the opportunity to control audiences increased—particularly in order to charge money for what primarily had been free. Yet, audiences became even more active, responsive, and vocal than they had been. In fact, audiences have become increasingly less active and responsive.

During the English Renaissance, all classes except the highest mingled together in such public **playhouses** as the Rose, the Fortune, or the theatre known as Shakespeare's, the Globe. Shakespeare, as did other playwrights of his day, included something for everyone in his plays, and this approach may have contributed to their lasting appeal. The Globe audience of approximately 3,000 could buy beer, nuts, and other refreshments from vendors moving about the theatre, contributing to an environment that must have resembled a sporting event today. Because of the **thrust** configuration of the theatre, most spectators were close to the stage. This fact, along with the largely circular shape of the spectator area that allowed much of the audience to see each other, must have created a wonderfully communal space (a conjecture that one of the authors experienced as fact at a production of *The Merchant of Venice* at the newly reconstructed Globe in London).

**FIGURES 3.9**

The development of theatre architecture for opera in Italy toward the end of the Renaissance signaled changes that would remain typical for theatre until the late nineteenth century also in Europe and America. The auditorium was divided into a **box, pit, and gallery** arrangement, designed to reflect the developing class structure in Europe and later in America. The boxes around the auditorium were the most expensive seats; above them, the gallery accommodated the working class in the cheapest seats in the house; and the pit (now referred to as the orchestra), the area on the ground floor in front of the stage, contained seats less expensive than the boxes, but considered more desirable than the gallery.

Although this arrangement remained typical for centuries, some variances occurred. One of the most interesting was the placement of audience members onstage with the actors. This occurred in such societies as neoclassical France—from the 1630s to approximately 1760—when the desire by spectators to be seen by other spectators reached a peak, and theatres realized that they could charge more for the onstage seats. The practice reportedly ended when an actor could not make his entrance because the stage was so crowded with spectators.

**FIGURE 3.10**

**IN DEMOCRATIC THEATRES**    The nineteenth century in Europe saw a significant shift in the audience, primarily due to the rise of the working class, which began to attend the theatre in such large numbers that some historians argue that the higher classes were driven away to such alternative forms as opera. The members of this rising class, looking for relief from their often harsh working and living conditions, in turn shifted the nature of what appeared on the stages, making **melodrama**, with its escapist entertainment, the most popular form of theatre, along with variety entertainment.

These events led to the development and increasing use of more "democratic" auditoriums, and most theatres built from the late nineteenth century to the present have abandoned box, pit, and gallery for a fan-shaped configuration that supposedly creates equally good seating for all (although many theatres today are divided into at least two tiers of seating: the more expensive orchestra and the less expensive balcony). Or, as noted in Chapter 4, prosceniums have been abandoned for other theatre configurations that offer more equal seating, such as the thrust and arena, or configurations that blur the line between actor and audience, as in **environmental theatre** staging.

**FIGURES 3.11 AND 3.12**

**IN NON-WESTERN THEATRES**    Clearly, audience behavior and expectations in the Western world have shifted over time; what of audiences at non-Western theatre? It is difficult to make generalizations about so many diverse cultures and societies, but certain conventions can be noted in audiences for classical Asian theatre forms, as well as for indigenous African performance and ritual.

Classical Asian forms, such as Indian **Sanskrit theatre, Beijing Opera** of China, and Japanese **Noh, Kabuki**, and **Bunraku**, have, as theatre in much of Western history, encouraged audiences to be vocal and immediately responsive with clapping, cheering, shouting, or booing. Audiences tend to be smaller, as in theatre of the English Renaissance, as opposed to theatre of ancient Greece. Eating and drinking in the theatre, as well as coming and going during what are often performances of familiar stories, have been the norm. In African ritual and performance indigenous to the continent, intimate spaces have most often been valued, as well as the blurring of boundaries between performance and spectator; audience participation is even encouraged sometimes.

Of course, as these cultures become—for better or worse—increasingly Westernized, the Western conventions of the more passive, quiet audience are affecting prior expectations of audiences.

**FIGURE 3.13**

### Contemporary Audiences

Audiences today bring myriad experiences and expectations to the theatre that were unheard of in the past. Foremost among these is their likely immersion in a mediatized world. One increasingly frequent hallmark of this immersion is a lack of awareness as to the ways in which their behavior may affect the performance.

One compelling (and alarming, to anyone who creates theatre!) example of this occurred during the 2010 World Cup, the "Super Bowl" of soccer. *The Wall Street Journal* reported, in an article on the spread of Broadway musicals around the world, that during a stage performance of Disney's *Mary Poppins* in Amsterdam, audience members were intermittently screaming in their seats. The disconcerted performers soon learned that the screaming patrons were watching a soccer game on their mobile devices.

**FIGURE 3.14**

Possibly dragged against their will to a performance to which tickets were purchased before the Dutch team was scheduled to play at that time, the audience members still should have observed proper theatre etiquette. Perhaps now more than ever, a sort of "Ten Commandments" of theatre etiquette is called for, and it might look something like this:

1. Thou shalt not be an ignorant audience member.
2. Thou shalt not be late.
3. Thou shalt not bring food and drink into the theatre unless otherwise notified.
4. Thou shalt turn off thy cell phone or other electronic devices (not merely silence it).
5. Thou shalt not text or instant message.
6. Thou shalt not take video or still pictures of the performance.
7. Thou shalt not talk during the performance.
8. Thou shalt not put thy feet on the backs of seats.
9. Thou shalt avoid leaving the theatre while a performance is in progress.
10. Thou shalt laugh, cry, gasp, or applaud as appropriate.

As an audience member, always approach the production with respect for the hard work that has gone into the creation of the performance and an awareness of how your presence impacts what happens on stage.

## THE CRITIC

In many ways, the audience serves in the role of critic for a production, analyzing, interpreting, judging, and describing it to others. Word-of-mouth can be extremely influential advertising, and audience critiques, largely as amateur endeavors, have happened throughout the history of theatre—although some audience members are more qualified to judge than others. In ancient Greece, when plays were presented at such dramatic festivals as the City Dionysia in Athens, prominent citizens were chosen to serve as judges at competitions in which the plays were presented. During the fifth century BCE, three tragic playwrights competed for the prize for best dramatist each year at the City Dionysia (Sophocles won at least 18 times). During the Restoration in England, in the late seventeenth century, Samuel Pepys wrote an extensive diary chronicling his frequent trips to the theatre; his judgments, albeit heavily biased, in that diary have provided historians with extensive—if not always accurate—information about the theatre of that period.

Technology has enabled a proliferation of amateur critics, particularly online on various websites and blogs; anyone can quickly, and sometimes quite widely, disseminate their opinions via cyberspace. Even so, a relatively small number of people actually work as professional critics, with a few making their living solely as such. Critics may write for newspapers, magazines, or academic journals, or they may disseminate their criticism in books, on television, on the radio, and/or online. The audiences for these media outlets differ, and critics adjust their content accordingly. For example, the scholarly critic, writing for academic journals or in books, and without the pressure of a tight deadline, is often able to analyze a play or performance in complex, deep ways, engaging in extensive research to contextualize the piece and often theorizing through a long lens, making larger connections, or closely reading the work in order to analyze it in minute detail. This section will focus more on popular criticism, because your experience with criticism as an audience member will most likely be through such venues as newspapers and magazines, either print or online.

**FIGURE 3.15**

Critics have an extremely difficult role; they are a part of the theatre scene in any given community, but often remain on the margins due to the nature of their job. They can be the butt of jokes and reviled by the creators of theatre. But although the term "criticism" has come to have negative connotations, it refers to the general act of making judgments, whether negative or positive. And the critic's work is much more complex than merely recommending to an audience whether or not a production is worth seeing. The best critics have extensive backgrounds in both studying and viewing theatre.

In communicating their experiences, good critics provide a balance of the four types of information mentioned earlier: description, analysis, interpretation, and judgment. Most reviews begin by describing what the critic saw, although he or she must be careful not to give away too much information. The description may be woven throughout the review, along with the analysis—the reviewer's examination of how what he or she describes worked. Usually, later in the piece, the critic includes both interpretation, or what the performance or parts of the performance mean, and judgment, or statements concerning the value of the work (although the judgment may be stated as early as the lede, or opening, of the review). Good reviewers consider context when determining value; for example, a critic should not hold a community theatre production of *Cats* to the same standards as a Broadway production. Likewise, a reviewer should not view a production of Japanese Noh theatre with the same expectations he or she would have for a production of the very American work of Neil Simon.

Critics can have an enormous amount of influence on the financial success or failure of a production. On the other hand, examples exist of reviews of a show having little to do with its popular success; largely disdainful reviews of Andrew Lloyd Webber's *Cats* did not stop it from becoming the second-longest running show in Broadway history (surpassed only by *Phantom of the Opera*, also by Lloyd Webber). Critics also can contribute an account of the production for historical record. Reviews are important evidence from which historians attempt to reconstruct an ephemeral art. The best critics work to connect the production to larger cultural concerns, forecasting trends in theatre and placing the show within the context of contemporary society. In this capacity, the critic works to further the field, holding theatre to a high standard and helping to ensure its survival as both art and entertainment.

## THE THEORIST

Critics, both scholarly and popular, often draw on the work of theorists for their reviews of specific plays and productions; sometimes, critics and theorists can be one and the same. But instead of examining a single work, a theorist looks for larger trends between and among works and theatre artists.

A **theory** is an intellectual construct created to explain or predict a phenomenon. A theatre theorist might explore the connections between theatre and the society in which it is situated. For example, one theorist might ask why women have been relegated to the margins of theatre history and practice. Another theorist might ask how a model of theatrical performance (Kenneth Burke's **Pentad**, for example) can be used to explain everyday life. Although each of these theorists asks very different questions, both use theories to guide their search for answers.

Throughout the history of theatre, theorists have sought to define and redefine such basic concepts as theatre, performance, drama, tragedy, and comedy. One of the first theorists in the Western world was Aristotle, who, in his *Poetics*, attempted to define comedy and tragedy (although his descriptions of the former are lost to us). In the non-Western world, Bharata Muni wrote the ancient Indian equivalent to the *Poetics*, the *Natyasastra*, in which the author attempted to codify classical Sanskrit theatre.

**FIGURE 3.16**

The basics have been redefined again and again, and new questions have arisen, depending on what one society or another considers important. For example, **feminist** theory has sought to explore the role (or lack thereof) of women in the history of theatre. One of the most influential feminist theorists in theatre has been Jill Dolan, who writes "The Feminist Spectator," a blog on theatre, performance, film, and television. This theory is typical of the application of theories to theatre, from other fields; much of feminist theory grew out of film theory and psychoanalytic theory.

The multiplication of theories by which to explain and explore various aspects of theatre is partly a product of the predominance of **postmodern** theory after World War II. Before then, in the modern age, assumptions about the world rested on reason, science, and objective, verifiable truths. But in the postmodern age, emphasis shifted to the relativity of truth and the importance of multiple perspectives in making meaning, as well as a perception of history as discontinuous and a breakdown of hierarchies and dualities. So, one can view a single event, such as a theatrical production, from multiple theoretical perspectives, opening up the possible meanings of that event.

Theorists are crucial to theatre practice in that they help audiences process what they see—and even affect what audiences expect to see. Debates have been raging for some time regarding which comes first, theory or practice. Some view both of them as existing on parallel planes, and some would even view them as inseparable. Bertolt Brecht's theories on epic theatre, for example, were developed in conjunction with his work as both a playwright and a director. Richard Schechner and Peter Brook are two more examples of artists whose theories—on environmental theatre and **performance studies** in the former case, on the "empty space" and **intercultural** theory in the latter—have grown out of their considerable practice as directors.

## THE DRAMATURG

The position of the **dramaturg**, although far from new, is often misunderstood. At its most basic level, it describes a specialist in dramatic analysis and literature, production research, and audience engagement. The odd name often raises brows; dramaturgs, because of the nature of the work that they do, can come under the same cloud of suspicion as critics.

The use of a dramaturg in the production process in the United States is relatively recent (in the past 30 years or so), but increasing. Although the work that a dramaturg does can be traced back to the beginnings of theatre, the formal position dates back to eighteenth-century Germany and the time of Gotthold Ephraim Lessing. In 1767 Lessing declined an offer by the Hamburg National Theatre to serve as resident playwright.

Instead, he proposed to serve a number of functions that have since become the work, partly, of the dramaturg: acting as in-house critic, reading and helping to select plays, and writing theoretical essays on theatre, which attempted to influence audience tastes. This position later became standard in many European theatres, long before it became more common in the United States.

**FIGURE 3.17**

Although the role of the contemporary dramaturg can shift depending on the context, the dramaturg often performs the following functions; those who specialize in the first two may be called literary managers:

- Assist in the selection of plays
- Work with playwrights on the creation of new plays
- Conduct research for productions
- Serve as the in-house critic, attending rehearsals as an "ideal audience member"
- Provide links between the production and the audience through program notes, lobby displays, lectures, and pre- or post-show discussions

In general, the dramaturg serves as the "questioning spirit" or "conscience" of the production, helping the creative team or playwrights constantly evaluate their choices—in relation to original goals for a production or a play as well as in relation to the potential audience or reader.

## THEATRE AS BUSINESS

Most people engaged in the creation of theatre like to think of it as art. Indeed, for the first two thousand years or more of its existence in the Western world, theatre was not largely a commercial enterprise undertaken by people attempting to make a living at it (i.e., professionals). It was usually a communal, free event and frequently had sacred functions.

However, since the English Renaissance, theatre has also been a business. Acting, directing, designing, and dramaturging—all of the tasks involved in the creation of theatre—are hard work, and artists in most cases deserve to be paid for it. Theatre can be a costly product, particularly due to what makes it unique: its live nature. In mediatized performance, once the creative work of the actors, directors, and others is complete on a film, that film can be reproduced and shown thousands of times, recouping the expense to create it with few ongoing costs. The same is not true for theatre, which must have its actors, technicians, and other staff (except for some members of the production team) on hand at each live performance in order for it to continue existing—and making money. And those actors and staff must continue to be paid, night after night after night.

The money for the perpetuation of such an ephemeral, but vital, product is usually obtained from two different general sources in professional theatre. First, funds may be generated to pay the artists and create the performance through ticket sales; thus, the audience pays for it, either through single ticket sales or subscriptions for the season. Second, money may be donated by some kind of a patron, a system of funding that became quite common from the Renaissance onward, when rich citizens or rulers would consider it their honor or duty to fund the work of artists. This system continues today in a couple of ways: Private citizens or corporations may fund theatre, most often through a foundation or board created to direct donations to various organizations; and governments may provide money for the creation of theatre. The latter is more common in Europe than in the United States.

**FIGURE 3.18**

Professional theatre can be divided into two categories: **commercial** and **nonprofit**. Commercial theatre must earn a profit for its investors. The money that is taken in through box office or raised from other sources in nonprofit theatre must be channeled back into the theatre, to support staff, productions, and facilities. The term "nonprofit" does not mean that these theatres cannot earn a profit; it means that money cannot be used to pay investors a return on their investment.

Along with money comes the issue of control; as with any enterprise, the source of the money often expects to exercise control over the product created with that money. Although contemporary American culture tends to dismiss theatre as mere entertainment, example after example throughout history exists to prove that various societies have recognized theatre's potential to affect morality, politics, religion—indeed, all aspects of that society. And because of this potential, those in power sought to control the theatre.

The English Renaissance and the period immediately after provide two excellent examples of this. When Elizabeth I came to the throne in 1558, England was experiencing considerable religious upheaval as the queen fought the Catholic Church to gain autonomy through the Church of England, the new religion created by her father, Henry VIII. Recognizing the power of theatre, Elizabeth passed a number of edicts controlling theatre: She forbade religious subjects (which had been the focus of the drama prior to her reign); all plays had to be approved by the Master of Revels, an office under the queen; and no playhouses could be built within the walls of London. The last edict served multiple purposes, including limiting fire hazards within the city proper and limiting rioting that might spill over into the city streets near the seat of the government. In the next century, during the Civil War in England (1642–1660), Puritans controlled Parliament. Because they viewed acting as "lying" and objected to the distraction caused by theatre from more "productive" activities like praying, the Puritans closed all theatres. When the theatres were opened again at the restoration of the monarchy, Charles II still maintained tight control.

Theatre often has been viewed as a threat to morality and has provided a home for people and ideas existing outside socially or governmentally accepted norms. For example, in many cultures, both Western and non-Western, actors were equated with prostitutes, either metaphorically or more literally. As a result, women were banished from the stage in a number of societies, paving the way for the development of the (often exquisite) female impersonator, as in the English Renaissance or in Beijing Opera in China and Kabuki in Japan.

In addition, playwrights have been imprisoned as a result of unpopular or threatening views. In the early 1980s, Vaclav Havel served four years in prison (1979–1983) for writing plays considered subversive to the Communist government in the former Czechoslovakia; after the fall of Communism, he served as the Czech Republic's first president. Wole Soyinka was placed in solitary confinement for two years during the 1960s for writing plays unsupportive of the dictatorship that controlled his native Nigeria. The first African Nobel Prize winner (for literature), Soyinka has lived in exile most of his life.

Censorship and control have often gone hand in hand with theatre, and theatre performed in the democratic United States is no exception. During the Great Depression of the 1930s, President Franklin Roosevelt created the Works Progress Administration (WPA) to provide work for poverty-stricken Americans, including theatre artists, many of whom were employed by the far-reaching Federal Theatre Project (FTP) under visionary director Hallie Flanagan. The FTP created theatre across the country, from musicals to children's shows, and from black theatre to vaudeville to "living newspapers," a documentary form of theatre that attempted to shed light on the plight of Americans during the period, in sometimes very honest ways. Plays such as the latter made some in the government uneasy, as did such children's shows as the musical *Revolt of the Beavers*, which some perceived as sympathetic to Communism. According to Hallie Flanagan in her book

*Arena*, among the last exchanges between the House Un-American Activities Committee (HUAC) and Flanagan included the following with Congressman Joe Starnes (Alabama):

> *Starnes* (reading from a magazine article that Flanagan wrote): "The workers' theatres intend to shape the life of the country, socially, politically, and industrially. They intend to remake a social structure without the help of money—and this ambition alone invests their undertaking with a certain Marlowesque madness."
>
> Starnes then challenged Flanagan, "You are quoting from this Marlowe. Is he a Communist?"
>
> After much laughter from the spectators in the balcony, Hallie Flanagan apologized for her own laughter and added, "I was quoting from Christopher Marlowe."
>
> *Starnes*: Tell us who Marlowe is, so we can get the proper reference, because that is all we want to do.
>
> *Flanagan*: Put it in the record that he was the greatest dramatist in the period immediately preceding Shakespeare.

Despite Flanagan's energetic defense, Congress voted to end funding for the project, while allowing the other "white color" projects, such as the writers, artists, and musicians, to continue.

**FIGURE 3.19**

In 1990, the National Endowment for the Arts (NEA), an office of the government created in the 1960s to follow the example of the FTP (and the governments of many European countries) in providing funding for the arts, rescinded money given to four artists due to the controversial nature of the performances that they created with the government's money. One of the performers, Tim Miller, used his work to explore his experiences as a gay man in America; Karen Finley was cited specifically for her performance in *We Keep Our Victims Ready*, in which, nude, she smeared her body with chocolate to represent the degradation of women. Their work, and the work of the other two artists, Holly Hughes and John Fleck, was deemed offensive by government officials who had never even seen it. The artists sued the government, and the subsequent court battles led in 1998 to the Supreme Court's upholding the 1990 law specifying that in granting awards the NEA could take into account "general standards of decency." However, they did not define "decency." What is labeled "decent," "moral," or "good" will continue to shift, depending on the perception of the one who is labeling theatre as such.

### The Producer

A key figure in theatre as business, primarily in the commercial (as opposed to non-profit) theatre, is the **producer**. The theatre producer, much like the producer in film, has the primary responsibility of raising money for the show, whether on Broadway, Off-Broadway, in the West End, or beyond.

In large, non-commercial theatres the person who functions as the executive director may also function as a producer. In university theatres the department chair often serves as the producer. The tasks of producing in settings such as regional theatre are considerably more diffuse, with a variety of people often carrying out the functions. Such theatres are more concerned with financing their institutions on an ongoing basis, not just for a single production. An artistic director or a managing director typically serves as the producer, usually under the guidance of the board of directors. He or she spearheads the mission of the organization, often helping to raise funds through government grants, foundations, corporations, and subscriber dollars; chooses plays for the season; and hires artists.

Regardless of the setting, the job remains largely the same: to assemble and provide for the resources and talent necessary to produce the show.

**FIGURE 3.20**

Although they have, in the past, been involved in the creative side of theatre-making (Oscar Hammerstein II and Richard Rodgers became producers after the success of shows that they had written, such as *Oklahoma!*), producers today tend to have experience in business. Also, whereas in the past a producer may have worked alone (Hal Prince solely produced *West Side Story*), the rising costs of creating theatre have shifted the model for producing. More often than not, the list of names next to the title "Producer" in the program is long (nine producers are listed for *Chitty Chitty Bang Bang*). Another ever-increasing model is the corporation-as-producer. Some producers do not invest money in the show themselves, but find various "backers" to invest.

Producers are responsible for hiring personnel for a show, including actors, the director, and designers. Although producers retain considerable power over the production process, most turn artistic control over to the director. Producers oversee marketing and publicity, because they must ensure that an audience comes to the show, thus providing investors a return on their money.

The corporate producer, such as Disney or Clear Channel Entertainment, is becoming increasingly common in the United States, particularly on Broadway and for touring shows. Corporate involvement in all aspects of our capitalist society seems American as apple pie, but its involvement in theatre is not without controversy.

**FIGURE 3.21**

For example, during the early 1990s, the Disney Corporation decided to develop musicals for the stage; their first, *Beauty and the Beast*, has been a huge hit, both in New York and on tour. But many critics labeled the show inartistic, because it primarily reproduces the Disney film on stage. For their next attempt, *The Lion King*, the company hired avant-garde theatre designer and director Julie Taymor, who moved beyond the animated film to create a visually stunning world, using innovative masks, costumes, and movement. Yet, new controversies arose over this critically acclaimed musical when Disney bought and renovated a run-down theatre, the New Amsterdam on 42nd Street, and moved the show into it.

**FIGURE 3.22**

This and other renovations (including the installation of a Disney store) were part of a wholesale effort to revitalize the Times Square Theatre District, which since the 1970s had become increasingly run-down, seedy, and crime-ridden. Then-Mayor Rudy Giuliani joined with Disney and other corporations to renovate the area, making it safer and more "family friendly." Critics of this "Disneyfication" of Broadway point to the disappearance of the character of the area that made it so uniquely New York; instead, they argue, it has an almost "theme–park-like" atmosphere. The Broadway of *Guys & Dolls* is now the Broadway of the Disney Store, the Nike Store, Applebees, and Target. And some worry about the control that Disney will wield over the theatre. So far, those fears seem unfounded as a new family audience flocks to *The Lion King*, *Chitty Chitty Bang Bang*, and other shows, and Disney's reach remains fairly limited (see also "What Is Producing?" in Chapter 6).

## The Marketing Team

In many theatres, the producer oversees the marketing and advertising of a production. This role is crucial for theatre as business: Its function is primarily to ensure that there is an audience. The marketing team must persuade people to come and see any show that its producer or theatre produces. This work may involve marketing a show that is free; or the stakes may be higher when ticket prices are over $100, as they frequently are on Broadway or in the West End. Therefore, how any given theatre goes about marketing and publicizing a production can differ radically. At a small community theatre, an intern may photocopy flyers created on a personal computer to post and distribute. A regional theatre, on the other hand, may advertise on local television and radio stations; take out an ad in the newspaper; put up elaborately printed posters and flyers; and send brochures to potential ticket buyers.

Marketing departments do not attempt to get everyone to see certain productions or buy tickets for all seasons. They must carefully target the appropriate audience. For example, they would not post flyers at an elementary school for a production of a David Mamet play, which usually contains mature themes and strong language. Instead, they would market the show to a more adult audience, saving the school flyers for their next production, Suzan Zeder's sensitive play for youth, *Step on a Crack*. If the theatre were producing a Mamet play, the marketing department, along with the dramaturg, would want to be sure to prepare the audience that they did attract, so that audience expectation is in alignment with the subject matter. This preparation can be accomplished through the ads for the show, as well as by items in the newspaper, pre-show talks, lobby displays, and program notes.

## The Agent

**Agents** in theatre, like producers, serve a function similar to agents in film; they connect theatre artists with the producers and directors who hire them. They are the links between theatre as art and theatre as business. Although theatrical agents most often represent actors and playwrights, they may represent other members of the creative team as well.

**FIGURE 3.23**

Agents earn a percentage (typically, about 10 percent) of their clients' earnings. They are extremely choosy about whom they agree to represent, selecting those clients with the most potential to succeed. As a result, procuring an agent—especially a well-connected one—is not easy for professional theatre artists. It is extremely beneficial, however, as the agent can help negotiate contracts or disputes, collect and distribute money, and connect the actor or playwright with appropriate people.

Agents are also helpful to those on the business side of theatre, because they serve as gatekeepers, directing only appropriate actors, playwrights, and others to producers or directors. However, as gatekeepers, agents may function as a barrier to unproven artists whose work lies outside of the mainstream of what is considered successful at the moment.

## For Further Information

Bennett, Susan. *Theatre Audiences: A Theory of Production and Reception*. 1997.

Blau, Herbert. *The Audience*. 1990.

Brook, Peter. *The Empty Space*. 1995.

"Censorship." *The Cambridge Guide to World Theatre*. 1988.

Dolan, Jill. *The Feminist Spectator as Critic*. 1988.

Flaagan, Hallie. *Arena*. 1940.

Gold, Sylviane. "The Disney Difference." *American Theatre*. December 1997.

Horwitz, Simi. "The Critic's Voice." *Back Stage*. June 12, 1998.

Houchin, John. *Censorship of the American Theatre in the Twentieth Century*. 2003.

Kalina, Stefanova-Peteva. *Who Calls the Shots on the New York Stages?* 1993.

Kattwinkel, Susan, Ed. *Audience Participation: Crossing Time and Genre*. 2003.

Kauffman, Stanley. *Theatre Criticisms*. 1984.

Marks, Peter. "As Giants in Suits Descend on Broadway." *New York Times*. May 19, 2002.

Schechner, Richard. *Performance Theory*. Rev. ed. 1988.

Spolin, Viola. *Improvisation for the Theatre*. 3rd ed. 1999.

Sontag, Susan. *Against Interpretation and Other Essays*. 1966.

Sauter, Willmar. *The Theatrical Event: Dynamics of Performance and Perception*. 2002.

Taymor, Julie. *Playing with Fire: Theater, Opera, Film*. Rev. ed. 1999.

## Suggested Films

*42nd Street* (1933): A Broadway producer struggles to make a comeback, and his hopes rest on the slim shoulders of an innocent girl from Allentown, Pennsylvania.

*Farewell My Concubine* (1993): Depicts the conflation of acting with prostitution in Beijing Opera, as well as the *dan*, or female impersonator.

*Moon Over Broadway* (1997): A behind-the-scenes look at the production of the Broadway comedy *Moon Over Buffalo*.

*The Producers* (2005): The well-known Mel Brooks "movical" adapted from his 1968 smash-hit movie shows the struggles of two hapless producers attempting to create the perfect flop.

*Shakespeare in Love* (1998): The scene at the opening of *Romeo and Juliet* is an excellent depiction of the audience at the public theatres of the English Renaissance.

*Stage Beauty* (2004): Depicts the transition from female impersonators to actresses on the English stage.

## Glossary

**agent**   Person who connects theatre artists (actors, designers, etc.) with the producers and others who hire them.

**backers**   Investors who help fund a theatrical production.

**Beijing Opera**   A classical, traditional Chinese form that combines music, dance, and speech with elaborate, codified costumes, makeup, and movement.

**box, pit, and gallery**   Auditorium arrangement common from the Renaissance into the nineteenth century, including the ground-level pit with boxes and galleries surrounding it, with the highest galleries that hold the cheapest seats.

**Bunraku**   Extraordinarily lifelike, classical Japanese puppetry form, in which each puppet is manipulated by three puppeteers.

**catharsis**   A release of tensions resulting from the climax of a tragedy.

**commercial**   In general, theatre that earns a profit for its investors; however, this term is increasingly difficult to define as its meaning continues to broaden.

**cycle, or mystery, plays**   Medieval plays based on stories from the Bible that were elaborately staged, often during Christian festivals.

**dramaturg**   A specialist in dramatic analysis and literature, production research, and audience engagement.

**environmental theatre**   A style of staging that involves flexible, found, or transformed performance space in which actors and audience share the same space; also involves variable focus, and emphasis on all elements of the performance as language (not just the written text) as formulated by Richard Schechner on the basis of the work of such groups as the Polish Laboratory Theatre, the Living Theatre, and the Open Theatre.

**feminist**   A term that, at its most basic, describes someone dedicated to equal treatment and rights for men and women under the law and in society.

**intercultural**   Between or among two or more cultures.

**Kabuki**   A classical Japanese form of music theatre developed in the eighteenth century that emphasizes spectacle.

**literary managers**   Dramaturg positions that include such tasks as assisting in the selection of plays at a theatre.

**liturgical dramas**   Performances developed during the Middle Ages by and within the Catholic church to communicate Christian teachings.

**mansion**   Term for a set piece in performances during the Middle Ages.

**mediated performance**   Performance that is mediated through technology, such as the lens of the camera or a microphone.

**melodrama**   A movement that developed parallel to Romanticism, but outlived it to become the most popular form of theatre in America and Europe during the nineteenth century. Some hallmarks include plots focusing on good versus evil, with clear-cut heroes and villains; exotic locales; plot devices such as hidden documents, disguises, and kidnappings; and musical accompaniment.

**Noh**   A classical Japanese form created in the fourteenth century; emphasizes minimalism as a reflection of the influences of Zen Buddhism.

**nonprofit**   A term largely related to the tax status of an organization; not-for-profit theatres must ensure that profits go not to investors, but back into the workings of the theatre, including staff salaries.

**pageant wagons**   Movable wagons carrying the set (mansion) and playing area for the cycle plays of the Middle Ages.

**paratheatricals**   Ancient Roman entertainments outside of the theatre structures that housed tragedies and comedies. During the empire they became increasingly common, replacing theatre as the primary form of entertainment. Common types were gladiatorial combats, chariot racing, venationes (animal fights), and naumachiae (recreated sea battles).

**Pentad**   Act, scene, agent, agency, and purpose. Kenneth Burke (1897–1993) argued that most social interaction and human communication should be analyzed as a form of drama where the "plot" is shaped by the interactions of the five pentadic elements. Such a method is called a "dramatistic analysis," and Burke saw the relationship between life and theater as literal rather than symbolic. In his view, all the world really is a stage.

**performance studies**   Discipline developed during the past 20 years that expands the notion of what can be considered performance; one of its primary theorists, Richard Schechner, posited a horizontal continuum of performative activities, with ritual on one end, play on the other, and such activities as games, sports, and theatre in between.

**playhouses**    Common term for theatres during the English Renaissance.

**postmodern**    Umbrella term for a philosophy, condition, or movement, depending on one's perspective, in the contemporary world that reflects such characteristics as pastiche, fragmentation, disunity, and suspicion of any one explanation for things, or "grand narratives."

**producer**    Primary individual (or, increasingly, group or corporation) responsible for raising money for a theatrical production.

**proscenium**    Theatre configuration in which the spectators are separated from the performers by a proscenium arch that acts as a frame through which the actors, perspective scenery, and so on are viewed. The audience thus views the production from only one side, the front.

**Sanskrit theatre**    An ancient Indian theatre form, in the language of Sanskrit, which avoided realistic practices and involved codified performance, including elaborate costumes, makeup, and a complex set of movements and gestures known as mudras.

**theatre-in-the-round**    Theatre configuration in which the audience views a performance from four sides; also known as "arena" staging.

**theory**    An intellectual construct created to explain a phenomenon; also termed a hypothesis.

**thrust**    Theatre configuration in which the audience views a performance from three sides, as the stage "thrusts" into the spectator space.

**willing suspension of disbelief**    An audience's willingness to become caught up in the "fantasy" world on stage.

## Key Concepts

- Although judging art can be subjective, standards by which art can be judged have been developed over time and within any given culture.
- There can be as many interpretations of a theatrical production as there are audience members; however, some interpretations may be more valid than others.
- Audience conventions and expectations have shifted over time.
- In today's world, one of the main factors that sets live performance apart from mediatized is the community that exists not only among audience members, but also between actor and audience.
- A good theatre review is a balance of four types of information—description, analysis, interpretation, and judgment—with an engaging lede at the start.

- Theories help to explain and explore various aspects of theatre.
- The dramaturg may serve several crucial roles in a theatre, but in general, functions as the "questioning spirit" or "conscience" of the production.
- Since the Renaissance, theatre has often operated as a business, with various positions created to help ensure that theater artists can make a living at their craft, such as the producer, marketing team, and agent.
- Since the beginning of theatre, those in power have attempted to control it.

# Where Can Performance Be Done?

## Chapter Outline

*To view the figures in this chapter, log on to www.pearsonexploretheatre.com.*

## INTRODUCTION

On a series of occasions in 1977, a group of actresses wearing white coffee-shop-style uniforms burst into the famous Brown Derby restaurant in Los Angeles, CA. Customers watched with bewilderment. What they didn't know was that the actresses were members of a feminist "guerilla" theatre troupe who would select a variety of "found" locations–most not originally intended for performance—in which to perform their protests. One woman posed as "Wonder Waitress," a variation of the Bionic Woman; another actress, armed with oversized radar equipment, ran through the restaurant reporting on hazards to waitresses spotted at fictitious restaurants such as "The Greasy Spoon," "The Hole in the Wall," "The Grinder," and "Mom's Kitchen." The actresses exposed these fake restaurants for discriminatory practices—hiring waitresses strictly for their looks, and then forcing them to run between tables in three-inch heels. Sometimes the group presented "Millie Awards" in an ironic, Oscar-like ceremony, to outstanding area waitresses.

**FIGURES 4.1 AND 4.2**

On another occasion in New York City on March 21, 2001, audiences stood outside of the St. James Theatre awaiting the first preview performance of the greatly anticipated Broadway musical of Mel Brooks's film *The Producers*, likely chatting excitedly among themselves at the prospect of seeing the first live production of a Mel Brooks work. Others, perhaps from out of town, may simply have been thrilled to be seeing a Broadway show. All were aware that they were attending a theatrical event. Although they had no idea whether or not the show would be a success, the expectation that the Broadway context would ensure some level of quality likely increased their excitement. They were not disappointed; the show went on to win a record number of Tony Awards and ran for over six years.

Still in another incident, one of the authors, conducting research for this textbook (really!), joined an Internet chat room for singles. Posing as "Good4U2," she interacted with others in the virtual environment, taking on an identity quite different from her own in "real" life. All performers in the space, also acting as audience for each other, seemed eager to impress, with offers to exchange emails, phone calls, even photos. Although the author physically sat at a computer in Tucson, Arizona, the location of her virtual persona in cyberspace was without limits. Unsure of where the physical manifestation of each performer was, many of the "interactors" seemed eager nonetheless to insure that at least one of the virtual encounters led to an actual encounter, or "date."

**FIGURES 4.3 AND 4.4**

As argued in Chapter 1, all three of these incidents represent performance, with all of the requisite characteristics: actor, action, audience, arena, and arrangement. And as these three episodes illustrate, performance can happen anywhere: in a restaurant, on Broadway, and even on the Internet. The space and location of a performance are crucial aspects of the event as a whole and can have an enormous influence on performers, production elements, and audiences alike. For example, the arrangement or configuration of the space where a performance occurs is important in that it defines the relationship between the actor and spectator, such as in the cyber-performance described above, in which the nature of the chat room location virtually erases distinctions between the two. The formality of the space itself can affect the performance as well. An event in a large hall constructed specifically for the purposes of performance, with a lobby, auditorium, and stage–as is the case in the St. James Theatre mentioned above—connotes quite different meaning than a coffee shop.

Furthermore, the size of the space can influence the event. The theatres of Ancient Greece, which could seat as many as 15,000 people (similar to our modern-day arenas), required quite different performance conventions–and demanded quite different things from the audience–than a performance at the Brown Derby restaurant, which seated about 150 people. Finally, the location of the space can affect the overall experience, from the excitement of attending a Broadway show in Times Square in New York City, to the comforts of sitting in a home office at a computer, to the awe inspired when sitting in the ruins of the Theatre of Dionysus in present-day Athens. Whether or not the space is indoors, as in the former two, or outdoors, as in the latter, can also have an enormous impact on the production.

This chapter explores these variable in more details, describing the four typical theatrical configurations as well as other spaces utilized to create performance, and differentiates between professional and amateur production contexts while considering the diversification of these contexts in America.

**FIGURE 4.5**

**LEARNING OBJECTIVES**

**After reading Chapter 4, our students should be able to:**

* Identify the four typical theatre configurations: proscenium, thrust, arena, and flexible space.

⁑ Recognize other spaces utilized in the creation of theatre.

⁑ Differentiate between professional and amateur production contexts.

⁑ Describe the diversification of theatrical production contexts in America beyond Broadway.

## THEATRE CONFIGURATIONS

The four typical configurations for theatres are the **proscenium**, the **thrust**, the **arena**, and the **flexible space**, with the thrust most common throughout history, and the proscenium most common today. Each configuration provides a different—sometimes drastically so!—viewing experience for its audience, with the first, the proscenium, forcing a separation between actor and spectator more than the others.

**FIGURE 4.6**

### Theatre Configurations: The Proscenium

Probably the most common type of theatre today, and the most formal, is the **proscenium**, also known as the picture-frame stage. The proscenium theatre consists of a raised stage outlined by what is called the *proscenium arch*. This arch is architectural in nature and serves as a picture frame surrounding the view of the action on stage.

Similar to most movie theatres, the audience in a proscenium theatre views the stage straight on, from the front only. In some cases, a part of the stage, called an **apron** or forestage, may extend beyond the arch into the auditorium; however, the actor and audience are typically clearly delineated and separated. Often the actor pretends as if there were a **"fourth wall"** between himself and the audience. This term comes from the idea that the proscenium is an invisible wall through with the audience can see into the other three walls of a room.

**FIGURE 4.7**

In a proscenium theatre, the auditorium is separated from the stage by an orchestra pit. The seats in the auditorium, or **"house,"** may all be on the same level, or, more likely, they are **"raked"** upward toward the rear to improve the view of the stage. Typically, there are multiple levels of seating; the upper level seats are commonly termed balconies or **galleries** and the lower level seats refer to the orchestra. Originally, **"orchestra"** was the term for the circular area in the Greek theatre reserved for the chorus, who acted as both an emotional and physical link to the spectators. (See the description of the thrust configuration, later.) This area literally was situated between the stage and the often large auditorium, just like the present day orchestra. But as the chorus eventually lost its important functions in theatre during classical Rome, so did the orchestra lose its original functions.

The proscenium's stage is often deep, with areas offstage to the sides (called **"wings"**) and behind, as well as above (called the **"loft"**) and under. This arrangement greatly affects the way that designers create the look of the production and offers opportunities for considerable spectacle. They are able to store and manipulate scenery before it is brought onstage, using ropes, cables, turntables, elevators, and other means, both mechanized and not. Because the scenery is only viewed from the front, it need only be two-dimensional; however, the designer can create the illusion of a complete room so that the audience members feel as though they are peering in through a peep-hole (the fourth wall). Costumes, while they may be elaborate, need not have minute details; lighting designers must use light to create three-dimensionality, but only so that it is perceived as such by the audience.

The proscenium was first introduced in Italy during the Renaissance in the sixteenth century in conjunction with the development of perspective scenery; the proscenium was an ideal "frame" through which to view the perspective. Historians are not sure exactly when it first appeared, but it may have been the theatre built in the Uffizi palace in Florence in 1586. However, that theatre no longer stands, and the oldest surviving structure with a permanent proscenium arch, also in Italy at Parma, is the Teatro Farnese, completed in 1618. The configuration began to spread to other parts of Europe, including both France and England, in the later seventeenth century and became the standard theatrical arrangement in the Western world thereafter.

The shape and size of the auditorium in the proscenium theatre since its inception in Italy has shifted over time to meet the needs of both productions and audiences. For example, the first proscenium theatres in England were fairly small spaces, accommodating "drawing room" comedies about intimate subjects and reflecting class divisions in society via special seating for the "elite." In the late seventeenth century, the Drury Lane seated just 650. As the middle class grew in size, so did these auditoriums, shifting even to a fan shape in order to provide better viewing for a larger number of people in a society increasingly concerned with equality. In spite of these changes to the auditorium, the proscenium arch separating that audience from the acting space has remained pretty much the same up to the present.

**FIGURES 4.8 AND 4.9**

## Theatre Configurations: The Thrust

The oldest theatre configuration is the thrust. In this arrangement, the audience sits on three (or even two) sides of the stage, which "thrust" out into the auditorium. The depth of the thrust can differ from theatre to theatre. Like the auditorium of the proscenium theatre, the audience space in a thrust theatre will likely be raked to improve the view of the stage and may include more than one level, although this is less common.

**FIGURE 4.10**

The thrust tends to provide a more intimate experience for the audience because spectators can be closer to the action on the stage. The thrust has more potential for three-dimensionality as opposed to the two-dimensional quality of the proscenium, because instead of merely viewing the production from the front, audiences can view it from two other sides as well. Flat scenery, unless placed far upstage, fails to work in this configuration. However, this arrangement presents certain limitations for the designer, who must avoid blocking **sightlines**. Mechanisms for shifting scenery in the proscenium, where they are easily masked, are generally unavailable in the thrust theatre; thus, scenery is usually shifted by hand, although such devices as elevators, turntables, and **traps** may be utilized.

The ancient Greeks, in the late sixth century BCE, first used the thrust for their tragedies and comedies. They built open-air **amphitheatres** into hillsides to take advantage of the natural rake. The audience sat on stone benches in a semicircle around the circular orchestra, home of the Greek chorus, and stage, nature often visible behind. In the middle of the orchestra, a **thymele**, or altar, signaled the religious importance of the theatrical event in Greek life. Behind the orchestra, the **skene**, or scene house, created a background for the action and provided a backstage area from which actors made entrances and exits. Theatres such as the **Theatre of Dionysus** on the Akropolis in Athens likely could seat as many as 17,000 spectators, although others were considerably smaller.

In the third century BCE, the Romans began to adapt the configuration of Greek theatres for their own dramas; however, because they reduced the orchestra to a semi-circle, their configuration was halfway between proscenium and thrust. Unlike the

Greek theatre, the elaborate scene house (**scaenae frons**) and auditorium were connected and the structure stood on flat ground, not on a hillside.

During the Middle Ages, no permanent theatre structures were built in Europe, most likely due to the transient, somewhat chaotic nature of society during the time, as well as the eventual close connection between theatre and the ubiquitous Catholic Church. But this did not mean that theatre did not happen. Although the church, originally, in its early days, did not condone theatre, a religious theatre developed, sanctioned by the Church, and performed by priests in the cathedrals. At some point later, these dramas moved outdoors and were produced by the **trade guilds**, forerunners to the modern unions, either on moving **pageant wagons**, similar to parade floats, or on stationary platforms set up outdoors.

**FIGURE 4.11**

When permanent theatres were again constructed, just before the time of Shakespeare in the sixteenth century in England, the thrust configuration came to the fore a third time. The playhouse of the English Renaissance was based on temporary theatres set up in the open, inner courtyards of inns. But more permanent theatres were needed to accommodate a growing professional theatre. The London theatres for which Shakespeare wrote, such as the **Globe** on the south bank of the Thames River and the Fortune north of the town walls, contained a roofed thrust and a platform stage with a multi-level façade behind with multiple entrances. Spectators stood in an open area, called the **pit** or yard, where there was standing-room only. Roofed galleries surrounded the pit. The 2,000 or more spectators likely felt a great sense of community within the space, not just with fellow spectators, but with the performers as well, who were no more than 60 feet or so away from any audience member.

**FIGURE 4.12**

In Spain a variation on this kind of thrust arrangement was utilized for the religious drama that continued there after it ended rather abruptly elsewhere in Europe as rulers attempted to gain autonomy from the Church. The use of the thrust gave way to the proscenium until attempts were made in the twentieth century to recreate the circumstances of the original productions of Shakespeare's plays. But the thrust has gained contemporary use beyond such intentions, perhaps as theatre has made attempts to differentiate itself from media such as television and film, the viewing of which recreates the proscenium configuration. Such thrust theatres include the Guthrie in Minneapolis, the Mark Taper Forum in Los Angeles, and the Kalita Humphries Theatre of the Dallas Theatre Center, designed by eminent architect Frank Lloyd Wright. Some classical Asian forms, such as Noh Theatre in Japan and Beijing Opera in China, also utilize the thrust. Both use platform stages, often covered by a roof, and little scenery, with actors making entrances and exits from doors at the rear of the stage. In Noh Theatre, the audience sits to one side and in front of the stage. The relative smallness of the traditional Noh and Beijing Opera stages makes for an intimate experience.

**FIGURE 4.13**

## Theatre Configurations: The Arena

The Arena theatre, or theatre-in-the-round, consists of a stage surrounded on all four sides by the raised audience. Both the benefits and the limitations of the thrust are multiplied in the arena. Spectators feel the greatest sense of intimacy because their seats surround the performance and there is no frame or formal separation between the performers and them. Further, spectators may experience a feeling of community, with their seats arranged in a circle, enabling them to look into the eyes of other spectators at any given time. However, this very set-up creates a real challenge for performers. Actors must always be mindful of the presence of spectators on all sides; they cannot turn their back to one side of the audience more than the other, a particularly difficult task for those used to performing in a proscenium theatre. Set designers have a challenge as well in that they must set the scene with little possibility for masking the mechanisms by which they do so. As a result, arena staging tends to avoid elaborate scenic effects and focuses on acting, costumes, and props.

The arena also places great demands on the director, who must ensure that all elements of the production are conveyed from every angle. Such demands have limited the use of the arena, although such theatres as the **Arena Stage** in Washington, D.C., and the Alley Theatre in Houston have embraced it successfully.

**FIGURE 4.14**

Although, historically, there haven't been many permanent arenas constructed, the circle configuration that is formed around the performers has been fairly common, particularly for more ritualistic performances, as in some Native American or African events, or in some productions of plays during the Middle Ages, performed in earthen "rounds." In ancient Italy, elaborate, large arenas like the **Coliseum** in Rome were constructed to house entertainments often referred to as **paratheatricals**: gladiatorial combats; venationes, or wild animal fights; even naumachiea, which were recreated sea battles in which the floor of the arena would be flooded to accommodate ships. Today the arena is a common configuration for some sports events, such as basketball and hockey, as well as such popular entertainments as concerts and circuses.

**FIGURE 4.15**

## Theatre Configurations: The Flexible Space

Some performances require a flexible space that can be manipulated to meet the needs of the production and its spectators. The most common of these is referred to as the "black box" theatre, and many amateur, educational, and even professional companies have all used this type of theatre. As the name suggests, it is simply an empty space, usually with four walls, often painted black or a neutral color.

The black box is flexible because it can be configured in any of the arrangements discussed earlier, or others, usually with some movable platforms for the stage area and seats for the audience area. It is also used in performances in which the audience is surrounded by the action or moves about the theatre, with scenes staged in various locales around the space (usually requiring a large space). This use of the black box is often referred to as **environmental theatre**, a technique embraced by Richard Schechner during the 1960s with the Performance Group, who still create and perform productions in a converted garage in New York City. During that same decade, Polish director and theorist Jerzy Grotowski explored a similarly innovative use of space with his Polish Laboratory Theatre. In addition, the Theatre du Soleil, led by Ariane Mnouchkine, performed *1789*, a play about the beginnings of the French Revolution, in an abandoned factory in Paris, surrounding the standing audience with platforms on which the action took place. All are examples of dynamic uses of the flexible space.

**FIGURE 4.16**

## Theatre Configurations: Other Spaces

It is important to note that the stage and auditorium are not the only areas utilized in the creation of a production. Besides the backstage spaces already mentioned, various spaces often exist within the larger theatre organization to house all of the varied people who collaborate on making the production happen.

Costumes are often created in a costume shop, which might also include storage areas, dye rooms, laundry facilities, and dressing rooms. The lighting designer and crew usually work in the "**grid**" above the stage and, possibly, the auditorium. There is almost always some kind of **control booth** in which the stage manager "calls the show" and the light and sound boards are housed. The audience usually stands in some kind of lobby or waiting area before the show and during intermission. Some lobbies are tiny or non-existent; others, such as the ornate, elaborate lobbies (note the plural) of the still-existent Opera Garnier in Paris (originally known as the Paris Opera when it was built in the nineteenth century) are nearly as important as the auditorium as places for spectators to see, and be seen, by other prominent citizens. Adjacent to the lobby is some form of box office, or counter that sells tickets. Many theatres even have business offices for all of the personnel who market the shows. Despite the extra space in most theatres, many artists still create theatre with just the bare minimum amount of space—and some with little more than the proverbial "two boards and a passion."

**FIGURE 4.17**

## PRODUCING CONTEXTS

Throughout the history of theatre, these configurations—and theatre in general—have usually been situated in one of two contexts: professional or amateur. **Professional theatre** is undertaken largely by artists who are making their living in theatre; because of this, profit may be the "bottom line." **Amateur theatre** is created by artists whose primary income is not generated or derived from box office sales. Some theatre is a hybrid of the two.

Both professional and amateur contexts can be found throughout the world. For example, theatre in Ancient Greece was largely an amateur endeavor, done relatively infrequently at religious festivals in honor of gods such as Dionysus. So, too, was the religious drama of the Middle Ages, produced by priests in the churches or by members of the trade guilds outside of the churches, members whose primary professions may have been as carpenters, shipbuilders, farmers, and so forth, with the money raised by productions often given to charities. But during the English Renaissance, theatre became more professionalized. Theatre lost its sacred and charitable functions when Elizabeth I, trying to maintain order in a society made chaotic by conflicts between Catholics and those who wished to be autonomous from the Catholic Church, forbade religious subjects in plays. As a result, theatre had little choice but to shift to for-profit functions, and producers built permanent theatres to control paying audiences. Such changes paved the way for artists such as William Shakespeare, who eventually was able to make his living in the theatre, first as an actor, then as a playwright, and finally as a producer. Theatre in the non-Western world has also shifted between professional and amateur, depending on the location, situation, and contexts.

**FIGURE 4.18**

Professional and amateur theatre continue to play a role in contemporary American theatre as well. Although the categories are not always clear, neat, and discrete, in general, professional theatre can be divided into commercial, including Broadway, Off-Broadway, and tours, and not-for-profit, including Off-Off-Broadway and regional theatre. Amateur theatre encompasses primarily both educational and community theatre.

### Producing Contexts: Commercial: Broadway, Off-Broadway, and Tours

In commercial theatres, profit is an important goal. The money earned pays back investors before any of the creative team sees any financial rewards. These investors, or "backers," hope to make a large return. However, as with any investment, risk is involved, and they may lose every dollar of their investment, or in the case of a long-running, award-winning show like *The Producers*, may become wealthy on one show alone. However, investors may also be passionate about supporting and nurturing the creation of new theatre.

**Broadway.**   When many people in the United States think of theatre, they often think of the New York theatre district in **Times Square**. (**Broadway** is actually the name of a street in Manhattan that runs through Times Square.) Broadway theatres are commercial, professional, for-profit organizations, and are therefore costly to attend (with top prices of over $100 per ticket). Audiences tend to be somewhat limited and homogenous—consisting largely of older, white, middle-class-and-above individuals. Some New Yorkers attend Broadway shows, but tourists make up a sizable part of the house.

**FIGURE 4.19**

Mounting a show on Broadway has become almost prohibitively expensive, for a number of reasons. There are a limited number of theatre spaces in the area, and Manhattan real estate prices are notoriously high; consequently, the cost of owning or renting a Broadway theatre is extremely high. Unions regulate the wages of personnel. And the costs of materials needed to build the show have escalated as spectacle becomes the norm rather than the exception.

Both producers and audiences, as investors and as ticket buyers, respectively, are unwilling to take risks due to the high costs. As a result, less and less new material and more and more revivals and shows based on existing, familiar material appear on Broadway. Musicals—the spectacle of which often gives the theatergoer the feeling that they are getting more "bang for their buck"—are more common than non-musical plays. Historically, typical Broadway musicals have followed a common formula, honed during the mid-twentieth century and designed to support and maintain the status quo of society at the time (and beyond). Romantic love between a man and woman, ideally ending in marriage, is emphasized, and characters are not extremely complex. "Blue" material like sex, profanity, and nudity are verboten. Although the creators may—and often do—communicate serious themes, optimism is the overriding tone, and entertainment is the primary objective.

However, there are exceptions to the focus on profits and "safe" material. The TKTS booth in Times Square offers half-price tickets for many shows on the day of the performance. The producers of the musical *Rent*, relatively young themselves at the time the show opened in 1996 and recognizing the opportunity to attract younger audiences, set aside $20 orchestra seats for purchase the day of the show. The producers of *Spring Awakening*, which appeals to young audiences with its cast of teenage characters, have offered similar deals. (However, lines for such cheap-ticket opportunities can be extremely long.)

Musicals such as *Rent* and the 1968 *Hair*, to which it is often compared, offer more challenging subject material (e.g. drug use, profanity, and in the case of *Hair*, nudity) than most musicals, as do a number of recent shows. The very title of *Urinetown* hints at its often tasteless, bathroom-humor subject material. Avenue Q, playing at the Golden Theatre, revels in profanity, sex, and generally raunchy, irreverent humor beneath its seemingly innocuous Sesame Street-like paradoxical veneer, with songs titled "The Internet Is for Porn," "You Can Be as Loud as the Hell You Want (When You're Makin' Love)," and "It Sucks to Be Me." *Spring Awakening* depicts masturbation. However, it is too soon to tell whether such shows signal a change in the tone of twenty-first century Broadway productions.

**FIGURES 4.20 AND 4.21**

**Off-Broadway.**    During the 1950s, artists in New York City seeking alternatives to the increasingly expensive, commercial, conservative Broadway, opened theatres near to, but outside, the Times Square theatre district. Referred to as **Off-Broadway** theatres, these houses were originally, by contract, smaller than their Broadway counterparts, and offered lower salaries for actors and others on the creative teams. Though they were still considered professional theatres, less emphasis was placed on commercialism, so artists could take more risks; new playwrights, directors, and designers could get their work seen. Still, audiences have been—and continue to remain—largely the same as those for Broadway.

In the past 20 years, however, most Off-Broadway theatres have become only slightly less expensive versions of Broadway houses, with Off-Broadway often viewed as a tryout for Broadway, as such with musicals as *Urinetown* and *Avenue Q*. Nonetheless, if it weren't for the opportunities available to artists at some of these theatres, such as the Phoenix Theatre or the Circle in the Square, the work of playwrights such as Tennessee Williams and directors such as Jose Quintero, who both started out in Off-Broadway theatres and became two of the most prominent artists of twentieth-century American theatre, might not have gotten the exposure that Off-Broadway deserves.

**Tours.** Productions of shows originating in New York City—usually, on Broadway—have traveled to cities across the United States since the nineteenth century. Although, historically, Broadway stars toured the country, and nonmusical plays were somewhat common in the repertoire, shows now rarely tour with the original Broadway cast intact and are usually musicals. Also referred to as **road shows**, these productions travel with complete sets and costumes. Although they are largely self-contained, local actors occasionally are employed in the ensemble, or the theatre architecture—usually, a large, proscenium performance hall—is altered to meet the specific needs of the production, as in the tour of *Phantom of the Opera*. Occasionally, a less successful musical finds its home not on Broadway, but on the road.

**FIGURE 4.22**

### Producing Contexts: Not-for-Profit: Off-Off-Broadway, and Regional Theatre

Not-for-profit does not mean that a theatre makes no money or is free; it simply means that all money earned goes back into the operations of the theatre—from personnel to facilities to future productions—instead of to investors. There is still an element of risk, as lack of profit can lead to the demise of the organization and loss of jobs. But this approach can allow more room for risk-taking than commercial theatre.

**Off-Off-Broadway.**    As costs of Off-Broadway shows escalated and restricted opportunities for artistic risk-taking, **Off-Off-Broadway** theatres developed during the 1960s to serve the purposes that Off-Broadway once served—to provide opportunities for artists to take risks and explore the limits of what theatre can be.

These theatres—sometimes in "found" spaces not originally intended for use as theatres—usually feature pared-down production values, with the emphasis often on the text, on the actor, or perhaps even on the audience members and their participation in the theatre event. Although some offerings can appear amateurish, others have been, and continue to be, exciting, stimulating, and even sometimes controversial. One of the most important groups of early Off-Off-Broadway is LaMama Experimental Theater Club, founded by Ellen Stewart in 1961. Still a working organization, LaMama e.t.c. has encouraged experimental techniques and nurtured the work of new playwrights, such as Sam Shepard, and directors, such as Tom O'Horgan, who went on to direct *Hair*. By 1970, the theatre was producing more plays than all Broadway houses combined. Other significant theatres Off-Off-Broadway include the Living Theater, the Open Theater, Mabou Mines, the Performance Group, and the Wooster Group.

**FIGURES 4.23, 4.24 AND 4.25**

**Regional Theatre.**    Nonmusical plays and, sometimes, original work, musicals or otherwise, have found a home in **regional theatre**, or resident theatre, which began as a movement to decentralize theatre from New York City in the 1940s. As a result of this decentralization, cities such as Chicago, Seattle, Atlanta, and San Francisco have thriving theatrical communities. Regional theatre helps make theatre accessible to audiences who might not be able to travel to New York City, and developing young audiences is often one of its missions. Private funding from corporations and foundations, such as the Ford Foundation, has contributed to its development and flourish.

**FIGURE 4.26**

Often organized as **not-for-profit** institutions, regional theatres, free from ties to a group of investors, for whom profit is the bottom and only line, can take more risks than more commercial professional theatre. (Such is the theory, at least: Not-for-profit does not mean that the theatre eschews financial gain; rather, that all profits must be put back into the theatre—e.g. capital improvements or to pay personnel—and not divided among investors.) Increasingly, this producing context serves the function once served by Off-Broadway: as a proving ground for new works. As a result, audiences far from Manhattan sometimes have the opportunity to get a first look at an exciting new work that may eventually play on Broadway.

Regional theatre provides employment for thousands of theatre artists; more actors now work outside New York City than inside. Regional theatres are also excellent training grounds, offering internships and programs for young artists in the profession. Theatres like the Guthrie in Minneapolis, the Dallas Theatre Center, Indiana Repertory Theatre, the Arena Stage in Washington, D.C., and the Mark Taper Forum in Los Angeles are part of a dynamic, important network now referred to by many as America's national theatre.

**FIGURE 4.27**

## Producing Contexts: Amateur Theatre: Educational and Community

Amateur theatre is created by artists whose primary income is not generated through box office sales. In educational settings, artists may make a living at theatre through their work as teachers; in community theatre, many involved make their living at jobs outside of the theatre. All—from students to teachers to a local businesswoman acting in a production as a hobby—tend to share a passion for theatre that supercedes their desire to profit financially from it.

**Educational Theatre**. Educational theatre can be found across the country, from elementary schools through colleges and universities. This type of theatre has become increasingly common in K–12 settings, particularly at the secondary level where theatre opportunities range from being small parts of larger arts classes to elaborate high school drama programs that produce several shows a year and offer a number of courses on acting, stagecraft, and so forth. The International Thespian Conference held each June in Lincoln, Nebraska, is a testament to the importance of theatre at many high schools in the United States.

Theatre programs in colleges and universities make up much of the amateur theatre being done in the United States. At most schools, a student first becomes involved in theatre through extracurricular activities. Later, the student may take some formal classes in drama, often offered through English or classics Departments. George Pierce Baker became one of the founding fathers of theatre training at universities when he offered classes in playwriting, and later, in production, in the early twentieth century at Harvard and Yale. Carnegie Institute of Technology offered the first theatre degree in 1914, and by the 1940s drama departments were becoming common. Now most often referred to as theatre departments, these programs are sometimes organized together with related disciplines such as dance, speech, or film.

The primary goal of many theatre departments is to educate and train future theatre artists on the undergraduate and/or graduate level, depending on the school; however, the mission of some schools, particularly departments housed in smaller liberal arts institutions, might be to utilize theatre as a tool to provide a broader, humanities-based education that could be the basis of any career.

**FIGURE 4.28**

University and college theatre programs provide employment for more theatre artists than any other context, artists who more often than not are individuals dedicated to the teaching profession and to passing on their own knowledge of and passion about theatre. Educational theatre can also serve an important function in the community, particularly in smaller cities without a professional theatre company, providing a wide range of offerings for local audiences. Although, as amateur endeavors, most college or university theatres can operate without the restrictions of professional companies, more and more are relying on box office income for their operating expenses, sometimes limiting the risk-taking other educational theatres might enjoy.

**FIGURE 4.29**

**Community Theatre**. The second most common context for amateur theatre is community theatre. The United States has a long, proud history of providing entertainment and theatrical opportunities for and by local communities. These theatres draw on local talent for all positions in the creation of a production, from the actors to directors, designers, and stagehands. Participants often work full-time jobs during the day unrelated to theatre, working on the show at night and on weekends for the sheer love of theatre.

Like educational theatres, **community theatres** may offer the only theatre available in an area; however, the quality of each show can vary greatly because of the voluntary nature of the participation. Further, because community theatre often offers the first opportunity for people to be exposed to theatre, it often gets a bad "rep" because of its amateur nature (as in the hilarious "mocumentary" film *Waiting for Guffman*). Despite this reputation, some of the world's greatest theatres, such as the Moscow Art Theatre, began as amateur, community endeavors.

**FIGURE 4.30**

## Producing Contexts: Hybrids

Although American theatre has diversified into the contexts already discussed, offering a wide array of options for audiences throughout the United States, in fact some theatres cross the boundaries of these categories, existing fluidly in several of the contexts. For example, a few theatres in Manhattan have managed to eschew geography and work across the three contexts of Broadway, Off-Broadway, and Off-Off-Broadway, blurring the distinctions—stylistically, economically, and contractually—between the three. One of the most influential of these hybrids has been the producing organization now known as the **Public Theater**.

In the late 1950s visionary director Joseph Papp founded the New York Shakespeare Festival to bring free productions to the play-going public, a program so successful that in 1962 the city built the Delacorte Theatre in Central Park as a permanent home for the festival. In 1967, Papp expanded the festival to a year-round, Off-Broadway producing organization at the former Astor Library in Greenwich Village, which he converted to five different performance spaces. Still one of the most vital American theatres, the Public continues to produce Shakespeare's plays in Central Park, but also nurtures the work of an extremely diverse group of playwrights, actors, directors, and other theatre artists. Several of its productions have been produced on Broadway, such as *A Chorus Line, Bring in 'Da Noise, Bring in 'Da Funk, Topdog/Underdog,* and *Take Me Out.*

Papp's practice of nurturing some shows to commercial success on Broadway has proved to be financial genius, as such shows as **A Chorus Line** have provided the funds to produce less commercial, more risky fare. When Papp died in 1991, he was succeeded briefly by JoAnne Akalaitis and then by George C. Wolfe.

**FIGURES 4.31 AND 4.32**

Children's Theatre, also known as theatre for young audiences, often crosses categories as well; whereas education may be a primary goal, a theatre may operate as a professional not-for-profit organization, yet reflect commercial theatre by touring a popular production. Three of the most prominent in the country are the Seattle Children's Theatre, Dallas Children's Theatre, and the Children's Theatre Company in Minneapolis. In amateur, educational university theatre, a professional, equity actor may be brought in for a production to both increase ticket sales and to help train the student actors with which he or she works. Blurring the boundaries between professional and amateur theatre may become more and more common as theatres must find creative ways to attract audiences.

One last area of hybridization that is important to mention here is the question of mediated, as opposed to live, performances. Many of the physical spaces and producing contexts discussed here so far apply to **mediated performances**, too. Although theatrical productions may actually be captured on film, many films and television shows utilize sound stages and studios that can be set up in configurations similar to theatres. Another example is the situation in which television and film may be created "on location," in nature or on streets; in office buildings, homes, or restaurants; and so forth. Mediated performances may occur in the intangible spaces of virtual reality, existing in bits and bytes on the Internet. In other words, mediated performance can occur in much the same—and as varied—spaces as live performance. Finally, just as theatrical professionals move between and among the various producing contexts of live theatre, causing many hybrid forms to emerge, so too do those same professionals move back and forth between mediated and live performance contexts (treated with greater depth in Chapters 9 and 13). In this sense, both the theatrical spaces and contexts and the theatrical artists themselves are thus "hybridized" by the constantly changing forces in the ages-old dance between performers and their audiences.

## For Further Information

Atkinson, Brooks. *Broadway*. Rev. ed. New York, 1974.

Brockett, Oscar G., and Robert R. Findlay. *Century of Innovation: A History of European and American Theatre and Drama Since 1870*. 2nd ed. 1991.

Carlson, Marvin. *Places of Performance: The Semiotics of Theatre Architecture*. 1989.

Charles, Jill, Ed. *Regional Theatre Directory*. 2002.

Jones, Margo. *Theatre-in-the-Round*. 1951.

Langley, Stephen. *Theatre Management and Producing in America: Commercial, Stock, Resident, College, Community, and Presenting Organizations*. 1990.

Roose-Evans, James. *Experimental Theatre: From Stanislavsky to Peter Brook*. Rev. ed. 1984.

Shank, Theodore. *Beyond the Boundaries: American Alternative Theatre*. 2002.

## Suggested Films

The Proscenium: *Stage Beauty* or *The Adventures of Baron Munchausen*

The Thrust Stage: *Shakespeare in Love*

The Arena: *Gladiator*

Broadway: *Broadway: The Golden Age* or *Broadway: The American Musical*

Experimental or Off-Off-Broadway: *Vanya on 42nd Street* or *The Goodbye Girl*

Community Theatre: *Waiting for Guffman*

Chinese Theatre: *Farewell My Concubine*

19th Century Parisian Theatre: *Les Enfants du Paradis*

19th Century English Theatre: *Finding Neverland*

## Glossary

**amateur theatre**   done by artists whose primary income is not generated or derived from box office sales.

**amphitheatre**   an outdoor performance space, often circular with seats sloping toward the stage.

**apron**   also termed the "forestage," it is the area closest to the audience, downstage of the proscenium arch.

**arena theatre**   configuration in which the audience views a performance from four sides; also known as "theatre in the round."

**Broadway**   a street in midtown Manhattan most famous for the concentration of commercial theatres located on and adjacent to it.

**Coliseum**   circular Roman entertainment structure, built in 80 CE to house paratheatricals; its remains still stand.

**community theatre**   theatre produced by amateurs in, by, and for the local communities in which the theatre is situated.

**control booth**   area, often enclosed and at the back of the house, from which the stage manager, light board operator, and, sometimes, sound board operator work to run a production.

**educational theatre**   theatre produced by schools, from K–12 to universities and colleges.

**environmental theatre**   a style of staging that involves flexible, found or transformed, performance space in which actors and audience share the same space; variable focus; and emphasis on all elements of the performance as language, not just the written text, as formulated by Richard Schechner based on the work of such groups as the Polish Laboratory Theatre, the Living Theatre, and the Open Theatre.

**flexible performance space**   a space in which the configuration can be changed from performance to performance; many are known as "black box" theatres.

**Fourth Wall**   an imaginary wall between the actor and audience in a proscenium theatre; a concept that developed in conjunction with realism, the conventions of which held that the stage space was like a room with one wall removed so that the audience could view the action in that room.

**galleries**   also known as balconies, these are audience areas in theatres that historically have been both the highest seats and the cheapest.

**Globe Theatre**   London theatre of the English Renaissance in which many of Shakespeare's plays were produced. Built in 1599, it was destroyed by fire in 1613, rebuilt the next year and then torn down in 1644. A reconstruction sits on the south bank of the Thames near, but not on, the original site.

**grid**   metal scaffolding above the stage and sometimes audience area on which lights are mounted, from which scenery is hung, or from which a follow spot is operated.

**house**   common term for the auditorium or spectator space in a theatre.

**loft**   area above the stage, often used to store scenery that is "flown in."

**mediated performance**   performance that is mediated through technology, such as the lens of the camera or a microphone.

**not-for-profit**   a term largely related to the tax-status of an organization; not-for-profit theatres must insure that profits go not to investors but back into the workings of the theatre, including staff salaries.

**Off-Broadway**   Manhattan theatres located outside of the Times Square district, once experimental but now quite commercial; these tend to be smaller than Broadway theatres.

**Off-Off-Broadway**   theatres outside of the Times Square district that have replaced Off-Broadway theatres as the primary purveyors of experimental, non-commercial theatre in New York City; limited seating capacities often exempt these from union rules and wages.

**orchestra**   1. Originally the circular or half-circular space in classical theatres between the stage and auditorium in which the chorus performed and, later, important people sat. 2. Today it is the audience area closest to the stage on the ground level; seats are often most expensive here.

**pageant wagons**   a movable wagon carrying the set and playing area for the cycle plays of the Middle Ages.

**paratheatricals**   ancient Roman entertainments outside of the theatre structures that housed tragedies and comedies; during the empire they became increasingly common, replacing theatre as the primary form of entertainment. Common types were the gladiatoral combats, chariot racing, venationes (animal fights), and naumachiae (recreated sea battles).

**pit**   also known as the yard, the ground level area in which the "groundlings" stood in theatres of the English Renaissance. This was the cheapest audience area.

**professional theatre**   undertaken largely by artists who are making their living in theatre; because of this, profit may be the "bottom line."

**Proscenium Theatre**   theatre configuration in which the spectators are separated from the performers by a proscenium arch that acts as a frame through which the actors, perspective scenery, etc. are viewed. The audience thus views the production only from one side, the front.

**The Public Theater**    Manhattan organization founded by Joseph Papp in the late 1950s; it has bridged successfully the differences between commercial, experimental, and not-for-profit theatre in its various producing arms

**raked stage**    stage slanted upwards from the apron area at the proscenium arch to the back of the performance area; enhances perspective scenery but can be difficult for actors to walk on.

**regional theatre**    theatre originated outside of New York City; the term usually refers to professional companies, often not-for-profit.

**road shows**    also known as touring shows, most often these are productions of shows originated in New York City that travel across the country after obtaining success on Broadway.

**scaenae frons**    the scene house of the ancient Roman theatre, which included a back stage area as well as the facade behind the stage; much more elaborate than the Greek skene.

**sightlines**    refers to how well the audience can view the stage; architectural columns and posts may sometimes exist that block the sightlines.

**skene**    the scene house of the ancient Greek theatre, which included a back stage area as well as the facade behind the stage.

**Teatro Farnese**    oldest surviving structure with a permanent proscenium arch, built in Parma, Italy, in 1618.

**Theatre of Dionysus**    ancient Greek amphitheatre in Athens situated on the hillside of the Akropolis; first site of tragedy. Its ruins still stand today.

**Times Square**    area in midtown Manhattan that has become synonomous with commercial American theatre, particularly Broadway, a street that intersects with the square. TKTS, the discount ticket "booth" for New York City theatres, is located here; it recently underwent extensive renovation and expansion.

**thrust stage**    configuration in which the audience views a performance from three sides, as the stage "thrusts" into the spectator space

**thymele**    the altar in ancient Greek theatre situated at the center of orchestra.

**trade guilds**    the Medieval equivalent to modern-day unions, which protected the rights of tradespeople and craftsmen throughout much of Europe. They served as producers of cycle plays at such events as the Corpus Christi festivals.

**trap**    area in stage floor through which actors, scenery, etc. can appear and disappear; may simply be an opening or include complicated macinery for raising and lowering.

**wings**    1. area offstage to the sides in a proscenium theatre; actors "wait in the wings" to go on. 2. The scenery used in this area, placed parallel to the front of the stage at the sides behind the proscenium; often combined with painted drops upstage in "wing-and-drop" scenery.

## Key Concepts

- Theatre can occur in a variety of spaces with a number of different configurations, such as proscenium, thrust, and arena.
- The thrust and proscenium configurations have been the most common historically.
- The stage space is only one among many utilized in the creation and viewing of performance.
- Theatre can occur in various producing contexts, both professional and amateur.
- Although American theatre has become, in many ways, synonomous with the commercial theatre produced in and around Broadway, there exists a vital American theatre in regional, educational, and community theatres.

# 5

# Playwrights

## Chapter Outline

Introduction

Learning Objectives

The Playwrights in History

Types of Playwrights

Playwriting Methods and Processes

Training and the Profession

For Further Information

Suggested Films

Glossary

*To view the figures in this chapter, log on to www.pearsonexploretheatre.com.*

## INTRODUCTION

Theatre is a handcrafted product in a world of mass production. The term for one of the most important players in much of theatre production, playwright, reflects this fact. The word "wright" means "maker"; a wheelwright handcrafts a wheel, a shipwright constructs ships, and a playwright makes a play by hand. And, unlike workers in a factory who may toil alongside thousands of other workers to create their product, the playwright's process is often a solitary, isolated one. (See the section "Types of Playwrights.") Her independence is somewhat ironic, given the collaborative nature of creating theatre, as is the fact that the other members of the production team—from the actors to the designers to the director—would have little to do without the blueprint that is often created by the playwright, in whatever form it takes.

**FIGURE 5.1**

The act in which playwrights engage, playwriting, correctly includes the word "writing," because playwrights do write. But this word is an incomplete description of their complex process, which perhaps is more accurately described as crafting a play. For, unlike the poet or writer of fiction or nonfiction, the playwright is creating words for actors to speak and for audiences to hear, as well as the silences and images that are communicated on stage, and he is more akin to the screenwriter for film or television. He creates actions, not just words. And the words that are spoken by the actors—**monologues** and **dialogue**—are never the same as everyday speech, but more intense, active, selective, and compressed.

Although playwrights may be viewed as poets (as in classical Western traditions) or literary artists in some contexts, playwrights are theatre artists and as such are quite different from other writers, having chosen, for one reason or another, to create in a medium that is never complete in and of itself.

**FIGURE 5.2**

### LEARNING OBJECTIVES

**After reading Chapter 5, you will be able to:**

* Explain the history of the playwright's role and status.
* Describe different types of playwrights: individuals; teams; collectives; playwrights who are also actors, directors, and/or designers; and "play doctors."
* Discuss some common methods and processes in playwriting.
* Describe some options for and benefits of formal training for playwrights.

## THE PLAYWRIGHTS IN HISTORY

Except for the actor, the playwright is the earliest role in the history of theatre and, historically, often has combined playwriting with other positions in the creative process. In ancient Greece, both Thespis and Aeschylus were actors, and most playwrights served as what we would today call directors for productions of their own plays. Playwriting during the height of ancient Greek theatre, the fifth century BCE, was not a profession, but instead was considered an important contribution to civic life, with great honor bestowed on playwrights who won festival competitions like the one at the City Dionysia.

Later in Greece, and then in the Roman world, playwriting was professionalized, but still relatively esteemed, and although the works of only a handful of these playwrights exist today, we know the names of many more. Not true for playwrights of the very Christian, Catholic Middle Ages, who—with a few exceptions, like the ninth-century German nun Hrosvitha—were anonymous, eschewing any individual honor, or identification and writing plays for the glory of God or the community. The **cycle plays** of the Middle Ages, in fact, are identified by the town or city that produced them, such as the York or Wakefield cycles. Likewise, perhaps due to similarly close religious ties, many plays of classical non-Western theatrical traditions such as **Noh, Beijing Opera**, or **Sanskrit theatre**, were written by anonymous authors. Some may have been scripted by extremely prominent citizens, such as King Sudraka, possible playwright of the celebrated Sanskrit work *The Little Clay Cart* (some scholars dispute his authorship).

During the Renaissance, as theatre became increasingly professionalized, so did the position of playwright, although few copyright laws existed to protect their works as commodities—and valuable commodities they sometimes were. Once a playwright such as Shakespeare sold a script to a company, he no longer retained any rights to it, and it could be altered at will. Furthermore, plays were not revered as literature and thus often were not "published" until much later, if at all. (Shakespeare's plays were not published until 1623, seven years after his death.) This system of flat fees for plays continued until the late eighteenth century, when the first law granting **royalties** (fees per performance) was passed in France, still, it took a while for such practices to become common.

In spite of the growing professional status of the playwright through the Renaissance and the **Neoclassical Age**, his or her position in society was one of contradictions; although playwrights were valued for their talents that contributed to the entertainment and enlightenment of society, their involvement with the stage often made them morally suspect, not unlike actors. This point of view made it particularly difficult for women to engage in the profession, although some did, such as Aphra Behn, the first professional female playwright in England, and Susana Centlivre, who wrote in the period after Behn.

**FIGURE 5.3**

The growing importance of the individual and "artist as genius" in the Age of Enlightenment and then the Romantic Movement lent some cachet to being a playwright. But the growing middle class of the nineteenth century and its demand for entertainment led to the perception of the playwright as "hack," someone churning out material for the masses, that was perceived to have little of the literary value of such writers as Shakespeare, Moliére, or Goethe. Not until the late nineteenth century, when writers such as Ibsen, Chekhov, and Shaw began to address socials ills, did the status of the playwright begin to rise. It has remained generally high ever since, although relatively few can afford to make their living exclusively as writers for the stage.

**FIGURE 5.4**

## TYPES OF PLAYRIGHTS

In a sense, we are *all* playwrights, constantly creating the scenarios of our lives. Our most theatrical scenarios are literally dreamed up each night as we sleep, our subconscious creating characters, dialogue, entire worlds—sometimes, bizarre ones. But not everyone can translate their dreams, or their own lives or the lives of others, to the page and then to the stage. And those who can are an extraordinarily diverse group.

**FIGURE 5.5**

Most play texts, at least initially, are written by individuals. Done frequently as solo work, playwriting can thus be quite isolating (albeit, perhaps necessarily so). American playwright Tennessee Williams wrote of the isolation he often felt: "We're all of us sentenced to solitary confinement inside our own skins, for life!" Rabindranath Tagore, an Indian playwright who won the Nobel Prize for Literature in 1913, once intoned, "Life's errors cry for the merciful beauty that can modulate their isolation into a harmony with the whole."Increasingly, though, in the contemporary process of play development, most playwrights, at some point, collaborate with others, including dramaturgs, directors, and others who may become involved in the play's journey to the stage. Tracy Letts's Pulitzer Prize- and Tony Award-winning *August: Osage County*, for example, is inextricably tied to its development at Chicago's Steppenwolf Theater Company.

Some playwrights choose to write as teams. For example, George S. Kaufman and Moss Hart collaborated on the popular American comedy *You Can't Take It With You*. Jerome Lawrence and Robert E. Lee together wrote *Inherit the Wind*, which enjoyed a critically acclaimed Broadway revival in 2007. More commonly, writers collaborate on the book, or libretto, of a musical, although the librettists are far less likely than playrights to work on an original idea, engaging instead in adaptation.

Taking the collaborative notion to its extreme are playwrights who write as collectives, or in groups (often, still dominated by one person). This type of playwriting became more common in the United States during the 1960s, as theatre artists and companies, such as the Living and Open Theatres, sought working methods alternative to those of the mainstream. Some feminist theatre groups in the 1970s also embraced **collective creation** as an alternative to perceived male isolationist models of playwriting. A contemporary example of collective creation is Moisés Kaufman's collaboration with the New York-based Tectonic Theater Project on the important piece *The Laramie Project*, a response to the 1998 murder of gay Wyoming college student Matthew Shepard.

Other types of playwrights include those whose work goes hand in hand with their work as directors, designers, or actors. The German playwright Bertolt Brecht, for example, also regularly directed his own work. Sam Shepard's plays have been informed by his work as an actor, just as French playwright Yasmina Reza's acting has influenced her works. Seventeenth-century French actor, director, and playwright Moliére died a few hours after performing the title role of a hypochondriac in one of his own plays, *The Imaginary Invalid*.

Finally, the work of some playwrights may fall into the category of what has been called the "**play doctor**" a writer called in at the last minute to fix a "flawed" play. This usually occurs at out-of-town tryouts of a play or musical and thus is a kind of pandering to audience tastes. Perhaps the most famous playwright of this type was Abe Burrows; in fact, the phrase "Get me Abe Burrows!" became Broadway shorthand for a script that needed repairs. (But it must be noted that Burrows won a Pulitzer Prize with his collaborator Frank Loesser for the popular musical *How to Succeed in Business Without Really Trying*.) Today, collaborations with dramaturgs are one way that playwrights can avoid the need for such last-minute changes.

**FIGURE 5.6**

## PLAYWRITING METHODS AND PROCESSES

Playwrights' methods and processes can vary greatly, but a look at playwrights who work largely independently can show some common elements. Any playwright's process must begin with an idea, with inspiration, and this can come from anywhere: one or more experiences in the playwright's life, contemporary socio-political or historical events, a story that the playwright has read, an object, a dream, an image, and so on. Suzan Lori-Parks, author of such works as *Topdog/Underdog* and *365 Days/365 Plays*, has written, according to the *New York Times*, about what she saw outside an airplane window! Almost anything can spark the playwright's desire to create.

**FIGURE 5.7**

Some theatre artists believe that it is necessary to write only about what you know (e.g., they would argue that a white playwright cannot write about the black experience, as a playwright like August Wilson can); others see no subject as off limits. Indeed, late British playwright Sarah Kane, who committed suicide in 1999, wrote of her mental illness in her final play *4.48 Psychosis*. Her *Blasted* confronts the brutality of modern warfare with scenes of rape and cannibalism.

Once a playwright is inspired, she might create a general plot outline. Some playwrights begin by writing the first scene. Others start with the final scene and work backwards. At some point, they must begin to construct dialogue and stage directions; a good working knowledge of all of the concepts outlined in Chapter 2 is essential. The writer may not even be conscious of overall themes and structure until later in the process. Regardless of an individual's methods, the oft-quoted axiom that playwriting is not about writing, but about *rewriting* is an apt one, and the creation of a "final" draft of the play can be a long-term laborious process, taking months or even years.

Even when a playwright deems a play complete and sends it off to theatres for potential production, if it is selected and the playwright is involved, the play still may be altered in the production process. The process called "new play development" may include readings of the plays—from actors sitting around a table **reading** the script to a "staged" **reading** during which actors move around, script in hand—and **workshops**, in which repeated rehearsed readings or performance give the playwright the chance to revise the play over time. The Eugene O'Neill Theatre Center in Waterford, Connecticut; the New York Theatre Workshop in Manhattan; the Victory Gardens Theatre in Chicago; and the New Harmony Project in Indiana are four sites that nurture playwrights and their work through workshopping.

Festivals of new plays such as the one at the Actors Theatre of Louisville also are important venues in which playwrights can get their plays heard and seen in order to obtain crucial feedback for further development of the work. Professional productions of new plays and musicals may require revisions right up to opening night. Even when a play is "finished" and disseminated in print form through publication, an author might alter it, as Tennessee Williams did years later with many of his early plays.

## TRAINING AND THE PROFESSION

As mentioned earlier in this chapter, few writers are able to engage in playwriting as their sole profession. Many playwrights also work in other areas of theatre, as well as screenwriting or other types of professional writing. The economics of contemporary theatre, particularly in the United States, dictate that a relatively small number of plays are ever professionally produced.

**FIGURE 5.8**

Membership in such groups as the Dramatists Guild ("the only professional association which advances the interests of playwrights, composers, and lyricists writing for the living stage," according to its website) and ASCAP, or the American Society of Composers, Authors and Publishers, can aid the playwright in negotiating this often complex profession. These groups can help a playwright navigate through the tricky system of copyrights and royalties that ensure that the playwright does get paid when her plays are produced.

Some playwrights receive little formal training, whereas others pursue general BAs in theatre, or professional training in BFA or MFA programs. Critics of such programs question the ethics of training playwrights for extremely limited job opportunities, but degree programs can provide the playwright with general information about theatre, specialized knowledge, and connections, and liberal arts degrees can provide a wealth of information from which the playwright can draw.

One important contact that professional training programs might lead to is an agent. More and more playwrights turn to agents for help in getting their work read by literary managers and producers, who at some theatres receive thousands of manuscripts each year. But without connections, obtaining an agent is difficult, because agents are paid based on a percentage of their clients' earnings, and thus choose to represent only those whom they carefully select on the basis of their perceived potential to succeed.

This potential can come from certain techniques that can be taught and learned. A playwright can learn the elements of a certain style, and he can choose to adhere to or rebel against that form. In order to be "successful" more than two hundred years ago in Europe, playwrights conformed to the dictates of the Neoclassical Rules, codified by the French Academy and disseminated throughout Europe. But author Victor Hugo consciously chose to flout those rules, and his play *Hernani* was so popular with audiences that neoclassicism became obsolete, paving the way for new styles.

**FIGURE 5.9**

The *art* of playwriting, however, is something that really can't be learned; it is based on innate instincts and talents. Through a combination of both art and technique, the playwright has the best chance of successfully engaging in one of the most rewarding actions a human can undertake: creating something from nothing.

**FIGURE 5.10**

## For Further Information

Bigsby, C.W.E. *Contemporary American Playwrights*. 1999.

Cohen, Edward M. *Working on a New Play*. 1997.

Cole, Toby, Ed. *Playwrights on Playwriting*. 2001.

Davis, Tracy C., and Ellen Donkin, Eds. *Women and Playwriting in Nineteenth-Century Britain*. 1999.

Euba, Femi. *Poetics of the Creative Process: An Organic Practicum to Playwriting*. 2005.

Hall, Roger A. *Writing Your First Play*. 2nd ed. 1998.

*The Internet Movie Script Data Base* (an electronic resource of film scripts that can be read and discussed).

Packard, William. *The Art of the Playwright*. 1997.

Savran, David. *In Their Own Words: Contemporary American Playwrights*. 1988.

Smiley, Sam. *Playwriting: The Structure of Action*. 1971.

Sweet, Jeffrey. *The Dramatist's Toolkit*. 1993/2000.

Wright, Michael. *Playwriting in Process: Thinking and Working Theatrically*. 1997.

Wright, Michael, and Elena Carrillo, eds. *The Student's Guide to Playwriting Opportunities*. 1998.

## Suggested Films

*Author! Author!* (1982): A working playwright balances a hectic life with the demands of his yet imperfect script.

*Bullets Over Broadway* (1994): A classic Woody Allen farce that skewers those playwrights willing to do anything to get produced.

*The Libertine* (2004): Based on historical figures, this provocative tale of power, art, and friendship showcases English Restoration theatre and several types of performance modes.

*Shakespeare in Love* (1998): Written by Tom Stoppard and Marc Norman, this film imaginatively depicts a possible path that might have guided Shakespeare to his famous tragedy *Romeo and Juliet*.

*Something's Gotta Give* (2003): A romantic comedy that shows how a successful playwright, Erica (Diane Keaton), uses her own life to create the plays that have made her famous.

## Glossary

**Beijing Opera**    A classical traditional Chinese form that combines music, dance, and speech with elaborate, codified costumes, makeup, and movement.

**collective creation**    The collaboration on the creation of a play and/or production by a group of writers, actors, directors, etc.

**cycle plays**    Medieval plays, also known as mystery plays, based on stories from the Bible and elaborately staged, often during Christian festivals.

**dialogue**    Actual words spoken between and among the characters.

**monologue**    A long speech delivered by a single character in a play.

**Neoclassical Age**    A period in Europe during and after the Renaissance characterized by a renewed interest in the "classics" of Greece and Rome, such as the philosophies of Aristotle or the plays of Seneca. During this period, many in positions of power urged artists and writers to follow the "Neoclassical Rules," a sometimes-distorted interpretation of classical culture.

**Noh**    A classical Japanese form created in the fourteenth century; emphasizes minimalism as a reflection of the influences of Zen Buddhism.

**play doctor**    A writer who fixes a "flawed" play at the last minute in a production process; no longer common as such.

**reading**    The script-in-hand verbal communication of the words of a play, usually early in the play's development. The actors or readers may sit or engage in a staged reading with blocking.

**royalties**    The fees per performance granted to the author (and his or her representatives) of a play.

**Sanskrit theatre**    An ancient Indian theatre form, in the language of Sanskrit, which avoided realistic practices and involved codified performance, including elaborate costumes, makeup, and a complex set of movements and gestures known as mudras.

**workshops**    "Tests" of new plays, more fully produced than readings, often conducted to gauge audience reactions of, or obtain financial backers for the project.

## Key Concepts

- Playwriting is often a solitary process that involves much more than just writing; playwrights create actions, not just words.
- Except for the actor, the playwright is the earliest role in the history of theatre.
- Although the position of playwright became more professionalized during and after the Renaissance, few are now able to make their full living at it.

- Playwrights usually begin with an idea or insipation of some sort, although their working methods from there can vary drastically.
- Although training is not necessary to write plays, it can help the author build on innate talents to become a better writer and theatre artist.

# Directors

## Chapter Outline

*To view the figures in this chapter, log on to www.pearsonexploretheatre.com.*

## INTRODUCTION

The concept of the director in theatre is a relatively recent one. Before the advent of an autonomous director, largely in the nineteenth century, actors and playwrights were the artists who most commonly attempted to control the creation of theatre; evidence suggests that Shakespeare served this function for productions of his own plays. Sometimes, no one supervised the overall process, leading to a lack of unity among the elements.

**FIGURE 6.1**

But before realism, this lack of unity was not a concern; neither did questions of stylistic interpretation or of the choice of acting method arise. Conventions were firmly set, from theatrical traditions in classical Greece, Rome, and Asia, to Europe during the Middle Ages and beyond. Greek playwrights such as Aeschylus served primarily organizational roles when staging their plays, as did the Medieval precursor to the director, the pageant master.

From the seventeenth to the nineteenth centuries, the **actor-manager** became the norm, in which a person whose primary role in a theatre was to act took over other duties related to directing as well. Moliére, for example, acted in, wrote, and oversaw the production of many of the plays in which his company performed in France of the late seventeenth century. During the eighteenth century, David Garrick became one of England's most popular actor-managers, and in Germany, Caroline Neuber became one of Europe's earliest.

**FIGURE 6.2**

But the term "director"—and its modern connotations—did not come into common usage until the late nineteenth century, when the advent of realism led to the need for someone to help oversee and unify the various aspects of the production.

Georg II, the Duke of Saxe-Meiningen, is considered by many to be the first modern director. At his German court theatre in the late nineteenth and early twentieth centuries, he created productions with an unheard of, until then, attention to historical accuracy, organization of crowd scenes, and ensemble work. His productions, which toured extensively, influenced some of the most significant modern directors, such as Konstantin Stanislavski.

**FIGURE 6.3**

**LEARNING OBJECTIVES**

**After reading Chapter 6, you will be able to:**

- Explain the main tasks of a director—working with the text, working with the designers, working with the actors, and coordinating all elements of the production—and what each task involves.
- Discuss the difference between directing and producing.
- Describe different types of directors, such as directors who work in service to the text; auteurs; "slash" directors (e.g., director/choreographer, director/designer); and directors who emphasize certain themes or influences (e.g., interculturalism).
- Describe some options for and benefits of formal training for directors.

## WHAT IS DIRECTING?

Three primary activities can be said to underlie everything that a director does: creation, collaboration, and problem solving. Creativity should be a the root of all decisions and choices made by the production team, and the director should guide them in this. But this creativity is always collaborative; directors rarely work in a vacuum, instead of pulling together the best ideas of the production team to support the success of the show, however that is defined. Inevitably various challenges arise during the process, and the director serves at the leader in meeting those challenges. Indeed, the modern director performs myriad tasks, most of which fall under four categories: working with the text, working with the designers, working with the actors, and coordinating all elements of the production (all of which often overlap).

**FIGURE 6.4**

## WHAT IS DIRECTING?: WORKING WITH THE TEXT

Most of the director's work with the text, if there is one, occurs early in the production process. She might be involved in selecting the play or at least approving the script, although this is not always the case. Plays are selected according to a number of factors that can depend on the context in which the play will be produced: the director's likes and dislikes, the pool of actors available for roles, the preferences of the targeted audience, and the educational value of the text (particularly at schools). Sometimes, plays are chosen by a director, a producer, or an artistic director; sometimes, a committee is involved. Once the play is chosen, the director often works to create an overall concept for the production. In order to do this, she must engage in very close analysis and interpretation of the text.

**FIGURE 6.5**

After several readings, a director may start with an assessment of the strengths and weaknesses of the play, paying particular attention to the challenges that the play may present—to the actors, the designers, the audience, and to himself—and may begin to brainstorm ways to meet the challenges. The director then should apply the basics of play analysis outlined in Chapter 2 in order to come to a better understanding of the text. This analysis must be both broad and deep, and the skills of a **dramaturg** may be utilized at this point. Dramaturgs are a relatively recent addition to the artistic team, but are found increasingly in both professional and academic theatre.The director must pay particular attention to mood or tone, the ideas he would like to communicate, location and period, and the progression of the action, as well as consider which of Aristotle's six parts to focus on. For example, will the production emphasize the characters and their relationships, with minimal sets and props? Or is spectacle most important, to communicate meaning visually through the set, lights, and costumes? Finally, a director often will conduct research, sometimes, again, with the aid of a dramaturg, in order to understand the context of the play—the author, the societal conditions in which it was written, earlier productions, and so on. If the play is new, the director may work with the playwright and dramaturg to understand both the text and the context.

**FIGURE 6.6**

The analysis and interpretation of the text is an ongoing process, but at some point early in the production process, most directors work to shape these into an overall concept for the show. Much has been written about the modern director's conceptualization of a play for production. The concept is a short, distilled statement that communicates the director's overall vision. The statement may be an image, an action, a philosophical statement, or a metaphor. Regardless of which form the statement takes, it guides all future decisions about the process, all of which are unified under the umbrella of the concept. (Not all directors work conceptually, with unification of elements as a goal. Alternatives will be discussed later.)

## WHAT IS DIRECTING?: WORKING WITH THE DESIGNERS

Once a concept is established, it is conveyed to the design team, and the director begins collaborating with artists like the scenic and costume designers. This process often starts months before rehearsals, with a series of design conferences in which the concept is honed with feedback from the designers, who then begin to play quite broadly with ideas and images. These ideas and images then begin to take shape into more specific choices, with all members of the design team consulting with each other, as each choice affects all the others.

For example, a director of Martin McDonagh's play *The Pillowman*, a "whodunit" about a storyteller and his brother, set in a totalitarian state in which a serial killer is at work, may decide that an overriding image for her production is "containment." The set and lighting designers might then work to create a cramped, confined space on stage to convey that concept.

**FIGURES 6.7 AND 6.8**

Once designs are agreed upon, each artist works somewhat independently of the others in order to realize her designs for the stage, consulting regularly with the director, often during regular production meetings. The director's ability to communicate with the design team, to shape the overall production, and attend to the practical aspects while still allowing the various artists the freedom to instill the show with their own aesthetic, is crucial. All of the design elements are integrated into the show, at the end of the rehearsal process, during a series of technical rehearsals.

## WHAT IS DIRECTING?: WORKING WITH THE ACTORS

The director's work with the actors begins with **casting** and may be done in conjunction with a producer or casting director. The director is scrutinizing the actors' physical appearance, vocal work, personality, potential, presence, and overall abilities in order to match an actor to a specific role. (See Chapter 9 for more information about auditions.) Casting is, arguably, the most important part of the production process, and although governed by some concrete elements, it is ultimately quite subjective and reliant on the director's instincts. Once the roles are cast, a director may post a cast list, as in university theatres, or contact the actors directly or through agents. Rehearsals usually begin shortly afterward.

**FIGURE 6.9**

The rehearsal process can be as brief as a few weeks for a play, or as long as eight weeks or more for a musical; some rare productions rehearse for longer periods. Rehearsals may begin with **table work**, in which the performers read through and discuss the text, often while sitting around a table. Soon comes the process of staging the play, or "getting it on its feet"; this is key because most plays were written to be produced, not merely read. Initially, the actors rehearse with scripts in hand, but are encouraged to memorize their lines, or work "off book," as soon as possible. Individual scenes are rehearsed until the director feels ready to run entire acts.

All the while, actors are exploring their characters' motivations and relationships with other characters, solidifying these as time goes on according to the director's constant feedback. Some directors may use **improvisation**, or exercises that that emphasize immediate responses as opposed to rehearsed behavior, in order to aid the actors in exploring their roles and onstage relationships.

Directors also guide the actors in moving about the space, in relation to each other and to the furniture, as well as entrances and exits. This process of directing the physical movement is known as **blocking**. Directors also coordinate **stage business** or activities in which the actor engages during the performance. Beforehand, the director and scene designer will have worked out a **ground plan**, or the dimensions of the playing area on stage, and the stage manager oversees the taping of an outline of that area onto the rehearsal room floor.

**FIGURE 6.10**

Some directors completely pre-block the play before rehearsals begin, making only minor adjustments throughout staging; others prefer to allow the actors to improvise their characters' movements and then "fix," or set, the blocking before the performances. Many directors employ a combination of both.

When blocking, the director uses a standardized stage vocabulary and shorthand for stage areas and certain movements. For example, on a proscenium stage, *upstage* refers to the rear of the acting area; *downstage* refers to the front, closer to the audience. *Stage right* and *stage left* are from the actor's perspective, facing the audience. The director can then use a combination of these to communicate: "Move down right" or "up center." Actors may be asked to "turn" or "cheat" out, meaning to face the audience more. To "take stage" means to make a small movement downstage, which puts the focus more on that actor. Because movements "pull focus," or draw attention to the performer moving—and can communicate as much as words do—they have to be used judiciously and with careful timing.

During staging, the director must pay attention both to the details of each actor's blocking and stage business and to the overall picture that is created by all of the actors at any given time on stage, sometimes called composition and **picturization**. This process can become considerably complex, particularly in crowd scenes, when the director's process is often jokingly referred to as "traffic control." Balance is important, to ensure that no one stage area is filled with actors more than another during the course of the production, as is height or level, because the most elevated performer is likely to pull focus.

The director is perhaps most often held responsible, by audiences and critics alike, for the pacing of a show, which involves more than how quickly or slowly actors say their lines. What does (or does not) happen between the lines is as important. Pacing can be intuitive, although certain styles of theatre may dictate it: Farce requires fast pacing, whereas a psychological drama requires slower pacing to enable the audience to grasp deep, complex motivations. But most productions vary the tempo throughout, depending on the mood of the scene or the character. Although the actors sometimes adjust the pacing during performance, a good director will instill in them a sense of appropriate tempo.

**FIGURE 6.11**

Throughout the rehearsal process, repetition is key in order to solidify lines, blocking, business, and other aspects of the production. However, these aspects should not be repeated so much that they become stale before an audience views them. In performance, the actors must appear fresh, as if they are engaging in the world of the character and the play for the first time.

The last phase of the rehearsal process is the technical rehearsals, in which all elements of the production are integrated. This is often the first time that the performers rehearse in the actual performance space, and the first time they get to act with costumes, sets, lights, real props, and sound. Because the focus in tech rehearsals is on these elements, not on the acting, the actors' choices should be solidified at this point. Still, many adjustments are made to all aspects of the production. Some directors invite select people to the final dress rehearsals in order to get a sense of audience response. But, once the show opens, the director's job is done.

## WHAT IS DIRECTING?: COORDINATING THE PRODUCTION

In general, the director oversees the planning and coordination of many aspects of the production, although she may have numerous people to help. Assistant directors may run some rehearsals, take notes for the director at others, or simply provide another eye to view the process. The dramaturg may assist with script analysis and preparation, and research, and, like the assistant director, also serve as a pretend audience member or in-house critic. The stage manager, discussed in Chapter 8, is indispensable to the director; he coordinates the rehearsals and the running of the performances. Furthermore, much of what the director does or does not do is determined by the presence—or absence—of a producer.

**FIGURES 6.12, 6.13, AND 6.14**

## WHAT IS PRODUCING?

As detailed in *Chapter 3*, the producer bears mentioning briefly here, as he or she plays a role similar to the director in seeing the big picture of the process of creating theatre. Producers oversee all financial and managerial aspects of the production. As Oscar G. Brockett and Robert J. Ball wrote: "The producer is concerned with the business of show business." There is always someone in a theatre in this role, even if he or she may not be called by this title. On Broadway, or in London on the West End, the producer is rarely an artist, but instead more of a business person—or, more commonly, persons—responsible for raising money to finance the show; overseeing the budget; hiring of the creating team and actors; dealing with unions; procuring the space and supervising those who run the theatre; and overseeing the advertising.

One of the most notorious, but successful, producers in recent American theatre history was David Merrick; winner of numerous Tony Awards, Merrick produced such hits as *Hello, Dolly!, Oliver*, and *Gypsy*. But his autocratic personality is suggested in the title of one unauthorized biography, *David Merrick: The Abominable Showman*, and in a quotation attributed to him, "It is not enough that I should succeed—others should fail."

**FIGURE 6.15**

In commercial theatre today, the producer is rarely an individual; instead, partnerships and conglomerates of individuals or corporations, like the Nederlander Group, Jujamcyn, or Disney, serve this function. The Shubert Organization owns at least 16 of 38 Broadway theatres, thus controlling a significant portion of production on Broadway.

Throughout the history of American theatre, such control has made many theatre artists nervous. For example, in 1896, a group of businessmen known as the Syndicate gained a near monopoly on production on Broadway, as well as across the country through the shows they toured. Concerned primarily with making money, they discouraged innovation, keeping American theatre stagnant. Individuals such as David Belasco worked against their monopoly, but it was not until around 1915 that the monopoly was broken—by the Shubert Brothers. Their goals differed little from those of the Syndicate, however, and, as mentioned, their control continues until today.

What makes artists even more nervous is the potential control of Broadway by such corporations as Disney, whose enormously successful productions of *Beauty and the Beast, The Lion King,* and *Mary Poppins* have been accompanied by the purchase of theatres and retail space, as well as the merchandising for which Disney is well known. Others argue that the Disneyfication of Broadway is revitalizing the area and attracting families to a district that had become increasingly unsafe and seedy. Despite artists' fears, someone or something must be in charge in the role of producer because creating the handcrafted product of theatre in a world of mass production has become increasingly expensive, and producers are a vital link in its creation.

**FIGURES 6.16 AND 6.17**

## TYPES OF DIRECTORS

Although modern directors tend to perform many of the same tasks, their methods and approaches can vary widely. Two of these stand in relation to the director's views on the text.

Since the late nineteenth-century beginnings of direction as a singular, leading position in the theatre, many directors have taken an almost worshipful view of the text, attempting to communicate the author's intentions to the audience through their production. The director's process is in service to the playwright, and respect for the play is of paramount importance. Such directors often translate quite literally the world of the play as written by the author. An example would be a director who sets *A Doll's House*—about a character named Nora who feels trapped, like a doll, in her husband's patriarchal house and world—in Norway in the late nineteenth century, as did the playwright, Henrik Ibsen.

Other directors take a more heretical approach; because they tend to view multiple interpretations of a work as equally valid, they are not as concerned with the author's intention. Often, their focus is how to make a work meaningful for the audience at hand, and in discovering how to do this, they may set the play in a period or location that is wildly disparate from the original. This director might set *A Doll's House* in a 1950s American suburban home, emphasizing themes of a woman's attempts to break free of the model of the ideal nuclear family.

Some directors, often called **auteurs** (French for "authors"), take this heretical notion to an extreme, viewing the text, if there is one, as a jumping-off point for their production, capturing the spirit, but not the letter, of the script. With this approach, the director, not the playwright, is the primary creative force in the theatre. Even if the creative process did begin with a play, the production often bears little resemblance to it, or may be combined with other texts in a "pastiche" of a final product.

**FIGURE 6.18**

For example, Robert Wilson's highly imagistic pieces include his interpretation of Euripides' *Alcestis*, in which he highlighted themes of death and rebirth, intermingling the ancient Greek play with the music of Laurie Anderson, an ancient Japanese play, a play by German Heiner Müller, and lasers. The Wooster Group in New York, led by Elizabeth LeCompte, is famous for its conceptual, highly stylized stagings of such classic works as Racine's *Phedre* and Chekhov's *Three Sisters*. Mabou Mines' *Dollhouse*, directed by Lee Breuer, placed Nora in a miniature world suited only to the men—played by dwarfs—in that world. Such directors may also develop pieces by working collaboratively with actors, as in Mary Zimmerman's adaptation of Ovid's *Metamorphoses*, based on Greek myths. This high-concept production, set partially in a pool of water, proved that such work can have popular appeal; it played on Broadway for two years and is frequently produced at regional theatres and in universities. The auteur approach, sometimes labeled postmodern, can be quite controversial, but can lead to inspiring, and inspired, interpretations of works.

The slash director is increasingly common: director/choreographer or director/designer, for example. Agnes De Mille, Jerome Robbins, Bob Fosse, and Michael Bennett directed and choreographed at some point in their careers and have paved the way for such contemporary artists as Graciela Daniele and Susan Stroman. The Argentinian Daniele is the first female director/choreographer to work on Broadway since Agnes De Mille in 1947. Daniele began her career as a dancer, appearing in numerous Broadway shows, as well as assisting Bennett and Fosse, which led to more jobs choreographing. Her work on such shows as *Once on This Island* and the popular revival of *Annie Get Your Gun* has garnered her numerous Tony nominations.

**FIGURE 6.19**

Susan Stroman, known as "Stro" by insiders, has emerged as the most prominent director/choreographer working on Broadway today, thanks in part to her work on *The Producers*, which won the most Tony Awards of all time for one play. Like Daniele, Stroman put in time as a dancer until her first choreographic assignment in 1987, *Flora, the Red Menace*. By 1995 she won her first Tony for *Crazy for You*. She garnered another Tony two years later for choreographing a revival of *Showboat* and a third for her dance play *Contact*. With *The Producers*, Stroman became the first woman to win Tonys in two categories (direction and choreography) for a single show.

The idea of the director/designer is not new. Early in the twentieth century, Edward Gordon Craig, who began his career as an actor, proposed theories regarding actors and acting as well as visual elements such as color and light. He emphasized height and grandeur in his designs and sought flexibility on stage through the use of mobile settings. Robert Wilson, trained as a visual artist, is one example of a contemporary director/designer. He uses actors as just one part of the pictorial element of his pieces, which he lays out in storyboards. The pictures he creates on stage are often so elaborate that his work is most commonly presented in state-supported European venues that can afford to house it.

Julie Taymor is perhaps the most prominent director/designer working in the United States today; in 1998, she became the first woman to win a Tony Award for directing. Her influences—from travels to and study in France, Eastern Europe, Japan, and Indonesia—include mime, puppetry, Javanese shadow puppetry, mask making, music, and even tai chi. After working in regional theatre for years, Taymor came to prominence in New York with a revised version of an earlier Off-Broadway work, *Juan*

*Darien*, a carnival-like spectacle about a jaguar cub transformed into a boy. The play was nominated for five Tony awards in 1997. Taymor won two Tonys the next year for her work as director and costume designer (she also designed sets) for *The Lion King*; Taymor's involvement in that project elevated it, many critics claim, above Disney's earlier musical, *Beauty and the Beast*.

**FIGURE 6.20**

Taymor also represents another type of director: those who emphasize **interculturalism**, particularly bringing together Western and Eastern influences, in their work. Renowned Shakespearean director Peter Brook founded the International Center for Theatre Research in Paris in the 1970s to explore just this kind of work. Gathering together an international group of actors and other artists, Brook created a variety of productions, including *The Conference of the Birds* (based on a twelfth-century Persian poem), Alfred Jarry's *Ubu Roi*, Bizet's opera *Carmen*, Shakespeare's *The Tempest*, and, most famously, *The Mahabharata*, a controversial 1986 adaptation of the sacred Hindu epic. Brook compressed the story into a nine-hour production in which he emphasized themes that he perceived as universal, but many were critical of this British director's adapting an Indian work, given the history of colonialism. Still, audiences were exposed to a work that they otherwise may never have had the opportunity to experience. More recently, Brook directed an abridged version of *Hamlet* that toured in the United States with a multinational cast, including Jamaican-born, British-trained Adrian Lester in the title role, and music composed by Japanese musician Toshi Tsuchitori.

French director Ariane Mnouchkine creates intercultural theatre with her troupe, Theatre de Soleil, at an abandoned munitions factory outside of Paris. More collaborative and democratic than Brook's International Center for Theatre Research, the Theatre de Soleil produced a Kabuki-inspired *Richard II*, a Kathakali-influenced *Twelfth Night*, and a *Tartuffe* that emphasized religious hypocrisy in North African Islamic fundamentalism. Tadashi Suzuki works from the perspective of a Japanese director borrowing from Western traditions to create his intercultural theatre. Based in traditional Japanese forms such as Noh and Kabuki, interpretations of such Western classics as The *Bacchae* and *Macbeth* have proven extremely effective. (For more on Suzuki, see Chapter 9.)

## TRAINING AND THE PROFESSION

With so many different approaches to directing, no one method of training will work for all aspiring directors. Although the image of the autocratic, dictatorial director—perhaps epitomized in Richard Wagner, the nineteenth-century opera creator who, in his quest for *gesamtkunstwerk* (total art work), sought to control every aspect of production—is pervasive, today the more successful director is one who can communicate and collaborate with her fellow artists, skills that all directors must have. Some attributes of a good director are inherent, such as patience, leadership, and organization, and others can be acquired.

For example, directors should have a general knowledge of all aspects of the production process, knowledge that can be gained in an undergraduate university a BA degree program in Theatre. Some directors go on to graduate school to specialize in directing, pursuing an MFA. However, somewhat paradoxically, many graduate programs prefer that students have considerable experience as directors before they enter the program. Apprenticeships are another training option, or they are used in addition to degree programs; prospective directors work with more experienced directors as assistants. Many directors began working in theatre as specialists in other fields including playwriting, designing, choreographing, dramaturging, and so on. For example, Kenny Leon is one of America's foremost African American directors working today, most recently as the acclaimed director of the Tony Award–winning Broadway revival of August Wilson's *Fences*, starring Denzel Washington and Viola Davis. He began his career as an actor at Atlanta's Academy Theatre and has extensive acting experience on stage, film, and television. Like most professional directors, he is a member of the Society of Stage Directors and Choreographers.

**FIGURE 6.21**

Unfortunately, unemployment for directors is as high as it is for actors; opportunities in both professional and educational theatre are few and far between. Many directors work in both (and other) arenas, piecing together a life. For all of the actors, designers, technicians, and others who come together to create a production, just one director is needed. But the rewards of engaging in the complex, challenging process of directing ensure that numerous artists will continue to undertake it.

**FIGURE 6.22**

## For Further Information

Ball, William. *A Sense of Direction*. 1984.

Bennedetti, Robert. *The Director at Work*. 1985.

Blumenthal, Eileen, and Julie Taymor. *Julie Taymor: Playing with Fire*. 1995.

Brockett, Oscar G., and Robert J. Ball. *The Essential Theatre*. 8th ed. 2004.

Brook, Peter. *The Empty Space*. 1968.

Brook, Peter. *Threads of Time: A Memoir*. 1999.

Clurman, Harold. *On Directing*. 1972.

Cohen, Robert, and John Harrop. *Creative Play Direction*. 2nd ed. 1984.

Cole, Toby, and Helen Krich Chinoy. *Directors on Directing*. 2nd ed. 1977.

Delgado, Maria, and Paul Heritage. *In Contact with the Gods? Directors Talk Theatre*. 1996.

Diamond, David, and Terry Berliner, Eds. *Stage Directors Handbook: Opportunities for Directors and Choreographers*. 1998.

Donkin, Ellen, and Susan Clement. *Upstaging Big Daddy: Directing Theater as if Gender and Race Matter*. 1993.

Marranca, Bonnie, Ed. *The Theatre of Images*. 1996.

Ostrow, Stuart. *A Producer's Broadway Journey*. 1999.

Quadri, Franco. *Robert Wilson*. 1997.

## Suggested Films

*A Chorus Line* (1985): A director casts a new show, and dancers sing to him about their lives, both onstage and off, as each attempts to win a part in the show.

*The Goodbye Girl* (1977): Richard Dreyfuss's breakthrough role as a struggling actor stuck in an apartment with an angry dancer and her daughter. Dreyfuss's character has several notable run-ins with his director.

*The Mahabharata* (1989): A brilliant example of the work of director Peter Brook.

*Moon Over Broadway* (1997): A documentary of the mounting of Ken Ludwig's *Moon Over Buffalo* on Broadway.

*Noises Off* (1992): A behind-the-scenes look at how a show gets directed and produced.

*Titus* (1999): A visually stunning adaptation, directed by Julie Taymor, of Shakespeare's violent play *Titus Andronicus*, directed by Julie Taymor.

## Glossary

**actor-manager**  An actor who serves as the head of a theatre or theatre company; a precursor to the director; common from the seventeenth to the nineteenth centuries.

**auteurs**  French term for the types of directors who work as the primary creative forces behind a production; the auteur emphasizes interpretation in the theatrical process.

**blocking**  The process of creating and fixing the actors' movements about the stage during rehearsals.

**casting**  The process of selecting actors for a theatrical production (or a film, a television show, etc.).

**concept**  A brief statement that communicates the director's overall vision for a production.

**dramaturg** A specialist in dramatic analysis and literature, production research, and audience engagement.

**ground plan** A diagram or map of the dimensions of the playing area on a stage.

**improvisation** Acting technique that emphasizes immediate responses as opposed to rehearsed behavior. Viola Spolin is a pioneer in "improv" techniques.

**intercultural** Between or among two or more cultures.

**Kabuki** A classical Japanese form of music theatre developed in the eighteenth century that emphasizes spectacle.

**Kathakali** A classical Indian form that developed from ancient Sanskrit theatre and combines elaborate movement, music, gesture, and facial expressions.

**Noh** A classical Japanese form created in the fourteenth century; emphasizes minimalism as a reflection of the influences of Zen Buddhism.

**picturization** The director's creation of pictures on stage, using the various visual elements, such as the actors.

**postmodern** An umbrella term for a philosophy, a condition, or a movement (depending on one's perspective) in the contemporary world that reflects such characteristics as pastiche, fragmentation, disunity, and suspicion of any one explanation for things, or "grand narratives," as outlined by such philosophers as Frederic Jameson and Jean-François Lyotard.

**stage business** Activities in which the actor engages onstage.

**table work** The initial read-through and discussion of the play text at the beginning of the rehearsal process, often literally done while the actors. stage manager, and the design team sit around a table.

**technical rehearsals** Also known as "techs," rehearsals in the last phase of the rehearsal process that involve the integration and honing of all of the design and technical aspects of the production.

## Key Concepts

- The concept of the director is a relatively recent one, but the director has quickly gained prominence as one of the primary creative forces in the theatre.
- The modern director performs four, often overlapping, functions:
  1. to work with the text
  2. to work with the actors
  3. to work with the designers
  4. to coordinate all elements of the production
- For many directors, their concept—or overall vision for a production—guides all choices related to the production.
- The production process often begins with casting and ends with technical rehearsals.

- The producer, whether an individual or a group and/or corporation, oversees all financial and managerial aspects of productions.
- Some directors work in service of the author's "intentions" in a play; others, such as auteurs, view the play as a mere starting point for more interpretive work.
- Although not new, the slash director—such as the director/choreographer or director/designer—has become increasingly common.
- Directors can be trained in a variety of contexts.

## Appendix

**FIGURE 1**

To view this video please visit www.pearsonexploretheatre.com

# 7

# Scenic Designers and Costume Designers

**Chapter Outline**

*To view the figures in this chapter, log on to www.pearsonexploretheatre.com.*

## INTRODUCTION

Because plays are usually written to be performed on a stage—whether proscenium, thrust, arena, or another configuration—it is important to visualize plays in production as they are being read. This visualization should include not only the depiction of the characters by actors, but also the clothes that the characters wear (unless they are naked!) and the environment in which the characters interact and "live," from the furniture they use, to the time of day, the weather, and so on. The playwright may explicitly suggest the environment in the script, or the readers may need to conjure up such things within their imagination. But, for an actual production, it is the designers' job, in collaboration with the director, dramaturg, and other members of the production team, to realize at least one interpretation of that environment and to help bring to life in three dimensions the world of the play. These aspects of the production are what Aristotle referred to as "spectacle," although he had no way of envisioning how far technology would take that spectacle in modern times.

Designers—from scenic to costume to lighting—use a variety of key concepts to communicate meaning through the pictures that they create on stage. Their basic building blocks are the **visual elements** of line, shape, space, ornamentation, color, and texture. The principles of design, including balance, variety, proportion, rhythm, focus, and harmony, determine how the artists use those building blocks. The world that the designers create with these elements and principles is never a copy of the *real* world, no matter how realistic the play is. Costumes must be durable enough to be worn night after night, regardless of how diaphanous a particular dress may need to appear; the actors must be seen by the audience, no matter how dark a night the play may call for; sets often are viewed under colored light, not sunlight. As designers consider such things, they must take into account a number of factors, such as tone/mood, level of abstraction, period and location, and aesthetics.

**FIGURE 7.1**

The general tone or mood of a piece can be immediately ascertained by a designer if the play is classified as either a tragedy or a comedy. The light tone of a musical used to be fairly clear-cut, but since the appearance of darker shows such as *West Side Story*, based on Shakespeare's tragedy *Romeo and Juliet,* or Stephen Sondheim's *Sweeney Todd* or *Assassins*, this has not always been the case. And many non-musical plays today do not fall into any one genre or category, meaning that a designer must be prepared to communicate a range of moods in a single production, often with great subtlety.

Designers, in conjunction with the director, must decide whether to create a world on stage that closely resembles real life or, instead, to create a world that is more abstract, symbolic, and evocative of life. The former more directly communicates meaning; the latter requires the audience to engage more actively in the making of meaning through the visual elements. Or a designer may choose a middle ground through a combination of the two. A good example of this approach is Jo Mielziner's set design for Arthur Miller's *Death of A Salesman*, which depicted the outline of a house through which the cityscape could be viewed as it loomed over the home.

**FIGURE 7.2**

Part of the director's **concept** involves the selection of the period and location in which to set the play. This period may be the same as prescribed by the playwright, or a director may choose to ignore such a prescription. The concept may involve the period in which a play was originally produced, such as fifth-century Greece for Euripides's *Trojan Women*, or the creative team may choose to set Euripides's play in contemporary Iraq. Most often, the selection of a period requires considerable research on the part of the designers. Lighting designers might need to explore the quality of light in late nineteenth-century Sweden for a production of Ibsen's *A Doll's House* set in its original location and period; sound designers, the quality of thunder for a production of *King Lear*; costume designers, the clothes of a Medieval shipbuilder for a production of a cycle play of the biblical story of Noah and the flood. However, a designer's choices go beyond research, complicated by the perceptions and expectations of the audience, whose understanding of a period and place may be conditioned through the lenses of contemporary media. Designers may have to determine whether to confirm or subvert such audience perceptions as they consider the importance of historical accuracy.

**FIGURE 7.3**

Finally, designers must consider aesthetics: the beauty of their work as art. Even a design meant to communicate "ugliness" to its audience—for example, two trash cans on stage for Samuel Beckett's *Endgame* or the orphan's clothes in the musical *Oliver!*—should be artfully and carefully produced. Indeed, it has become somewhat common for the work of designers, particularly scenic and costume, to be exhibited outside the context of a theatrical production, in a gallery setting, as art for its own sake. Theatrical design is, in a sense, art you can walk on (and in) and wear.

This chapter will focus on the earliest designers, scenic and costume. Historically, their art has been less dependent on new technologies (although this is changing). Chapter 8 will examine designers (lighting and sound) and technicians who rely on technologies developed in the (relatively) recent past.

**LEARNING OBJECTIVES**

**After reading Chapter 7, you should be able to:**

* Identify the visual elements and principles of design
* Describe how scenic and costume design contribute to the theatrical power of a play or musical.
* Apply the terms and vocabulary to specific examples of live theatre to identify and differentiate the effects of scenery and costumes on a production.
* Discuss the tools and processes that scenic and costume designers use to accomplish their art.
* Discuss the contributions made by other related personnel to a theatrical production.

## SCENIC DESIGNERS

Scenic design is a complex art, and the designer is part visual artist, part sculptor, and part engineer.

**FIGURE 7.4**

### Scenic Designers: History

Until relatively recently, in both Western and Asian traditions, scenery onstage was usually quite minimal, the location having been suggested either by the architecture of the theatre (as in the **skene,** or scene house, of the ancient Greek *theatron*) or by the words of the playwright, as in Kalidasa's ancient play *Sakuntala* or Shakespeare's work. It is quite likely that some scenic pieces elaborated on these, such as the **periakoi**, or triangular painted prisms of ancient Greece, or the **mansions**, such as the "hell mouth," of the theatre of the Middle Ages. But it was not until the creation of the indoor European theatres during the Renaissance that scenery came into focus as a design component as crucial as costumes, makeup, and masks. A great period of painted, illusionistic scenery began, aided by protection from the elements that indoor theatres afforded, increased control of lighting (albeit candlelight) to illuminate the scenery, and above all, the development of perspective painting.

**FIGURE 7.5**

**Perspective** painting, as discovered and perfected by great Renaissance artists such as Leonardo Da Vinci,, paved the way for elaborate, illusionistic scenery and thus for a significant development in both scenery and theatre architecture: the **proscenium**. Historians argue as to which came first, the perspective scenery or the proscenium. Either way, the proscenium provides a perfect frame or lens through which to view perspective painting. The art of the scenic painter became legendary through the work of Italians Sebastiano Serlio (1475–1554) and Giacomo Torelli (1608–1678), as well as the Englishman Inigo Jones (1573–1652) and others. Over the next 200 years, flat scenery became more and more elaborate, with devices created to move the scenery, a combination of **wings** (flat scenery pieces placed on the left and right sides of the stage), **borders** (scenery pieces placed above the stage to mask changing mechanisms and/or the proscenium), and **drops** (short for "backdrops" at the rear of the stage).

The proscenium format is still the most widely used today. However, the two-dimensional flat perspective scenery, which attempts to give the illusion of three-dimensionality, gave way in the nineteenth century to actual three-dimensional sets, as the dramatic form of realism rose to prominence. The "**box set**" is a series of hard **flats** interconnected to give the appearance of three walls of a room. The "room" is then filled with furniture and props to give the appearance of a real-life environment. Often, the actors in the space act as if there is a **fourth wall** downstage, ignoring the audience, in order to give the spectators the feeling that they are voyeurs peering into a slice of real life.

**FIGURE 7.6**

As soon as the realism of such dramatists as Ibsen, August Strindberg, or David Belasco came to prominence in the late nineteenth century, artists rebelled against it, advocating working more metaphorically and abstractly—particularly as film developed, its technology seeming even more appropriate for capturing a "slice of real life." The modern abstraction of scenery is perhaps best embodied in the work of Adolphe Appia and Edward Gordon Craig. Appia advocated, above all, unifying the various elements on stage:—the three-dimensional actor, the two-dimensional vertical scenery, and the horizontal floor into one harmonious and fluid entity. This could be accomplished by replacing flat scenery with steps, platforms, and ramps; and light could fuse all of the elements into a whole. Craig's sometimes controversial theories included the unification of simplified décor, moving scenery, and directional lighting by a single, autonomous artist, as well as the replacement of the actor with an "Übermarionette"— a nebulous concept that might have referred to using a mechanical "super" puppet, instead of a live performance figure. Regardless of the precise meaning, both artists sought to replace representational elements on stage with abstractions.

In the United States, these European innovations later developed as a movement known as the **New Stagecraft**, began when designer Sam Hume, who had worked at the Moscow Art Theatre, organized an exhibit of such designs in Boston and New York in 1914–1915. The use of simplified, nonrealistic settings and lighting as a major design component and the search for alternatives to the proscenium influenced American designers like Norman Bel Geddes, Lee Simonson, and Robert Edmond Jones, who wrote the still influential *The Dramatic Imagination*. The New Stagecraft became the dominant design mode in the United States by the 1920s.

**FIGURE 7.7**

The abilities of such designers to build a more abstract world for the play would grow with the development of new technologies, first most prominently embraced by renowned Czech scenographer Josef Svoboda. Advocating the notion of **scenography** over design to suggest the conceptualization of space in three dimensions, Svoboda first gained recognition in 1958 through his theories and work on *polyekran* and *laterna magika*. The former involved projections on multiple screens to avoid "visual paralysis"; the latter combined live action with recorded action projected on screens. These experiments with multimedia became the hallmarks of Svoboda's work, which included the use of closed-circuit televisions, the manipulation of various materials as screens on which to project images, and the use of light as an integral part of scenography.

A kind of modified American realism developed out of a combination of **realism** and the early twentieth-century dominance of New Stagecraft, and this has become the norm on many mainstream Western stages, as can be seen in the work of such contemporary designers as Ming Cho Lee and Scott Pask. Born in China and educated at UCLA, Lee assisted Jo Mielziner, then one of America's foremost designers, early in his career. Lee's first Broadway design was for *The Moon Besieged* (1962). Since 1980, many of Lee's designs have leaned more toward realism, as in his design for *K2*, set on a ledge on a mountain in the Himalayas. Through his work in opera, theatre, and dance, as well as through his teaching at the Yale School of Drama, Lee has had a greater influence on American scenography than any other contemporary designer. In fact, Scott Pask, one of the most successful young scenic designers working today, studied with Lee at Yale. In 2005, three Pask-designed shows lit up the marquees on Broadway: a revival of the musical *Sweet Charity*, the new musical *Urinetown*, and the play *The*

*Pillowman*, for which Pask won a Tony Award. The stark, simplified, institutional scenery for *Pillowman*, set in two interrogation rooms of an ambiguous modern-day police state, was enhanced by expressionistic shadowboxes that were eerily lit for scenes in other locales—a combination of realism and abstraction at its best. Pask's extensive designs on and off Broadway, in regional theatre, and in London make him one of today's most prominent designers.

**FIGURE 7.8**

Although realism—or a form of it, sometimes called "selective realism"—continues to be the dominant mode for scenic designers today; for some, **postmodernism** and **interculturalism** are strong influences. Postmodernism, in some ways, represents a departure from Appia and Craig's desire for unity; instead, disunity is the key, with pastiches of seemingly unrelated periods, styles, or objects. For example, British director Jonathan Miller's 1989 production of Bertolt Brecht's *Mahagonny*, designed by Robert Israel, included a boxing ring, the walls of which were painted with murals influenced by Renaissance painter Giotto's *Massacre of the Innocents*. Intercultural artists draw on design elements from outside their own dominant cultural experience, with West often meeting East. Many actor-centered Eastern performance traditions, such as Indian **Sanskrit theatre**, Chinese **Beijing Opera**, and Japanese **Noh**, utilize sparse sets (unlike Kabuki scenery, which is quite elaborate), but some scenic artists draw on design elements from those cultures at large. Director Julie Taymor's *The Lion King*, for example, borrows from Asian shadow puppetry and Japanese **Bunraku**, another form of performance that uses puppets. Her collaboration with a number of designers created a truly intercultural world of both Asian- and African-inspired elements.

**FIGURE 7.9**

## Scenic Designers: Materials, Methods, and Processes

The *technical director* takes the designs and oversees their creation into actual sets on stage, from determining costs to purchasing building materials and constructing the sets. Although the materials he or she uses to create scenic elements and realize a scenic design can vary depending on the designer's style and approach, there are several basic building blocks. The **flat** is a wooden or metal frame onto which canvas or other material has been stretched and attached, then painted. Flats may be combined with platforms, steps, or ramps to add levels and to isolate locations. Other three-dimensional objects on stage may include trees, columns, or architectural fragments. Drapes can serve a number of purposes: as decoration, to transform the stage into neutral space, to define a playing area, or to mask other elements or actors. Painted canvases, called **drops**, can be hung at the back of the stage to help define locale. And **scrims** are made of thin, gauzy fabrics through which light can pass. Light from the front makes the material opaque, and from the back, transparent to reveal previously unseen scenic pieces. A **cyclorama**, or cyc, is a series of stretched-taut curtains—or one long curtain— that surrounds the stage on three sides; these can be used to represent the sky or infinite space. Furniture and props may complete the scene. Today, more and more designers follow Svoboda's lead and work with newer, less tangible "materials," such as projections, lasers, televisions, film, or even virtual reality.

**FIGURES 7.10, 7.11, AND 7.12**

Designers' working methods and processes, obviously, can differ from one designer to the next. Most begin their work with careful readings of the text in order to inform discussions with the director and other members of the creative team, while compiling images and other research to contribute to the overall concept. During the readings, the designer must ask a number of questions of the text, such as the following:

- How many settings are required?
- What size and shape will the stage be?
- How will the scenery be moved or shifted?
- What materials will be used to build the scenery?
- Are there any special effects?

The scenic designer then might create preliminary, rough sketches of his or her ideas based on the basis of feedback at meetings, eventually producing more finalized renderings, or drawings, of the set—including a **ground plan**, a "map" of the shape of the playing area as seen from above—and, ultimately, a three-dimensional, often minutely detailed, scale model. The media used for the **renderings** vary: pencil, paint, watercolor, collage, or more commonly, computer-assisted design (CAD) programs. CAD systems have all but replaced the most common drafting tools—compasses, triangles, T-squares, and rulers—and, like much computer software, they greatly enhance the abilities, flexibility, and efficiency of the user without replacing the human creativity still needed.

**FIGURE 7.13**

After the designs are finalized and approved, extensive, detailed, working drawings provide the technical director with the information needed to realize the set; good drafting skills are essential. Drawn-to-scale **elevations** from the front, rear, and side indicate suggested materials and methods for construction. Paint elevations communicate specifics of color and texture. Once these are complete, construction begins, supervised by the technical director in conjunction with the designer. Once rehearsals begin, the set designer usually attends periodically in order to make any adjustments necessary, also regularly visiting the scene shop where the set is being constructed. Once most or all of the pieces are built, the set is **loaded in**—moved to the theatre, where the designer can finally see the set in the actual performance space. There, he or she makes any final adjustments and may dress the set, adding final touches. But in most contexts, at this point, it is too late to make any major changes.

## Scenic Designers: Related Aspects: Props

The scene designer usually supervises the creation of the **properties** (props), which are the items, separate from the scenery, that are used by the actor, including furniture, hangings, and hand props such as weapons, fans, and glasses for beverages. In some theatres, there may be a props master in charge of the creation and collection of these items. Some props may be built from scratch (some theatres have entire shops devoted to this), whereas others are rented, bought, borrowed, or found. All props must be selected carefully for their aesthetics and ability to fit in with the scenery, as well as for their functionality. Designers must work meticulously to ensure that the entire environment on stage is conducive to the event. Some even go so far as to design the audience spaces, including the lobby and the exterior of the theatre. When the musical *Rent* was moved uptown to Broadway from its original downtown space, scenographer Paul Clay and his collaborators designed the entire theatre to evoke the industrial grunge of the East Village, Alphabet City neighborhood in which the show is set. But even if the scene designer focuses primarily on the space on stage, he or she must draw on visual art, architecture, engineering, and other disciplines to realize this art, making the scene designer one of the most well-rounded contributors to the creative process of theatre.

**FIGURES 7.14 AND 7.15**

## COSTUME DESIGNERS

Costumes have helped audiences identify and understand characters since the earliest historical efforts at performance.

**FIGURE 7.16**

### Costume Designers: History

The costuming of actors is as old as theatre itself, practiced by the Greeks as they presented the first tragedies and comedies in their outdoor amphitheatres, starting in the sixth century BCE. In some periods and cultures, as in ancient Greece, costumes were based on the dress of the time; in others, dress on stage has been a wild departure from that of everyday life. Until the twentieth century, the actor was largely responsible for the creation and upkeep of his or her own costumes, so the *art* of the costume designer is relatively recent.

In ancient Greek and Roman theatres, actors typically wore a tunic-like garment, called a **chiton** in Greece and a **toga** in Rome, often enhanced by embroidery and symbolic colors. Pieces may have been added, such as a draped cloth, to indicate some aspect of character. All actors wore masks, and at least in the state-supported, institutional theatres, cross-dressing was common because men played all the roles. In ancient Greek comedies, most male actors sported the **phallus**, used to great comic effect, and often emphasized by a too-short *chiton*. The utilization of clothing in common use continued on stages throughout Europe during the Middle Ages, unless the character, such as an angel, called for a religious robe (borrowed from the church) or the costume, in the case of a devil, had to be specially made. These practices largely continued during the Renaissance. And although masks continued to be utilized in the Italian-based form of **commedia**, they fell out of use in Western performance.

**FIGURE 7.17**

Meanwhile, in much of the non-Western world, masks and highly elaborate, symbolic costumes continue to be the norm in classical theatrical traditions. For example, in Japanese Noh performance, approximately half of the actors wear masks. The masks are smaller than the face, focusing the energy of the actor and transforming him upon his donning the mask. The rich, colorful, embroidered fabrics of the Noh kimonos are symbolic of character; both the masks and costumes are works of art in and of themselves. Similarly, the Beijing Opera actors of China wear elaborate costumes, although around 1000 CE they eschewed masks for colorful, detailed face painting, of which hundreds of patterns exist to indicate the myriad characters that people the form. Cross-dressing is quite common in many Asian forms. The female impersonator in **Kabuki**, the **onnagata**, historically has been said to better personify images of womanhood than a woman could, herself! And in Africa, masks are an important, powerful part of ritual performance, with much secular theatre borrowing from such forms.

**FIGURE 7.18**

In the West, the practice of utilizing off-stage dress onstage, albeit more elaborate in some cases, continued until the advent of **romanticism**, **melodrama**, and **realism**, when, as with scenery, more attention was paid to detail and historical accuracy (and concurrent innovations in lighting made the details easier to see). By the twentieth century, the need for a person to oversee such detail and accuracy developed and the position of costume designer was born.

**FIGURE 7.19**

One of the most successful and acclaimed American designers has been Theoni V. Aldredge. Born in Greece in 1932, she studied at the Goodman Theatre School in Chicago. After moving to New York in the 1960s, she began her illustrious career at the New York Shakespeare festival. Her Broadway credits include *Annie, La Cage Aux Folles, A Chorus Line,* and *Follies*. At one time, five of her designs were running on Broadway simultaneously, and she has won numerous Tonys and an Academy Award. Other costume superstars include Irene Sharaff, Patricia Zipprodt, and Florence Klotz. Although costumers have been primarily women, some men have entered the field, such as Paul Tazewell and William Ivey Long, who, like Scott Pask, studied set design with Ming Cho Lee at Yale. (A number of designers create both sets and costumes.) Long has designed the costumes for such acclaimed musical revivals as *Chicago, Cabaret, Guys and Dolls, Annie Get Your Gun*, and *The Music Man*, as well as original works, including *Contact, The Producers*, and *Hairspray*. He has also created costumes for opera, rock concerts, dance performances, and a Siegfried and Roy show in Las Vegas.

**FIGURE 7.20**

## Costume Designers: Materials, Methods, and Processes

The primary materials utilized by the costumer to dress the performer are somewhat more limited than those utilized by the scene designer to set the stage. The basic building block is fabric, but there are, obviously, a wide array of choices available in terms of color, weight, texture, and pattern. And certain characters may call for certain special effects, such as distressing, fur, hair, dye, and feathers. Like the set designer, the costumer ascertains the specific needs of the show and characters within it by first closely reading the text several times, asking questions such as the following:

- How many costumes and costume changes are required?
- What is the appropriate line, shape, and silhouette for each costume?
- How much do the costumes need to alter the actor's appearance?
- How might the costumes reflect the mood or tone of the piece?
- How can the costumes help clarify the relationships of the characters, including the characters' status?
- How should the costumes affect movement, and how will the movement affect the costumes?

**FIGURE 7.21**

After analyzing the script, the costumer works in conjunction with the creative team—particularly, the scenic designer—to discuss the concept and ways in which the costumes will communicate that concept. Working from visual research, he usually creates preliminary, rough sketches; after more consultation with the rest of the creative team, the sketches are finalized as color renderings. Often, the designer attaches **swatches**, or small pieces, of fabric to the rendering. If there are special effects or features, the designer may include detailed drawings, sometimes in the margins of the rendering. Most costumers, or their assistants, also construct a **costume chart** that maps out what each character wears in each scene so that the overall organization of the show can be seen at a glance. This chart later may be used as a dressing list to aid the actors and their dressers in keeping track of the costume pieces and changes.

**FIGURE 7.22**

Once the designs are finalized, the costumer decides which costumes will be borrowed, rented, pulled from existing stock, or newly constructed. Creating new costumes is ideal for ensuring that the costumes will best fit the concept of the specific production (and the actors), but not all theatres can afford to construct all of the costumes, particularly for a large-cast musical. A number of rental houses cater to the needs of theatres, although the costumes usually arrive only in time for one or two dress rehearsals and hence cannot be altered in any significant way. If the theatre maintains a collection of wardrobe items from past productions, or **stock**, items may be selected, or pulled and altered to suit the needs of the present production. Some costumers on a limited budget may even design with the available stock in mind. Few costumers have the luxury of an unlimited budget, so most engage in a combination of these methods. The process can vary if costumes are to be created from scratch. In commercial theatres such as Broadway or West End houses, construction is "jobbed out" to a professional costume house, such as Barbara Matera's in New York, and designers have little direct involvement in the process beyond occasional fittings and final approval. But in other contexts, the costumer may oversee all aspects of construction, sometimes in conjunction with a costume shop manager.

**FIGURE 7.23**

The process of making a costume usually begins with measuring the actor and then shopping for materials. Next, patterns are drafted and/or the material is draped, or hung on a mannequin to determine construction. The material is cut, and the components are sewn loosely together, or basted. Sometimes, a **mock-up** in an inexpensive material, such as muslin, is made first, before cutting expensive fabrics. Either way, the costume is fitted on the actor at this point. Once the designer is satisfied with the fit and appearance, the garment is permanently sewn together and ornamentation is added, with a final fitting before the costume makes its way to the stage.

Once the costumes are finished, the actors will usually participate in a **dress parade**, in which they appear onstage in the costume so that the director and creative team can see each garment under the light and against the set. This usually occurs during technical rehearsals just before dress rehearsals. During the latter, the performers have the chance to move in their costumes, providing the actors with a much-needed final layer to complete their complex characterizations. Once performances begin, there is often a wardrobe running crew to help with costume changes, upkeep of the garments between performances, and striking of the garments once the show closes.

**FIGURE 7.24**

## Costume Designers: Related Aspects: Masks, Makeup, Wigs, and Hair

The creation of masks, makeup, wigs, and theatrical hairstyles are arts in and of themselves; indeed, some theatre artists specialize in one or more of these apart from costumes. Many costumers also design all aspects of the actor's appearance, and these various aspects are so intertwined as to warrant consideration together here. The importance of masks to some traditions—particularly classical non-Western forms such as Noh and Beijing opera, as well as much indigenous African performance—has already been noted. In Western theatre, masks have been a crucial component in ancient Greece and Rome, as well as the commedia dell'arte of Renaissance Italy and beyond. But the contemporary costumer may still be called on to create masks for select productions, as Julie Taymor has been for shows such as *The Green Bird* and *The Lion King*.

**FIGURE 7.25**

Makeup is ubiquitous in theatre, ranging from wildly fantastical and elaborate to realistic, but even for realistic productions, most actors *are* wearing *some* makeup to enhance their features. Makeup is often divided into three categories: straight makeup, character makeup, and special effects. Straight makeup enhances facial features, ensuring that the actor's expressions can be read by the audience, often at a distance. Character makeup further alters the appearance of the actor, as when an actor wants to appear older. Special effects makeup is often used to create scars and bruises, or can be used to radically alter the appearance of the actor, as in the musicals *Cats* or *Beauty and the Beast*. Wigs factor heavily in those two shows as well. An actor's own hair may be modified to fit a role, particularly if the production budget is limited. However, even if the character's hair is similar to the actor's, wigs can be useful to eliminate wear and tear on the actor's own hair, not to mention to save the time it might take to style or color the hair. In the musical *Hairspray*, exaggerated bouffant wigs suggest period and communicate the attitudes toward ideals of beauty during the period.

**FIGURES 7.26 AND 7.27**

Indeed, throughout the history of theatre, hair and makeup have sometimes been deeply symbolic, signaling certain meanings to audience members. The highly elaborate makeup of Beijing Opera and Kabuki is completely non-realistic; bold colors and patterns signify very specific character traits. In the former, for example, red indicates loyalty; white, treachery; and green, a demon. The burnt-cork blackface of American **minstrelsy** performance is fraught with complicated meanings. Originally used by white actors in the nineteenth century to enhance performances imitative of slave culture, blackface came to symbolize a host of racial stereotypes perpetuated by the performances. Ironically, when blacks eventually took to the stage in these events, they used burnt cork to blacken their faces as well. By the twentieth century, blackface performers still could be seen on stage, as well as in the burgeoning film and, later, television industries. By the time of the mid-century Civil Rights movement, the practice fell out of favor, but it has been revisited in a number of critiques of the practice, as in Spike Lee's film *Bamboozled*. That critique is occasionally turned on its head in the use of whiteface as in Suzan-Lori Parks's acclaimed 2001 play *Topdog/Underdog*, in which one of the two black characters works at a carnival as Abraham Lincoln, replete with white makeup.

**FIGURES 7.28 AND 7.29**

## TRAINING AND THE PROFESSION

Scenic and costume designers should be both artistic and technically proficient. They need to have the creativity, imagination, and talent, as well as the skills. Although aspects of these can be learned, successful designers need to have some innate aptitude and talent.

Designers must find a setting in which to become proficient in the skills required of *all* designers: play analysis; basic design elements; rendering and drafting, including computerized techniques when appropriate; research methods; and theatre history. Beyond these general skills and knowledge sets, each designer must learn aspects of his or her specific field—or fields, if the designer is interested in pursuing more than one area, as do more and more designers, such as Scott Pask and Julie Taymor. Scenic designers must learn basic construction and engineering, often including such special skills as carpentry and welding. Costuming requires knowledge of sewing, pattern making, and draping, often including special skills such as millinery.

**FIGURE 7.30**

Historically, designers gained this knowledge and skill, honing their talents and techniques, through apprenticeships with artists and theatres. Now, designers often pursue college degrees, such as the BFA or MFA, to gain proficiency in their field as well as to develop contacts, and they often seek out internships in the summers or immediately following graduation. Many also seek out the protections and benefits of union membership, primarily with the **United Scenic Artists**. Designers can network, hone their skills at workshops, and pursue employment through the **United States Institute for Theatre Technology**, which holds an annual conference and stage expo. The job market in design and, particularly technical theatre, is currently much more promising for young, aspiring designers than aspiring actors, playwrights, and directors. Although the designer may not be as prominent or as well-known to the average audience member, scenery and costumes are crucial. Without them, actors would stand naked in an empty space (which is the goal for some performances, but that's another discussion).

## For Further Information

Aronson, Arnold. *American Set Design*. 1985.

Bowman, Ruth Laurion. "Postmodern Design." *Theatre Journal* 43, 1–13. 1991.

Bay, Howard. *Stage Design*. 1974.

Corey, Irene. *The Face Is a Canvas: The Design and Technique of Theatrical Makeup*. 1990.

——. *The Mask of Reality: An Approach to Design for the Theatre*. 1968.

Corson, Richard, and James Glavin. *Stage Makeup*, 9th ed. 2000.

Ingham, Rosemary, and Liz Covey. *The Costume Designer's Handbook: A Complete Guide for Amateur and Professional Costume Designers*. 1992.

Izenour, George C. *Theatre Design*. 1977.

Jones, Robert Edmond. *The Dramatic Imagination*. 1987.

Maier, Manfred. *Basic Principles of Design*. 1977.

McAuley, Gay. *Space in Performance: Making Meaning in the Theatre*. 2000.

Mielziner, Jo. *Designing for the Theatre*. 1965.

Svoboda, Josef, Ed., and J.M. Burian, Trans. *The Secret of Theatrical Space*. 1993.

## Suggested Films

*San Francisco* (1936): Nineteenth-century scenic design, costumes, opera.

*Singin' in the Rain* (1952): Costumes, early filmmaking, talkies.

*Mephisto* (1981): Pre-WWII European theatre, costumes, sets, Nazi Germany.

*The Dresser* (1983): Makeup, wigs, costumes, 1940s London during WWII, King Lear.

*Bamboozled* (2000): Makeup, minstrel show, blackface.

*Noises Off* (1992): Contemporary farce, sets, costumes, backstage.

*An Awfully Big Adventure* (1995): General theatre, backstage, 1947 Liverpool.

*Slings and Arrows* (2003, TV series): Costumes, makeup, set design, lighting design, contemporary performance of Shakespeare.

*The Libertine* (2004): Seventeenth-century costumes, makeup, special makeup effects, Restoration Theatre, sets, early theatrical illumination.

*Finding Neverland* (2004): Victorian theatre, sets, lights, costumes, flying effects (Peter Pan), J. M. Barrie.

## Glossary

**aesthetics**   The study of the nature of beauty.

**Beijing Opera**   A classical, traditional Chinese form that combines music, dance, and speech with elaborate, codified costumes, makeup, and movement.

**box set**   A series of hard flats interconnected to give the appearance of three walls of a room. The "room" is filled with furniture and props to give the appearance of a real-life environment.

**Bunraku**   Strikingly lifelike, classical Japanese puppetry form, in which each puppet is manipulated by three puppeteers.

**chiton**   A draped garment that served as the basis for costumes (and dress) in ancient Greece.

**commedia**   A popular form of comedy that developed during the Renaissance in Italy; based on improvisation and stock characters.

**concept**   A brief statement that communicates the director's overall vision for a production.

**costume chart**   A "map" of what each character wears in each scene, developed so that the overall organization of the costumes can be seen at a glance. This chart later may be used as a dressing list to aid the actors and their dressers in keeping track of the costume pieces and changes.

**cyclorama, or cyc** A series of stretched-taut curtains—or one long curtain—that surrounds the stage on three sides; and are used, to great effect, to represent the sky or infinite space.

**dress parade** An event in which actors appear onstage in their costumes so that the director and creative team can see each garment under the light and against the set, before it is finalized for wear in a production.

**drop** Painted canvas hung at the back of the stage to help define locale.

**elevations** Drawings for the stage from the front, rear, and sides—all drawn to scale—that indicate suggested materials and methods for set construction.

**flat** A wooden or metal frame onto which canvas or other material has been stretched and attached, then painted.

**fourth wall** An imaginary wall between the actor and audience in a proscenium theatre; a concept that developed in conjunction with realism, the conventions of which held that the stage space was like a room with one wall removed so that the audience could view the action in that room.

**ground plan** A diagram or map of the dimensions of the playing area on a stage.

**interculturalism** Between or among two or more cultures.

**Kabuki** A classical Japanese form of music theatre, developed in the eighteenth century, that emphasizes spectacle.

**load-in** The movement of the set from the construction area to the performance space, usually supervised by the technical director.

**mansion** Set piece in the theatre of the Middle Ages. The most common were often elaborate mansions representing heaven and hell (the latter often called the "hell mouth," as the entrance to hell was often depicted as the mouth of a large beast).

**melodrama** A movement that developed parallel to romanticism, but outlived it to become the most popular form of theatre in America and Europe during the nineteenth century. Some hallmarks include plots focusing on good versus evil, with clear-cut heroes and villains; exotic locales; plot devices such as hidden documents, disguises, kidnappings; and musical accompaniment.

**minstrelsy** Controversial form, popular during the nineteenth century, in which white performers in blackface performed their impressions of slave music, dances, and culture. Eventually, black performers in blackface performed as well.

**mock-up** A temporary costume created before the final one, as a "test run."

**New Stagecraft** A movement in the United States in the early decades of the twentieth century, in which designers advocated the use of simplified, nonrealistic settings; lighting as a major design component; and the search for alternatives to the proscenium.

**Noh** A classical Japanese form created in the fourteenth century; emphasizes minimalism as a reflection of the influences of Zen Buddhism.

**onnagata** The female impersonator in Kabuki.

**periaktoi** Painted triangular prisms used as scenery in ancient Greek theatre.

**perspective** A technique of depicting volumes and spatial relationships, such as the simulation of distance, on a flat surface.

**phallus** A reproduction of the erect male penis commonly worn by comic actors in ancient Greece.

**postmodernism** An umbrella term for a philosophy, a condition, or a movement (depending on one's perspective) in the contemporary world that reflects such characteristics as pastiche, fragmentation, disunity, and suspicion of any one explanation for things, or "grand narratives," as outlined by such philosophers as Frederic Jameson and Jean-François Lyotard.

**principles of design** Principles—balance, variety, proportion, rhythm, focus, and harmony—on which a designer bases her use of the visual elements.

**properties, or props** Items separate from the scenery that are used by the actor, including furniture, hangings, and hand props such as weapons, fans, glasses for beverages, and so on.

**proscenium** Theatre configuration in which the spectators are separated from the performers by a proscenium arch that acts as a frame through which the actors, perspective scenery, and so on are viewed. The audience thus views the production only from one side, the front.

**realism** A movement that developed as a reaction against the escapism of melodrama, seeking to confront the social ills of nineteenth-century industrialized society. Realism has outlived melodrama to become the most prevalent form of non-musical theatre during the twentieth and twenty-first centuries in the Western world.

**renderings** Designers' completed drawings or paintings that indicate how a set or costume (or even lights) should look on stage.

**romanticism** Developed in part as a reaction against the restrictions of Neoclassicism and the intellectualism of the Enlightenment, a late eighteenth, early nineteenth-century movement, influenced literature, music, visual art, philosophy, and theatre; emphasized subjectivity and emotions; and brought Shakespeare back into favor.

**Sanskrit theatre** An ancient Indian theatre form, in the language of Sanskrit, that avoided realistic practices and involved codified performance, including elaborate costumes, makeup, and a complex set of movements and gestures known as mudras.

**scenography** Scene design that emphasizes the conceptualization of space in three dimensions, combined with time.

**scrim** A sheet of thin, gauzy fabric through which light can pass. Light from the front makes the material opaque, and light from the back makes the material transparent and reveals previously unseen scenic pieces.

**skene** The scene house of the ancient Greek theatron.

**stock** Refers to scenery or costumes that a theatre has on hand, from which they may draw for productions.

**swatches** Small sample pieces of a fabric.

**toga** A draped garment that served as the basis for costumes (and dress) in ancient Rome.

**visual elements** Basic building blocks of a designer's work, including line, shape, space, ornamentation, color, and texture.

**wings, borders, and drops** Scenic pieces that aid in the creation of perspective on a proscenium stage.

## Key Concepts

- The scenic and costume designers help bring to life in three dimensions the world of the play, taking into account tone or mood, level of abstraction, period and location, and aesthetics of the play being produced.
- Set and costume design are as old as theatre itself.
- Although today, illusionism, or realism, is the dominant mode for set design, throughout history it has shifted from realistic to abstract to combinations of the two.
- Designers' working processes may differ, but most utilize a similar set of building blocks and working methods. The materials used by the costume designer are somewhat more limited than those used by the scenographer.
- Both scenic and costume design involve an elaborate multi-step process, from play analysis to realization on stage.
- Careers in scenic or costume design require extensive training, either through apprenticeships in theatres or, more commonly, through more formal educational environments.

# 8

# Lighting Designers, Sound Designers, and Technical Production

*To view the figures in this chapter, log on to www.pearsonexploretheatre.com.*

## INTRODUCTION

Although the costume and scenic designers discussed in the previous chapter may utilize newer technologies to both create and implement their work, from computers to projections to new materials such as lycra or lasers, lighting and sound designers rely on a variety of technologies developed almost exclusively in the past and present centuries. Lighting and sound designers usually still approach design with the same basic building blocks of the visual elements (line, shape, space, ornamentation, color, and texture) and principles (balance, variety, proportion, rhythm, focus, and harmony) as costumers and scenographers do, yet their work, along with that of a number of technicians, is significantly different. It is interesting that the integration of new technologies into modern and contemporary theatre has stirred up some thought-provoking controversies, which this chapter will later revisit and that are visible in the production of *Two Character Play*.

**FIGURES 8.1, 8.2, 8.3**

### LEARNING OBJECTIVES

**After reading and watching Chapter 8, you should be able to:**

* Describe how lighting and sound design contribute to the theatrical power of a play or musical.

* Apply the terms and vocabulary to specific examples of live theatre to identify and differentiate the effects of lights or sound on a production.

⁂ Discuss the tools and processes that lighting and sound designers use to accomplish their art.

⁂ Discuss the contributions made by other technical personnel to a theatrical production.

## LIGHTING DESIGNERS

Of all the design elements in theatre, lighting is usually the last one added to the rehearsal process—yet, lighting design has a significant impact on the final quality of most shows.

**FIGURE 8.4**

### Lighting Designers: History

In the great outdoor **amphitheatres** of classical Greece, Rome, and Renaissance England, plays were performed during the day, so the lighting was the sun. Once theatre began to happen indoors, as early as the Middle Ages in the **liturgical dramas** of the churches, candles and oil lamps became the chief source of lighting, as they were during the Italian Renaissance and into the nineteenth century. Therefore, for 2,000 years, theatrical lighting remained relatively static. There were attempts to control the light, but these attempts could go only so far, as anyone who has tried to set a romantic mood with candlelight or suffered a power outage can attest. This is not to say that lighting was unimportant. It always has been crucial to theatre. (The meaning of the Greek word *theatron* as "seeing place" suggests the importance of light to make the "seeing" possible.) The ancient Greeks very likely timed scenes in their plays to coincide with the changes in the sunlight, and the theatre structures themselves were oriented to take advantage of the light. Colored glass, torches, polished reflectors, huge numbers of candles and lamps, and even fireworks were utilized to create special effects from the Middle Ages on. It is important to note, however, that until the nineteenth century, in the indoor theatres, both the stage *and* the auditorium were lit, unlike our present practice of darkening the auditorium.

Around 1672, **footlights** came into use, candles placed along the apron, or front edge of the stage, to illuminate the actors specifically. Because several of them were usually clustered at the center, actors tended to move there for important speeches. In 1785, Argand oil lamps were developed, producing a brighter, steadier light and generally replacing candles, which tended to flicker.

**FIGURE 8.5**

But it was the introduction of gas and limelight to the theatre that significantly enhanced lighting and the ability to control it. First introduced in 1816 at the Chestnut Street Theatre in Philadelphia, gas stage lighting was not widely adopted until the 1840s, when gas was more readily available to most cities. Still, it had its disadvantages, such as unpleasant fumes, high heat, carbon pollution, and fire danger. But the advantages overruled, particularly the ability of one person to control numerous gas lights through the invention, in the 1840s, of the **gas table**, a precursor to the modern control board. The **limelight**, also known as calcium or Drummond light, the latter after its inventor, produced a focused, intense light through the combination of gas, hydrogen, oxygen, and lime, making it the prototype for the modern spotlight. These inventions revolutionized stage lighting during the nineteenth century.

**FIGURE 8.6**

In England, director/producer Henry Irving (1838–1905), using gas exclusively, was one of the first to make an art of stage lighting. He experimented with colored glass, masking to prevent light spill from off the stage, and darkening the auditorium. However, by the time gas was in wide use, Thomas Edison's 1879 invention of the incandescent light bulb provided the impetus for more long-lasting innovations using electricity. Theatres quickly abandoned gas in favor of the first illuminant without fire danger, with London's Savoy Theatre leading the way in 1881. But because early incandescent lamps were low in wattage, they often were used alongside the more intense limelight (which by 1920, fell out of use, thanks to improvements in wattage), as well as the somewhat harsh **carbon arc**, which combined electricity with sticks of carbon and is still in use. Electric lighting paved the way for both subtlety and special effects that had never been seen before; one cannot overestimate its affect on the development of realism. In one famous New York production, *Madame Butterfly* (1901), created by David Belasco (1853–1931), the title character waits from sunset to sunrise for her lover; the lighting effect simulating both involved a series of lighting cues that took fourteen minutes to complete.

However, nearly as soon as the innovations were adopted to create realistic theatre, artists, such as Adolphe Appia (1862–1928), co-opted electric lighting for non-realistic, more abstract use. Appia is considered the father of modern stage lighting theory and design; he argued that light, the visual counterpart to music, should be the guiding artistic principle behind all design. Appia viewed the stage as having three conflicting elements: the horizontal floor, the vertical scenery, and the three-dimensional actor. For him, lighting was one of the primary tools to unify these.

Edward Gordon Craig espoused these and other theories on lighting in his designs and productions. Stanley McCandless, a professor at Yale University, is credited with creating the first comprehensive method for stage lighting, which he developed in the 1920s. Today theatre artists call him the "father of modern lighting design," and his book *A Method of Lighting the Stage* is still in wide use as a text today. Since McCandless, a number of designers have come to the fore in the Western world, including Rainer Casper, Jules Fisher, Chris Parry, Richard Pillbrow, Kenneth Posner, and Robert Wilson. Although men have participated widely in this relatively young profession, women have had illustrious careers as lighting designers, including Jennifer Tipton, Natasha Katz, Peggy Eisenhauer, Tharon Musser, and Jean Rosenthal.

The latter is considered by many to be the originator of the field of lighting design. When Rosenthal began working in the theatre in America during the 1930s, scenic designers were usually responsible for lighting the stage. Rosenthal is perhaps best known for her work with the Martha Graham Dance Company, as well as on such landmark musicals as *West Side Story* and *The Sound of Music*.

Tharon Musser is the lighting equivalent to scenic designer Ming Cho Lee in terms of her influence on the field. Like so many of America's outstanding designers, she graduated from Yale, and then she worked on José Quintero's Broadway production of Eugene O'Neill's *Long Day's Journey Into Night*. Her long, innovative career on Broadway, lighting over 125 productions, included all of Neil Simon's plays, *Follies*, *Dream Girls*, and *A Chorus Line*; she won Tony Awards for all three musicals. (See Figure 8.8.) For *A Chorus Line*, one of the longest-running Broadway shows, Musser introduced computerized lighting to the Broadway stage (which will be discussed in more detail later).

**FIGURES 8.7 AND 8.8**

### Lighting Designers: Materials, Methods, and Processes

Obviously, the main "material"—light—utilized to realize a lighting design is much less concrete than most of the materials manipulated by the set and costume designers. (And this is true for sound as well.) However, the many ways in which light is created and projected can differ widely. As noted before, the electric incandescent bulb has become the basic unit of stage lighting design. For most of the last century, the two main instruments that utilized the bulb were the **fresnel** (pronounced *fruh-NEL*), or spherical reflector spotlight, so named for the inventor of the lens—Augustine Jean Fresnel; and the **ellipsoidal** reflector spotlight, sometimes referred to as a "leko" after its two inventors, Joe Levy and Ed Kook. The fresnel gives a soft edge to the light; the ellipsoidal, a sharper, more defined edge.

**FIGURES 8.9, AND 8.10**

**Gobos** may be used on the latter; these are metal plates with stencils cut out so that the light projects a pattern, such as leaves, onto the stage. **Gels** short for gelatin, from which gobos were originally made, are colored sheets of plastic, Mylar, or acetate used widely on all instruments to change the colors of the light projected. **Follow spots**, as the name suggests, follow actors around the stage, and unlike the other instruments, require individual operators for each instrument. The other instruments are controlled on dimmer and control boards. The dimmer controls the intensity, varying the amount of power that goes to the light, and the control board "communicates" the timing and level to the dimmer. Other common instruments are the floodlights and "scoops" that provide general, much less concentrated illumination. Each instrument fulfills a different purpose.

**FIGURE 8.11**

Recently developed technologies have further revolutionized stage lighting. Innovations in bulb and instrument design have led to new types of lighting instruments, most notably par lamps and Source Fours. Par lamps, or par cans, have a bulb modeled after a car's sealed beam headlight and function much like a fresnel. Source Four instruments are similar to, but much in advance of, lekos. Control boards are now often computerized, allowing the designer or operator to program hundreds of cues (timed changes) for an entire show. In the past, these changes were performed manually by the board operator, allowing for a considerable degree of human error that was unacceptable, particularly for heavy-cue shows such as megamusicals (or rock concerts!).

**FIGURE 8.12**

With computerized boards, the changes happen automatically. More and more designers also are working with **automated lighting** (or "intelligent" lighting). Initially developed for rock concerts in the 1980s, automated lights provide much more flexibility with a single instrument than those listed previously, all of which require a human to move them. With automated lighting, one single light can be programmed to change its direction, focus, and color throughout a production. Computerized boards reduce both the inventory of lights needed and the human power needed to install so many lights (and in the case of the follow spot, to operate it). However, they are much more expensive to purchase and maintain, and can be distracting due to their movement; some designers resist the new technology, just as a photographer may prefer a single-lens reflex camera over a digital camera.

**FIGURE 8.13**

The methods through which designers utilize these various instruments to light a production can vary. As mentioned before, Stanley McCandless was a pioneer in the creation of a working method for lighting designers, but his is by no means the only method. Still, most designers engage in similar processes, beginning their work, as all members of the creative team, with careful readings of text, while compiling images and other research to contribute to the overall concept. Throughout the process, the lighting designer must provide or assist in providing the following:

- visibility
- mass, form, and texture
- focus
- creation of mood
- establishment of environment and atmosphere (place, time, weather, etc.)

- rhythm of visual movement
- special effects and practicals (e.g., table lamps or chandeliers to be turned on during the show)

Quite pragmatically, the designer must ensure that the actors and their costumes, the scenery and props, and so on, are visible. (Or not, if this is a requirement of the moment or scene. The first scene of Peter Shaffer's *Black Comedy* is played entirely in the dark.) But the job of the lighting designer goes far beyond the pragmatics of visibility, and whereas the audience may not be consciously aware of her craft, the designer is always cognizant of the subtler, unconscious effects of light. She must carefully work to creatively address the four controllable qualities of light: intensity, color, movement, and distribution. There are no set rules regarding how to do this, although the designer may be limited by issues related to safety, the available instruments, and the size or configuration of the theatre space itself.

**FIGURE 8.14**

The lighting designer's process is somewhat delayed when compared with those of the scenic and costume designers; she must wait for costumes and scenery to be designed in order to have something to light, and then she must complete a large amount of work only late in the rehearsal process when actors are blocked and working in the performance space. Some designers might create preliminary **renderings** of their initial ideas to indicate color and direction, working with colored media on black backgrounds.

Still, the two primary tools of the lighting designer are the **light plot** and **instrument schedule**. Designers usually will create two types of plots: floor plan and vertical section. The floor plan is a view from above the stage, and, often, the auditorium, that indicates the type and position of every instrument and the area it will light. The vertical section provides a side view. Usually, a separate light plot is created for each setting, along with one composite plot showing the settings, and thus, the lights, in relation to one another. The instrument schedule is a detailed list of each instrument used, including its specifications, position, color filter, area lit, circuit into which it is plugged, and dimmers that control it.

**FIGURE 8.15**

The designer occasionally will attend rehearsals to get a sense of the blocking. But the first important activity of the designer and his assistants is the hanging, or mounting, and focusing of the lights, usually done right before technical rehearsals. During technical rehearsals, he fine-tunes the lights in response to the finalized blocking, set, and costumes. Then he writes the cues for the show, notating each change in light and programming the light board (if it is computerized).

Throughout technical rehearsals, the lighting designer works closely with the director to finalize the design. The majority of the work of a lighting designer is done during brief, intense periods. Therefore he must be able to work under a great amount of pressure and remain calm and even-tempered (a personality requirement of all who work in theatre, yet it is sometimes absent!). He must also have a good working knowledge of physics and electronics in order to understand the general properties of light, electricity, and the instruments with which he works. Computer programming skills are increasingly necessary as well.

Just as scenic and costume designers do, the lighting designer also needs skills similar to those of the visual artist, including a basic understanding of composition, light, shadow, and color. Because the work of the lighting designer is often a unifier in the production, his approach is somewhat similar to the director's, requiring an ability to see the overall picture.

**FIGURE 8.16**

**Lighting Designers: Related Aspects: Assistants and Technicians**

Lighting designers often utilize one or two assistant designers, who may create light plots and instrument schedules and locate equipment, among other duties. Crucial to the stage lighting process is the Master Electrician (ME), who works closely with the designer to install the instruments, oversee safety procedures, and check and maintain the equipment during the run of the show. (In some theatres the technical director, described later, serves as the ME.) A lighting crew helps during the hang and focus, with maintenance, and with moving any lighting equipment during performance. As mentioned, a control board operator executes cues under the guidance of the production stage manager. In professional theatre, these technicians belong to the International Alliance of Theatrical Stage Employees (IATSE) union.

**FIGURE 8.17**

## SOUND DESIGNERS: HISTORY

Sound is almost as crucial to theatre as light. The Ancient Greeks recognized this, building their outdoor amphitheatres into the slopes of hillsides to take advantage of the acoustics inherent in such configurations. Playgoers during the English Renaissance recognized this as well; they would refer to attending the theatre as going to "hear," not "see," a play.

**FIGURE 8.18**

The preservation of play texts attests to the importance that many cultures place on words—and the speaking of those words—in theatre, but sound can mean much more than words. Music has always been an important component of theatrical sound; Aristotle considered it one of the six components of tragedy. Sound effects such as thunder have been used to augment productions. In Elizabethan theatres, thunder was simulated through such devices as "thunder machines" (wooden troughs down which cannonballs would roll) and "thunder sheets" (sheets of tin that were rattled). Cannons were fired from roofs to indicate the sounds of battle, trumpets announced the arrivals of important characters, and so on.

However, until the twentieth century, live sound was the only possibility. Now both recorded and amplified sound have increased the audio possibilities in the theatrical event, particularly thanks to innovations developed during the past 30 years, making live sound—to the detriment of an inherently live event, some argue—rarer and rarer.

Whether live or recorded, sound is often used in contemporary theatre to set the mood of the play, particularly through the use of pre- and post-show music, as well as music and other sound between acts, or even to underscore dialogue during scenes. Indeed, the use of music in theatre today seems to increasingly mirror its uses in film, harkening back to its ubiquity in classical Greece all the way up to melodrama. Regardless, sound in general is an extremely evocative technique on which many directors rely today.

## SOUND DESIGNERS: MATERIALS, METHODS, AND PROCESSES

The "material" of the sound designer is obviously as nebulous as that of the lighting designer. But the sound designer today uses a variety of technologies to create, record, control, manipulate, augment, and amplify sound in the theatre. (See Figure 8.19.) Since the advent of electricity, stage crews have employed a number of manual devices to create sound, such as telephones or doorbell ringers, and a door slammer, which is a smaller version of a door frame and door. Increasingly, such sounds are pre-recorded, now primarily digitally. Most designers maintain an extensive library of recorded sounds; today many can be downloaded from the Internet. Synthesizers also aid in the creation of sounds. Although reel-to-reel tapes were the norm for many years, today most designers record and manipulate digital sound on their computers, with the help of a variety of software programs such as Avid/Digidesign's Protools and Adobe's Audition.

**FIGURES 8.19 AND 8.20**

Stage microphones, which pick up sounds and then amplify them through speakers, are becoming an increasingly prevalent tool of the sound designer. Area mikes pick up general sounds, while body mikes, worn by actors, capture sounds emitted specifically from the wearer. Area mikes may be hung from above or mounted on the sides of the stage or elsewhere. Body mikes, often wireless, are usually either worn at the back of the costume or mounted to the head, which keeps the mike near the performers' mouth. Mounting the mikes to the performers' heads sometimes involves attempting to conceal them under makeup or wigs, but other designers leave them visible, as Kurt Fischer did for *Rent*.

**FIGURE 8.21**

The use of mikes is the primary source of controversy surrounding the ubiquity of such technologies in theatre today. The mediation of sound through mikes and speakers is anathema, some would argue, to the liveness that makes theatre unique. A well-trained actor it might be said, should be able to project his or her voice in any acoustically sound space, and there is no substitute for the quality of the unmediated voice (or, say, musical instrument). Others decry the increasingly extensive musical underscoring in plays, criticizing what they view as an attempt to mirror cinema. And some theatregoers quite simply complain that the sound is too loud.

Supporters of sound amplification counter that if it is done well, no one notices the reinforcement and the voice sounds better. And with advancements in home audio technologies, audiences will expect better sound everywhere, including in the theatre. Other proponents point out that the demands on actors' voices—particularly during musicals—in theatres which produce eight shows a week, as most professional theatres do, new technologies ease the demands on their voices. These productions also now often demand that a blues, rock, or pop sound is produced, which leads to the need for amplified instruments.

However one feels, technology is an integral part of theatrical sound design, and the increasing complexity of audio in theatre requires another important tool, the **sound mixer**, a device that allows the designer to layer multiple sounds, merging them into one stream of sound. More and more audiences find themselves sharing space with this control board and its operator, who often mixes a master sound recording with the less predictable sound coming through the mikes and speakers, making adjustments throughout the performance accordingly.

**FIGURE 8.22**

As all other designers do, the sound designer begins her process with close readings of the play, identifying the potential sound requirements, such as effects. For some productions, she will begin to consider the number and types of mikes required and the placement of speakers; if needed, the orchestra; and monitors projecting an image of the conductor on a screen only visible to the actors if he is not in full view of the performers. As she analyses the script, she may consider the four main functions of sound:

- to evoke mood and atmosphere
- to tell the story and reinforce the action
- to reinforce the style of production
- to reinforce voices and orchestra

Sound can have powerful effects on the mood or tone of the piece; music particularly can elicit emotional responses in the audience. Or the effects can be more direct, as when a gunshot is heard offstage. Without such a sound, a crucial component of the action or story could be missing.

**FIGURE 8.23**

In consultation with the director, the sound designer creates a sound score, indicating the sound, its duration, its source, and how it will be treated. Then the crucial work of collecting the sounds, using the various resources described previously, begins. A **sound plot** is developed, similar to the score but much more detailed, indicating such things as cue number, playback system, and source direction. Also developed is a "show tape" (likely, digital) containing all sound effects, pre-recorded music, and so on. The designer will periodically attend rehearsals to get a feel for points at which she will need to integrate the sounds, as well as to discover any additional sounds needed. During technical rehearsals, sound levels and lengths of cues may be adjusted, and the show tape updated accordingly. Often, a sound engineer will aid the designer in implementing the designs, working with actors and mikes and hooking up equipment. During the run of the show, the responsibility shifts to the sound board operator and the production stage manager, who "calls" the show (see subsequent discussion of technical direction and stage management).

Thanks to new technologies (for better or worse depending on one's perspective) sound has become an extremely complex part of the theatrical event, and the sound designer a crucial contributor to the production team. Men have tended to dominate the field, led by pioneer Abe Jacob, whose career began with rock bands and continued on Broadway with such shows as *Jesus Christ Superstar* and *A Chorus Line*. The craft of the sound designer is gaining more and more respect, thanks to designers such as Jacob, who was instrumental in encouraging IASTE to charter its first sound designers' chapter in 1986. John Gromada was awarded an Obie (Off-Broadway award) for sound design for *Machinal*, and in 1993 the Yale School of Drama admitted its first sound designers to the design program. Women are making inroads into the professions, such as Janet Kalas, who has pioneered the field for women at such Off-Broadway theatres as Playwrights Horizons, the Public Theatre, the Vineyard Theatre, and Circle Repertory Company.

## MIXING ART AND TECHNOLOGY

Both lighting and sound designers must mix artistry with a high degree of technical knowledge and sophistication, especially as new technologies expand and change what is possible.

**FIGURES 8.24, 8.25, 8.26, 8.27, 8.28, 8.29, AND 8.30**

## TECHNICAL PRODUCTION

The glue that holds together the work of all of the designers is, in many ways, the production/stage manager and the technical director. Alone or together, they oversee much of what is created behind the scenes; without them, theatre as we know it could not happen, particularly given the increasing complexity of elements that come together in production. In many theatres, a production manager coordinates all aspects of production in consultation with the creative teams of various productions in a season, setting the rehearsal schedules, presiding over production meetings, coordinating the overall budget, and many other tasks. One of his/her primary functions may be to oversee the stage management team.

**FIGURE 8.31**

A stage manager acts as the director's right-hand wo/man, in many cases, organizing rehearsals, communicating with actors, and making sure that the show maintains its overall look and integrity after opening. The stage manager's many functions include the following:

- managing rehearsals and readying the rehearsal place (including taping an outline of the ground plan of the stage and set to the floor)
- keeping a **prompt book** (a copy of the text noted with all rehearsal work, such as blocking)

- writing and disseminating rehearsal reports, a memo with changes needed to the set, props, costumes, and so on
- communicating with actors
- running, or "calling," the show by telling the light and sound board operators, as well as the stage crew, when to initiate a change

The stage manager may have one or more assistants, some or all of whom may stay backstage during a production to help there, communicating over headsets with the production stage manager, who sits in a booth with the board operators at the back of the auditorium. The stage manager must be organized, level-headed, diplomatic, and quick thinking. A sense of humor is a must as well for this position, which is considered by many to be the most demanding in all of theatre. However, some of the best job opportunities in theatre exist for a well-trained stage or production manager.

**FIGURE 8.32**

This is also the case for the technical director, or TD. His or her duties can vary considerably, depending on the context, but they primarily consist of maintaining and preparing the space, overseeing the construction of the set, and ensuring that all equipment and machinery are in working order. The TD works closely with the set designer to realize the design, creating technical specifications, "costing" and ordering materials, and overseeing the scene shop in which the scenery is built, although larger theatres may have a shop foreman for the latter duty. The TD also supervises the **load-in** of scenery, in which the set is moved from the construction area to the performance space, as well as the opposite of the load-in, the **strike**, following the show's closing. In small theatres, the TD may actually build sets himself. Large theatres such as Broadway or West End houses often contract with scenic studios to construct sets; in this case, the TD's primary job becomes writing technical specifications from the designs and serving as a liaison between the designer and the studio.

**FIGURES 8.33, 8.34, AND 8.35**

The TD may have a number of assistants, such as the shop foreman or carpenters, at her aid, as well as stagehands to help move scenery during the performance. However, the latter are becoming less necessary as more automation is utilized in theatre; today's technical directors must have a knowledge not only of hydraulics, but also of computerized motion-control systems, which is, not surprisingly, becoming more and more common, particularly in larger theatres. Indeed, the increasing technological complexity of theatre is driving the TD to be more of a full-fledged artist and creator than a mere implementer and technician.

## For Further Information

Appia, Adolphe. *Music and the Art of the Theatre*. Robert W. Corrigan and Mary Douglas Dirks, 1962.

Gillette, J. Michael. *Designing with Light*. 4th ed. 2002.

Izenour, George C. *Theatre Design*. 1977.

Jones, Robert Edmond. *The Dramatic Imagination*. 1987.

Keller, Max. *Light Fantastic: The Art and Design of Stage Lighting*. 2006.

Lebrecht, James, and Deena Kaye. *Sound and Music for the Theatre: The Art and Technique of Design*. 1998.

Leonard, John A. *Theatre Sound*. 2001.

Maier, Manfred. *Basic Principles of Design*. 1977.

McCandless, Stanley. *A Method of Lighting the Stage*. 1958.

Pillbrow, Richard. *Stage Lighting Design: The Art, The Craft, The Life*. 1997.

Reid, Francis. *The ABC of Stage Technology*. 1995.

Reid, Francis. *The Stage Lighting Handbook*. 1996.

Rosenthal, Jean. *The Magic of Light*. 1972.

## Suggested Films

*The Jazz Singer* (1927): The first talkie (sound).
*Singin' in the Rain* (1952): Phonetics for actors, sound, and movie sound.
*Cabaret* (1972): Lights, sound, singing, and dancing.
*All That Jazz* (1979): Lights, sound, singing, and dancing.
*Slings and Arrows* (2003): TV series. See, especially, Season Two, the *Hamlet* episodes.

*The Libertine* (2004): Eighteenth-century staging, lights, etc. (adult language).
*Finding Neverland* (2004): Lights, sets, and staging.
*Me and Orson Welles* (2008): Theatre scenes show examples of lighting, staging, and sound.

## Glossary

**amphitheatres**   Outdoor performance spaces, often circular with seats sloping toward the stage.

**automated lighting**   Also known as "intelligent" lighting, can be computer programmed to change direction, focus, and color for more flexibility, with fewer instruments and fewer human operators.

**carbon arc**   A harsh, noisy light that combines electricity with sticks of carbon. Invented in the early nineteenth century, but not used widely until the 1880s, when it was utilized in spotlights.

**ellipsoidal**   An electric lighting instrument, also known as the leko, that gives off a much sharper-edged light than the fresnel.

**follow spot**   Sharp-edged lighting instrument used to follow an actor with light.

**footlights**   Lights housed at the front of the stage along the edge of the apron that throw a rather unflattering light upward; common from the seventeenth through nineteenth centuries—using candles, oils, or gas—but rarely used today.

**fresnel**   Also known as a spherical reflector spotlight, an electric instrument that produces a soft-edged light and is widely used today.

**gas table**   Precursor to the modern lighting control board, enabling one individual to control all the gas lights in a theatre. Invented in the nineteenth century.

**gels**   Short for gelatin, from which they were originally made, today they are colored sheets of plastic, Mylar, or acetate, used widely on all instruments to change the colors of the light projected.

**gobos**   Metal plates with stencils cut out so that the light projects a pattern, such as leaves, onto the stage.

**instrument schedule**   A detailed list of each instrument used, including its specifications, position, color filter, area lit, circuit into which it is plugged, and dimmers that control it.

**light plot**   A map of lighting instruments, their positions, and their connections, that a lighting designer will use on a production; usually includes an instrument schedule.

**limelight**   Also known as calcium or Drummond light, produces a focused, intense light through the combination of gas, hydrogen, oxygen, and lime; the prototype for the modern spotlight. Identifies someone at the center of attention (e.g., "in the limelight").

**liturgical dramas**   Performances developed during the Middle Ages by and within the Catholic Church to communicate Christian teachings.

**load-in**   The movement of the set from the construction area to the performance space, usually supervised by the technical director.

**prompt book**   A copy of the play text, used by the stage management team, noted with all rehearsal work, such as blocking.

**renderings**   Artistic drawings of scenery, costume, or lighting designs that indicate line, color, media, direction (for lights), and so on.

**sound mixer**   A device used by the sound designer to layer multiple sounds, merging them into one stream of sound.

**sound plot**   A detailed list of cue numbers, playback systems, and source directions for all sound cues for a production.

**strike**   Removal of the set from the performance space after a production closes.

## Key Concepts

- Designers rely more and more on new technologies in their work.
- For nearly 2,000 years, theatrical lighting remained fairly static, utilizing natural light, candles, and oil lamps.
- The advent of the use of gas, electricity, and computers during the past two centuries revolutionized stage lighting.
- The craft of the lighting designer goes far beyond ensuring visibility.

- Because the work of the lighting designer often unifies all aspects of the production, it is similar to that of the director.
- The growing use of recorded and amplified sound in the theatre has increased the need for sound designers, as well as the complexity of their job.
- The "glue" that holds the work of the designers together—as well as other members of the production team—is the stage manager and the technical director.

# Actors

**Chapter Outline**

*To view the figures in this chapter, log on to www.pearsonexploretheatre.com.*

## INTRODUCTION

Everyone is an actor in some respects. Whether role-playing or imitating (mimesis, a Greek word meaning "imitation," is at the heart of Aristotle's definition of theatre), acting is an integral part of most people's daily lives. For example, a college student attempting to persuade another student to go out on a date with him may act more confident than he actually feels, pushing out his chest, swaggering, speaking more loudly, or in other ways adjusting his usual physical and vocal traits in order to impress. However, acting on the stage, for any theatrical tradition or style, is considerably different from everyday acting. It requires a consciousness that one is being watched—always. Although others may observe us at various moments in our daily lives, there are usually times, when we are alone or even when we are with others, that we are not the center of attention. This is not true for the actor, who must always consciously maintain a certain level of energy that many call "stage presence." However, that energy must be under control at all times. Although our emotions may get out of control in real life, leading to unexpected actions on our part, the actor onstage rarely engages in the unexpected, except in **improvisation**, which is still controlled.

**FIGURE 9.1**

Furthermore, acting is more than imitation; it is interpretation. Actors frequently are asked to play roles that they would never play in real life. Role-playing for most people is limited to a fairly small range of characters. Although actors may get typecast into certain roles, particularly in traditions like **commedia dell'arte**, **Bejing Opera**, or **Kabuki**, the best actors avoid this. For example, Denzel Washington is widely respected and liked in Hollywood, and roles such as Melvin Tolson in *The Great Debaters* capitalize on that perception, but playing killers like Frank Lucas in *American Gangster* or Alonzo in *Training Day* requires him to interpret characters who are very different from himself.

In this chapter, after defining the concept of acting, we will explore those tools, from rehearsal to performance, in which an actor engages in order to create a role. We also include a description of the similarities and differences between acting for the stage and acting for the camera, and then briefly discuss acting as a profession. Throughout, we consider changing methods and processes in various historical contexts.

## LEARNING OBJECTIVES

### After reading Chapter 9, students should be able to:

- Explain the differences between "acting" in everyday life and acting in a performance.
- Identify the key differences between presentational and representational acting, and discuss how each appears in different times and cultures.
- Describe the typical journey actors undertake in their training and preparation.
- Discuss the similarities and differences between acting for the stage and acting for the camera.

## ACTING DEFINED

Acting is the heart of theatre; without at least one actor, theatre cannot exist. Before there were playwrights, directors, or designers, there were actors. Thespis, from whom we get the word "**thespian**," meaning "actor," is the first known Western actor, who also created the plays in which he appeared. Acting is the most visible aspect of the collaborative theatrical process; most audience members never think of producing, playwriting, designing, or directing when they see a show.

**FIGURE 9.2**

Defining "acting" may at first seem to be a simple task. At its most basic level, as Aristotle pointed out, acting is imitation, but it is also transformation, because actors always undergo some form of change from their everyday selves to become a character. And how one defines "acting" can shift dramatically depending on the context—the culture and the period. Still, acting can be divided into two main types: **presentational** (or external) and **representational** (or internal). Debates regarding the comparative merits of the two have been waged since Ancient Greece and Rome, when most actors embraced a presentational style; however, much acting today is a combination of both.

**FIGURE 9.3**

## FROM PRESENTATIONAL TO REPRESENTATIONAL

The idea that acting is something which the actor presents to the audience originates in an emphasis on the external tools at the actor's disposal—facial expression, gesture and movement, and other aspects of the actor's physicality—as well as on imitation. Presentational actors work to illustrate a character "from the outside in." They may carefully study the outward manifestations of human behavior and then work, in a disciplined way, to reproduce them. Presentational actors often learn by imitating other actors or teachers whom they consider role models. They attempt to artificially re-create emotions. In contrast to presentational actors, who present to the audience, representational actors attempt to live real emotions, to truly feel them, and to even be the character. They work "from the inside out," searching for emotional experiences from their own lives to translate into the lives of their characters. The physical aspects of the character grow from the inner life, which is created first.

Up until about 1750, classical theatrical traditions, whether Western or non-Western, seemed to have called primarily for a presentational style. Acting in both Greek and Roman theatres would hardly look natural or realistic to us today; all actors, at least on the institutionalized stages, were men who tended toward types, specializing in playing young women, kings or queens, comic older servants, and so forth, and the plays themselves were not realistic, sprinkled as they were with ghosts, fairies, and other supernatural elements. Because of the large size of the theatres at the time (the theatres often were comparable to modern-day baseball parks), any subtlety of movement, gesture, or emotion would have been lost on most of the audience. As a result, presentational acting trained actors to project their voices and use their bodies to communicate to the vast crowd (an important detail, given that masks were worn at the time). Vocal delivery was probably declamatory, with a mixture of speech, recitation, and song, not unlike the vocal delivery of today's opera.

**FIGURES 9.4 AND 9.5**

In Asian cultures such as India, China, and Japan, classical theatrical traditions were based largely on a type of presentational acting called **codified acting**—a complex system of signs, including movement, facial expressions, and gestures, set by tradition and handed down from teacher to student, often for generations. Performances would often integrate dance, singing, acrobatics, mime, and music in complex, detailed, precise interpretations of well-known myths. Elaborate costumes and makeup would complete the system of signs, which can be difficult for the uninitiated to read. In other words, one needs some sort of training, albeit usually informal, in order to be able to understand the meanings communicated in these performances. Some examples of codified acting have appeared in Sanskrit Theatre, Kathakali, Beijing Opera, Noh, and Kabuki, which still exist today.

**FIGURES 9.6 AND 9.7**

Representational acting first surfaced during the early seventeenth century in England. Although the presentational style of acting still dominated, English playhouses were much smaller than those typical in Ancient Greece or Rome, seating around 2,000 if public, even fewer if private. This smaller space enabled a more intimate, realistic theatrical experience to develop, one in which audiences could witness the actors' detailed movements and facial expressions. Shakespeare's *Hamlet* suggests the notion that a representational style of acting was valued when Hamlet gives the following advice to the players, as actors were called in Elizabethan England:

> Speak the speech, I pray you, as I pronounced it to you, trippingly on the tongue; but if you mouth it, as many of your players do, I had as lief the towncrier spoke my lines. Nor do not saw the air too much with your hand, thus, but use all gently; for in the very torrent, tempest and, as I may say, the whirlwind of your passion, you must acquire and beget a temperance that may give it smoothness.
>
> . . . suit the action to the word, the word to the action; with this special observance, that you o'erstep not the modesty of nature: for anything so overdone is from the purpose of playing, whose end, both at the first and now, was and is, to hold, as't were, the mirror up to nature.

Shakespeare, via the words of the character Hamlet, is calling for a more natural tone of voice than the declamatory style a "towncrier" would use. He seems also to suggest that gestures should flow from, and be appropriate to, emotions. In general, he is warning against exaggerated acting and advocating what could have been closer to our representational acting. But, of course, we have little idea exactly what may or may not have appeared overdone to the Elizabethan audience member.

One hundred years later, in France during **Neoclassicism** and in England during the **Restoration**, the presence of women on stage may have provided an even greater impetus for a more representational style of acting, because the playing of women as stereotypes, interpreted by male actors, no longer was acceptable. Audiences expected more realistic depictions of women on stage. (See the film *Stage Beauty*.) In addition, the smaller size of the theatres, the subjects of plays such as those of Congreve, Wycherley, and Molière, and the indoor drawing-room settings of many productions of the time led to an intimacy that called for a more realistic acting style. In France, Molière spoke out against excessive acting practices in his short play *The Impromptu of Versailles*. And during the first half of the eighteenth century, David Garrick, often considered the greatest actor of the English stage, and Michel Baron, the leading tragic actor of his day in France, advocated for a more realistic approach, intent on communicating the complexities of a role. Still, aspects of the presentational style persisted. Actors played at the front of the stage (partly so as not to spoil the perspective in the scenery behind them), rarely showing profile, and exchanging stage positions after speeches; furthermore, evidence suggests that many delivered verse in long, intoned chants, prolonging certain exclamations for dramatic effect. Many, like Thomas Betterton, retained an oratorical style that would hardly sound natural to us today.

**FIGURES 9.8 AND 9.9**

The major shift from presentational acting to representational acting occurred after 1750 when Western theatre began to emphasize specificity and historical accuracy; both emphases were the result of increased attempts to make art copy life, which is at the heart of **realism**. **Romanticism** of the late eighteenth and early nineteenth centuries gave way to **melodrama**, the most popular form of theatre in the nineteenth century. The characteristic spectacle of melodrama included more and more elaborate detail in scenery. Technology paved the way for better, more controlled lighting, setting the stage for a more realistic production. Gradually, throughout the nineteenth century, representational acting increased the ability (beyond presentational acting) of performers to depict the inner life and complexities of characters, mirroring the complexities of real-life individuals.

**FIGURE 9.10**

The movement to representational acting was solidified when realism in playwriting began to appear in the mid-nineteenth century. The perfection of realism in drama in Europe rested largely on the shoulders of three playwrights: Henrik Ibsen of Norway, August Strindberg of Sweden, and Anton Chekhov of Russia. Chekhov became the resident playwright of the Moscow Art Theatre, cofounded in 1898 by Vladimir Nemirovich-Danchenko and actor and director Konstantin Stanislavsky. There, the basis for most methods of actor training for representational, realistic styles was born.

## ACTING METHODS

In non-Western, presentational acting traditions, formal training begins at a very young age, and the demands on the actor's instruments—the body and voice—are considerable. A student often prepares to perform a certain role, carefully learning all of the codes passed down to communicate that role, but eventually, after years of practice, making it his or her own (most likely his, since many of these forms have historically excluded female performers). In classical Sanskrit performance, for example, the actor has to learn six movements of the nose, six of the cheek, seven of the eyebrows, nine of the neck, seven of the chin, thirty-six of the eyes, and, even, five of the chest. For Beijing Opera, actors typically enter a school before the age of 10, studying for over a decade and eventually specializing in a particular role.

**FIGURE 9.11**

Although, as mentioned previously, representational acting began to develop in earnest before the eighteenth century, there was no system of training for it until the late nineteenth century. Historically, Western potential actors learned on the job as apprentices, moving from small roles to larger ones. Russian director Konstantin Stanislavsky set out to develop a system of training for representational acting in plays such as those of Chekhov. Stanislavsky's system is complex and difficult to summarize, partly due to various misinterpretations of Stanislavsky's original intentions, but there are some characteristics that can and should be described.

Using some theories from the newly developed science of psychology, Stanislavsky sought a means by which the actor could present situations, actions, and emotions closely similar to those in everyday life. He emphasized the importance of **given circumstances** in a play, to which the actor, using the first person, must explore ways by which the character would react to those circumstances. Considering the details of the play—the location, the period, and the conflicts—the actor asks, "Where am I? What has happened before the play begins? What is happening now? Why am I here?" and, perhaps most important, "Who am I?" Through careful analysis of the play, the actor begins to build a character. Once he or she outlines the given circumstances, the actor uses a concept called the "magic if" to explore how he or she would behave in such circumstances: "If I were Nora (in Ibsen's *A Doll's House*), how would I react?" The actor then divides the play into **objectives**, or statements of what the character wants to achieve, and determines an overriding superobjective. The objectives are expressed as active verbs—"to listen," "to leave." As the character works to achieve the objectives, the actor makes adjustments to shifting circumstances, each of which marks a **beat** in the play.

## EMOTIONAL MEMORY TO INTERCULTURAL

One of the most controversial techniques advocated by Stanislavsky is **emotional memory**, also referred to as emotional recall or affective memory. This method requires the actor to recall episodes in her own life that are similar to the character's experiences, utilizing within the performance the memory of the emotions and sensations from that time. Acting teachers have disagreed on how strongly this technique should be emphasized, because it can take the character outside the world of the play; critics argue that it encourages actors to go to the brink of an emotional breakdown by forcing them to recall negative incidents and emotions from their past. Proponents argue that it is the best way to achieve the most realistic representational acting. Stanislavsky himself eventually recanted his emphasis on this method. Still, most of his techniques remain the cornerstone of much Western representational actor training, particularly in the United States, where they were initially disseminated by the Group Theatre, a company of actors who created realistic, socially relevant theatre in the 1930s. When the company disbanded in the early 1940s, a number of members, such as Lee Strasberg, Sanford Meisner, Robert Lewis, and Stella Adler, founded studios to teach variations of "the Method," or "method acting," as it has come to be known.

**FIGURE 9.12**

In spite of its nickname, **the Method** is not the only training technique to be utilized in the twentieth century, and many actors and directors employ methods that bridge both presentational and representational acting. In Poland in the 1960s, for example, Jerzy

Grotowski developed a method based on his belief that theatre should counter the development and use of technologies on the stage; he advocated "**poor theatre**"—theatre pared down to its essence, as opposed to a technologically "rich" theatre. Decrying stage spectacle, he placed the emphasis on the actor in his innovative productions at the Polish Laboratory Theatre. With little in the way of sets or costumes, actors moved freely and acrobatically about the **black box** space, often integrating music, but only that which the actors could create themselves. Grotowski's system required them to be in complete control of their instruments, because performances were often physically and vocally demanding. Grotowski's methods utilized both a focus on the inner life of characters and an emphasis on a detailed physicality that mirrors techniques in non-Western classical acting.

Still another method was developed by British director Peter Brook, famous for his innovative pared-down interpretations of Shakespeare's plays. In the 1970s, Brook shifted his focus to the International Center for Theatre Research in Paris. There, he gathered a group of actors from around the world to create and adapt texts for the stage. His method focused on transcending different languages and cultures to produce an international theatre. Actors brought whatever technique by which they trained and worked—presentational or representational, Asian or Method, and so forth—to the table, and Brook made little attempt to integrate the various styles. Actors learned other methods by working side by side with their fellow actors. This **intercultural** approach was perhaps most successful in Brook's adaptation, with writer Jean-Claude Carrière, of the Indian epic, the *Mahabharata*. Despite the controversial opinion of many Indian artists that a British director and French writer had no business adapting the sacred Indian text, actors from 16 countries, including Ryszard Cieslak, formerly an actor at Grotowski's Polish Laboratory Theatre, toured with the piece throughout Europe and America.

**FIGURE 9.13**

## INTERCULTURAL TO NON-WESTERN

Although intercultural theatre often involves Western artists borrowing acting techniques from the East, more non-Western artists are ensuring that the exchange goes both ways. Japanese director Tadashi Suzuki's intercultural theatre is grounded in acting techniques borrowed from such Japanese forms as Noh and Kabuki in an effort to counter the realistic (*shingeki*) style of theatre becoming increasingly popular in that country. As in Noh and the Buddhism that influenced it, Suzuki's techniques, called appropriately the "Suzuki Method," emphasize energy in stillness, as well as breathing and a connection to the earth. Utilizing a series of exercises that involves stomping and walking, the actor becomes aware of her connection to the ground and creates a strong core for breathing. Suzuki views his company of actors as a family, with everyone participating in all aspects of running the theatre, which is based in Toga, where he created the first international theatre festival in Japan. Suzuki's techniques require complete dedication, physically, emotionally, and personally; from these techniques, powerful, highly stylized productions of ancient Greek plays such as Euripides' *Trojan Women*, and Shakespeare's work such as *Macbeth*, have been created.

In 1993, Suzuki cofounded the Saratoga International Theatre Institute (SITI) in New York with controversial director Anne Bogart. Their goal has been to "revitalize the theatre inside and out." Bogart's most prominent work has been her collaboration with dancer–choreographer Mary Overlie to create an acting method, called "**Viewpoints**," that counters the dominance of Stanislavsky-based methods. Described as a **postmodern** approach to acting and designed to mirror the fragmentation that is a hallmark of postmodernism, Viewpoints includes six elements: space, time, shape, movement, story, and emotion. Each nonhierarchical element contributes to a strategy for the actor in rehearsal, applying to gesture, the use of theatrical space, duration of movement, tempo, and so forth.

**FIGURE 9.14**

In spite of the dominance of Stanislavsky-based acting methods in the Western world, even Stanislavsky himself advocated the utilization of different methods for different plays, arguing that no one technique is appropriate for every production. In the United States, colleges and universities have become the primary training grounds for actors, from general, liberal arts BA programs to more focused, professional BFA degrees. Some actors prefer, instead of—or in addition to—degree programs, actor-training studios and conservatories, the most famous of which probably is the **Actor's Studio** in New York City. Thanks to artists such as Strasberg, Grotowski, Bogart, playwright and acting theorist David Mamet, and many others, the actor has a myriad of methods, Western, non-Western and intercultural, from which to draw.

## THE ACTOR'S PROCESS

Although all actors should be constantly working and honing their craft—from making simple observations of everyday life around them, to doing regular workouts to tone and strengthen the body, to taking care of the voice by avoiding smoking and excessive alcohol—their training becomes particularly focused when they are preparing to perform as a character on stage. Despite the fact that the actor's method or technique may vary from role to role, the process or routine for most contemporary stage actors in the United States is the same. First, the actor successfully auditions for a role; next, the actor begins preparing or rehearsing for the role. Finally, the actor performs the role for an audience.

**FIGURE 9.15**

### The Audition

For all but the most prominent actors in theatre, an **audition** is required before one is even considered for a role. Although requirements can differ from production to production, most actors must first submit a resume of their roles, with their "stats" (height, weight, etc.) and a list of their special skills (dialects, juggling, burping), along with a "**headshot**," or a professionally produced photograph of the face, neck, and shoulders. Depending on what type of actor the director or **casting** agent is looking for, he may then call in the actors to demonstrate their talent. Typically, actors audition one at a time, but there are many occasions on which actors may encounter hundreds of other actors at one audition; this is referred to as a "cattle call."

**FIGURE 9.16**

In auditions, first impressions can be *everything*. The actor's goal is to prove to the director or casting crew that he is most suited to capture a given role. Actors often are required to perform one or two monologues of their choosing, usually a one- or two-minute speech from a play similar to the one for which they are auditioning (e.g., a comic monologue if they are auditioning for a comedy). For musicals, actors typically must sing a brief excerpt of a selection from the musical theatre repertoire (one notable exception was the audition requirements for the musical *Rent*: those auditioning were required to sing a rock song); they also have to participate in a dance audition. Most actors memorize numerous monologues and, when appropriate, songs for possible auditions; these must be carefully developed and rehearsed. For some productions, actors are asked to do a prepared or impromptu "cold reading" from the play in addition to, or as a replacement for, the monologue.

What the director (or anyone else involved in the audition process) is looking for differs from show to show and may be as intangible as that elusive concept, "stage presence," which is a charismatic energy possessed by some actors that gives them the ability to command the attention of their audience. But more tangibly, they often are looking for experience (which they glean from the resume), preparedness, ease and confidence, and physical and vocal appropriateness for the role. Musical theatre composer and lyricist Stephen Sondheim claims that he can determine whether or not an actor is appropriate for a role that he has written in as little as four bars of a song. Actors may be cast immediately following their audition or, more commonly, be asked to a "callback," a more intensive audition, as the person responsible for casting narrows the field.

The audition process is perhaps one of the harshest, most difficult aspects of the highly competitive profession of acting. The number of actors seeking work at any given time far outweighs the roles available. Rejection is a hallmark of the life of an actor, who may audition for hundreds of roles in any given year and be thrilled to be cast in one.

## THE REHEARSAL

When the actor receives the joyous news that he has been cast in a production, he begins extensive preparation for the role. First, the actor starts building a character through careful analysis of the text—on explicit information, the subtext beneath, and the actor's own interpretation of the role. For example, in the play *Art*, by Yasmina Reza, the character Yvan's trips to his therapist, Finkelzohn, are explicitly outlined in the dialogue. *Why* he goes is implied in the subtext below the lines, and the actor, in conjunction with the director, may decide that the reason is because of his conflicted friendships, his relationship with his mother, his doubts about his impending marriage, or all of these. After this careful analysis, the actor starts memorizing the lines, although the deadline for when he must be off book—performing without the text in hand and with the lines memorized—can vary from production to production. Most directors prefer that actors be off book early in order to facilitate the focus in rehearsal on **blocking**, or the setting of movements of the actors about the space, and business, which is directed stage actions, such as drinking a cup of tea or reading a book.

**FIGURE 9.17**

Rehearsals, which usually begin with a read-through of the play, may involve discussions, the building of relationships, improvisations, and, in general, much experimentation, risk-taking, and exploration. A key to rehearsal is *trying*. Few details (except, often, the lines) are actually "set in stone" until fairly late in the rehearsal process. But at some point, repetition becomes key—of lines, of actions, of objectives—so that each actor can duplicate, in performance, the agreed-upon aspects of the production. (The French word for rehearsal is *repetition*.)

The end of the rehearsal process brings together the technical and design elements of the production—costumes, set, lights, and so forth—with the actors, who previously have been working only with minimal rehearsal props. More often than not, the end of the rehearsal process will be the first time that actors perform in the actual performance space; prior to this time, they are likely to be working in another room with an outline of the set taped on the floor. Four weeks is the average time for rehearsal in the United States, with musicals and more elaborate productions requiring more.

**NOTE**: Many of the actors interviewed in this chapter appear in *Two Character Play*, the one-act play that can be read in Chapter 10, "The Play." Readers can watch several documentaries on that rehearsal process as part of Chapters 6 and 11. The process began with casting, as seen in Chapter 6, "Directors." The regular rehearsal process was next and is documented in Chapter 11, and the very difficult and complex technical rehearsal process followed and is documented in Chapter 11.

## THE PERFORMANCE

Rehearsing a play or musical can be challenging, fun, and rewarding in and of itself, but many would argue that until all the work that has gone into rehearsals is tested in front of an audience, it is not truly theatre. Inevitably, the director, actor, and other members of the creative team can't be sure of the success of their work until the work has been performed. Although, for the most part, the actor should duplicate in performance what has been rehearsed, the stress of being in front of an audience can often change the performance. Stage fright can make the actor unable to remember lines, listen to fellow actors, or play actions and objectives determined in rehearsals. But actors must avoid the mechanical acting that can result from performing night after night, particularly if, as sometimes happens on Broadway, a show runs for years. Boredom can set in for the actor in such situations. But every audience deserves as high a quality performance as the actors are able to give.

Fortunately, systems of actor training such as Stanislavsky's are methods not simply for preparation and rehearsal of a role and production, but also for mining the emotions of a character night after night while remaining in control *and* still capturing in each performance the immediacy of opening night. Ultimately, the actor can prepare and rehearse until she is blue in the face, but without an audience, she is never truly *acting*. Laughter, applause, a barely audible gasp from an audience member, and so forth likely will cause the actor to adjust her performance, even if imperceptibly. This adjustment based on response to the audience shouldn't deviate in major ways from what has been rehearsed, but can help alleviate the mechanical acting and boredom mentioned previously. The exchange that occurs between the actor and the spectator—even if it is just an exchange of *energy*—can be nothing less than magic.

**NOTE**: A documentary on the eight performances of *Two Character Play* can be found in Chapter 11.

## ACTING FOR THE STAGE VERSUS ACTING FOR THE CAMERA

Since the advent of film, and then television (and now video games), performance opportunities for actors have expanded. Many actors have moved from acting for the stage to acting for the camera and back again. And although the techniques for both are similar, there are some significant differences. The primary difference, of course, is the presence of the camera, which completely transforms the ephemeral aspect of the stage performance to an event forever captured on film or video. The second most important difference is scale; acting for the camera requires a subtlety of action and emotion not always required for the stage. The camera comes to the actor, whereas a stage actor must reach out to the spectator. The camera picks up every tiny movement, gesture, and facial expression, which would not likely be observed by the spectator of a live performance, except in the most intimate of settings. Representational, realistic acting methods, such as those which are Stanislavsky based, are obviously, then, best suited for acting in most mediatized performances (see Chapter 1). Presentational performances would come across as false (although they are appropriate for some exceptional films). Finally, as mentioned earlier, stage actors must re-create the same performance again and again, perhaps only for a few nights, but sometimes for years, as in the case of a long-running show on Broadway or in the West End in London. By contrast, once filming has wrapped (ended), the film actor moves on to other roles, even while her performance has been captured on celluloid for future viewings.

**FIGURE 9.18**

Many film and television actors, such as Marlon Brando, Robert De Niro, and Meryl Streep, have undergone extensive formal training but some mediatized acting is undertaken with little or no training—consider Leonardo DiCaprio, Keanu Reeves, and Kirsten Dunst. This is rarely the case for the stage actor, who must learn to project the voice (although this is less of an issue with the increasing use of microphones in the theatre) and, most important, communicate with a live audience, typically in a large space. Neither of these tasks comes naturally to most actors.

Actors who are successful on stage are not always able to tranfer that success to film or television, and it may have nothing to do with talent. Chita Rivera, the original Anita in the stage version of *West Side Story*, was dismayed when she was passed over for the film role, which went to Rita Moreno, because she had a less obvious Latina look (in spite of the fact that the character was from Puerto Rico). Film actor Audrey Hepburn won the role of Eliza Doolittle in the film *My Fair Lady*, instead of Julie Andrews, the original stage Eliza; ironically, Andrews went on to enormous success as Maria in the film of *The Sound of Music*. (The original Maria was played on the stage by Mary Martin.) More recently, Cady Huffman, the original Ulla in the stage rendition of *The Producers*, was passed over for the role in the film, which was first given to Nicole Kidman and then to Uma Thurman, both primarily film actresses whose more conventional beauty and subtle acting were probably considered more appropriate than Huffman's rather strong, masculine features and broad acting, which both "read" fine in the theatre.

The financial rewards for acting for the camera can be much more substantial than those for acting on the stage, but film and television actors must deal with the fact that mediatized acting can involve a lot of waiting around—for appropriate light or weather, for stunts to be set up, for extras to be organized, and so forth. Furthermore, films are often shot out of sequence, so the actor is without the benefits of the logical building toward a climax that happens in realistic stage plays.

## THE PROFESSION

Whether on stage, film, or television, the life of an actor can be extremely difficult. Only a small percentage of those who consider themselves actors actually make a living at it. According to the U.S. Department of Labor, Bureau of Labor Statistics, fewer than 70,000 actors find regular work as a performer each year. There are over 230,000 performers who are members of one of the three professional acting associations (AEA, SAG, or AFTRA, described subsequently), and hundreds of thousands more who are not yet union members. Thus, only between 5 and 7 percent of all actors find work, and an even smaller percentage make their living as an actor, because many acting jobs last only a few weeks or months. Some may graduate from a training program and get cast immediately after their first audition in a show that runs for years. Others may audition for 10 years without ever being cast, working as a waitress, a construction worker, or a temp in order to make ends meet.

**FIGURE 9.19**

The misconception that actors are somehow unstable people is belied by the necessity that successful actors be healthy physically and emotionally, necessary in part due to the constant rejection that an actor may face. But even the life of a steadily working theatrical actor can be grueling; eight performances a week, late nights, and the constant care of the voice and body can take their toll and leave time for little else. Film actors can face the difficulty of being away from family and friends for months while on location for a film shoot, and even when they are filming in their home city, such as Los Angeles, 18-hour workdays are not uncommon. The development of unions for actors, such as **Actor's Equity** and the **Screen Actor's Guild** in the United States, has gone a long way to protect the actor from exploitation, who historically has been viewed as little better than the prostitute. Furthermore, because there are so many would-be actors, those who are working can easily be viewed as dispensable, with another actor always "waiting in the wings."

Although many actors aspire to perform in live theatre on Broadway, or on film or in television in Los Angeles, few actually will. Work is available, however, throughout the United States, in regional theatre and other local venues. Some actors choose to pass along their craft as teachers. Others explore alternative uses of their talent and training, such as performing in corporate shows and films. With passion, patience, and persistence, actors often can carve out a life for themselves in spite of the odds against them.

## For Further Information

Bogart, Anne, and Tina Landau. *A Practical Guide to Viewpoints and Composition*. 2004.

Brook, Peter. *The Empty Space*. 1968.

Caine, Michael. *Acting in Film: An Actor's Take on Movie Making*. Rev ed. 1997.

Carnicke, Sharon M. *Stanislavsky in Focus*. 1998.

Cohen, Robert. *Acting Professionally: Raw Facts About Careers in Acting*. 5th ed. 1998.

Cole, Toby, and Helen Krich Chinoy, Eds. *Actors on Acting*. 1970.

Frome, Shelly. *The Actors Studio: A History*. 2001.

Grotowski, Jerzy. *Towards a Poor Theatre*. 1968.

Stanislavsky, Constantin. *An Actor Prepares*. Reprint ed., 1989.

Stanislavsky, Constantin. Elizabeth Reynolds Hapgood, Trans. *Building a Character*. Reprint ed., 1989.

Stanislavsky, Constantin. *Creating a Role*. Reprint ed., 1989.

Suzuki, Tadashi. *The Way of Acting*. 2000.

Watson, Ian. *Performer Training: Developments across Cultures*. 2001.

## Suggested Films

Elizabethan Acting: *Shakespeare in Love* (1998)

Restoration Acting: *Stage Beauty* (2004)

Beijing Opera Actor Training: *Farewell My Concubine* (1993)

Method Acting: *A Streetcar Named Desire* (1951)

## Glossary

**Actor's Equity**    Union that protects actors' rights in relation to such aspects of their profession as pay, benefits, working hours, and safety.

**audition**    Process by which an actor displays his talent in order to secure a role in a production; may involve singing, dancing, presenting a monologue, and/or reading a scene.

**beat**    The most basic unit of a play, defined by actors and directors.

**Beijing Opera**    Classical, traditional Chinese form that combines music, dance, and speech with elaborate, codified costumes, makeup, and movement.

**black box**    Flexible theatre space, usually with four walls, often painted black or some similar neutral color.

**blocking**    The process, during rehearsals, of creating and fixing the actors' movements about the stage.

**casting**    The process of selecting actors for a theatrical production (or film, television show, etc.).

**codified acting**    A complex system of movement, facial expressions, and gestures that are set by tradition and handed down from teacher to student, often for generations. Typically utilized in classical theatre traditions of non-Western cultures, but sometimes used in the West, as in Delsarte's methods.

**commedia dell'arte**    Popular form of comedy that developed during the Renaissance in Italy and was based on improvisation and stock characters.

**emotional memory**    The recollection of episodes in an actor's life similar to those of the character she is playing; also known as emotional recall or affective memory.

**given circumstances**    The basic information communicated by the playwright: period, location, class, etc.

**headshot**    A photograph of the actor's head and shoulders, usually used in conjunction with a resume as the actor's "calling card" or "application" before or at an audition.

**improvisation**    Acting technique that emphasizes immediate responses as opposed to rehearsed behavior. Viola Spolin is a contemporary pioneer in "improv" techniques.

**intercultural**    Between or among two or more cultures.

**Kabuki**    Classical Japanese form of music theatre, developed in the eighteenth century, that emphasizes spectacle.

**Kathakali**    Classical Indian form that developed from ancient Sanskrit theatre and combines elaborate movement, music, gestures, and facial expressions.

**melodrama**    A movement that developed parallel to Romanticism, but outlived it to become the most popular form of theatre in America and Europe during the nineteenth century. Some hallmarks include plots focusing on good versus evil, with clear-cut heroes and villains; exotic locales; plot devices such as hidden documents, disguises, and kidnappings; and musical accompaniment.

**Method acting**   The version of Stanislavsky's method of acting developed in the United States and first disseminated by members of the Group Theatre in the 1930s.

**Neoclassicism**   A movement in Europe during and after the Renaissance based on a renewed interest in the classics of Greece and Rome, such as the philosophies of Aristotle or the plays of Seneca. During this period, many in positions of power urged artists and writers to follow the Neoclassical Rules, a sometimes distorted interpretation of classical culture.

**Noh**   Classical Japanese form created in the fourteenth century; emphasizes minimalism as a reflection of the influences of Zen Buddhism.

**objectives**   Statements regarding what characters want to achieve in any given play; there are usually many objectives, one for each beat or scene, but one overriding superobjective.

**poor theatre**   Minimalistic style of theatre developed in the 1960s by Jerzy Grotowski and the Polish Laboratory Theatre, in opposition to technologically "rich" theatre.

**postmodern**   An umbrella term for a philosophy, condition, or movement—depending on one's perspective—in the contemporary world that reflects such characteristics as pastiche, fragmentation, disunity, and suspicion of any one explanation for things, or "grand narratives," as outlined by such philosophers as Frederick Jameson and Jean François Lyotard.

**presentational**   Production style that emphasizes presenting theatre to the audience without necessarily trying to reproduce real life. Often involves a more active audience.

**realism**   Movement that developed as a reaction against the escapism of melodrama, seeking to confront the social ills of nineteenth-century industrialized society; has outlived melodrama to become the most prevalent form of nonmusical theatre during the twentieth and twenty-first century in the Western world.

**representational**   Production style that emphasizes the reproduction of actual life on the stage; often involves a more passive audience.

**Restoration**   Period in England, beginning in 1660, resulting from the restoration of King Charles II to the throne, after his royal line was ousted by the Puritans earlier in the century.

**Romanticism**   Developed in part as a reaction against the restrictions of Neoclassicism and the intellectualism of the Enlightenment, this late-eighteenth, early-nineteenth century movement influenced literature, music, visual art, philosophy, and theatre; emphasized subjectivity and emotions; and brought Shakespeare back into favor.

**Sanskrit Theatre**   Ancient Indian theatre form, in the language of Sanskrit, which avoided realistic practices and involved codified performance, including elaborate costumes, makeup, and a complex set of movements and gestures known as mudras.

**thespian**   Term for an actor, derived from the Greek performer Thespis, considered by some historians to be the first Western actor.

**Viewpoints**   Acting method developed by Anne Bogart and Mary Overlie to counter Stanislavsky's technique; involves six elements: space, time, shape, movement, story, and emotion.

## Key Concepts

- Although everyone "acts," acting for the stage involves more than mere imitation; it requires interpretation, an awareness of being watched, "stage presence," and control.
- How one defines acting can depend on the context.
- Acting can be divided into two types—presentational (common in classical traditions) and representational (more recent)—or can be a combination of the two.
- Stanislavsky's acting techniques, involving such concepts as objectives and emotional memory, have become the most commonly utilized for representational acting.
- Alternatives to Stanislavsky's methods include poor theatre, interculturalism, the Suzuki Method, and Viewpoints.

- The actor's production process often begins with the audition, moving through rehearsals, from blocking to techs, to the actual performances.
- Acting for the stage is considerably different than acting for the camera.
- Training is not necessary to become an actor, but is quite essential for classical theatrical traditions.
- Although no two actors' experiences will be the same, an actor's life is difficult and demanding.

# The Play

## Chapter Outline

*To view the figures in this chapter, log on to www.pearsonexploretheatre.com.*

## INTRODUCTION

Of the 94 definitions for the word "**play**" displayed on Dictionary.com, from gambling to playing games or music to "playing possum," the number-one definition is "a dramatic composition or piece." This definition has served as the basis for theatre throughout the history of the world, with emphasis placed on the written text to varying degrees, depending on the context.

**FIGURES 10.1 AND 10.2**

In many theatrical traditions in the Western world, the play has held status as a work of art and literature in and of itself, apart from its use in production. In some contemporary Western and classical non-Western performative forms, it serves as a mere outline for a much more elaborate performance and is considered relatively insignificant as an object apart from a production context. Either way, plays rarely are written to be appreciated only as literature; if that were the goal for the author, he would likely write in another genre, such as fiction or non-fiction. Although there are examples throughout history of plays that failed, for one reason or another, to find their way to the stage (often referred to as "**closet dramas**"; see Figure 10.3) and thus have been only read and never performed, most can truly come to fruition and completion only when they are presented in front of an audience.

**FIGURE 10.3**

Chapter 2 explored the elements that most plays comprise and provided the tools to analyze, interpret, and understand those elements. But in order to understand any given play, it is important also to grasp the context in which it was written, including why it was written, how, and for whom. Furthermore, the answers to these questions have changed, sometimes drastically, over time. Thus, this chapter will explore the various ways that playwrights, through historical trends and methods, have chosen to present their stories in front of an audience. The chapter ends with two examples of the play script written for this text, *Two Character Play*, the work that forms the basis for both Chapter 11 and the adaptation into a film for Chapter 13.

### LEARNING OBJECTIVES

**After reading Chapter 10, you should be able to:**

- Define the term "play" and place it in its theatrical context, apart from its identification as literature.
- Identify the main historical contexts and trends in and by which plays have been written.
- Trace the development of the play in the Western world from nonrealistic to realistic and back again.
- Describe the similarities and differences between scripts written for live performance and those written for mediated performance, using *Two Character Play* as an example.

## ELEMENTS OF THE PLAY IN CONTEXT

As with musical theatre, which will be discussed in Chapter 12, the play *is* difficult to define, as Dictionary.com demonstrates. Although it is known as a "dramatic composition," these two words are extremely general, and the ways in which various playwrights go about composing their drama can differ widely. However, Aristotle, writing in ancient Greece in the fourth century BCE, does delineate six elements of the play that have wide, if not universal, application throughout history and world cultures (although he was discussing them only in terms of ancient Greek theatre). These six—**plot, character**, thought (or **theme**), **diction (or language), music**, and **spectacle**—are explained in more detail in Chapter 2.

**FIGURES 10.4 AND 10.5**

Playwrights may differ on which elements they choose to focus on. Some write plays that are more character driven, whereas others focus more on plot. Some eschew music and spectacle while others assume these to be basic components of the theatrical context in which the play will be produced. (For example, in his play *Homebody/Kabul*, Tony Kushner includes the lyrics to Frank Sinatra's song "It's Nice to Go Trav'ling," emphasizing an important theme—travel juxtaposed with the concept of "home"—in the play).

Furthermore, the goal of the play may not always be the same. For example, as was explained in Chapter 2 and will be reviewed later in *this* chapter, what became known as the "**well-made play**" format, or the "climactic" or "cause-to-effect" format, is as old as Greek theatre and is the most common form in Western theatre (as well as film and television; see Chapter 13). Its goal is to lead to a single climactic moment of crisis. However, in the later part of the twentieth century, some feminist playwrights argued that this form is a "male" form, and they advocated instead, the goal of which was *multiple* climaxes. Others pointed out inherent problems in such a perspective, arguing that there can be no one "male" or "female" form. Other, alternative goals are represented by playwrights who create by using an **episodic play** structure, in which plays are composed of multiple episodes, each of which can stand alone, or by playwrights writing for classical **Sanskrit drama**, in which the goal of the plays is not to reach a climax, but to induce the appropriate **rasa**, which can be translated as tone, mood, or flavor.

**FIGURE 10.6**

## CLASSICAL AND MEDIEVAL ANTECEDENTS

This section and the next examine trends in plays and methods for writing them, leading up to the birth of the modern play in illusionist staging practices. This introductory sketch is necessarily brief, but your own curiosity or your instructor's efforts can lead you toward a fuller understanding of any of these topics. Although performative traditions likely are as old as humans themselves, the practice of writing scripts for these traditions did not become common in the Western world until the civilization of Ancient Greece, where playwrights wrote drama possibly as early as the eighth century BCE. The tragedies of Thespis in the late sixth century are the first known written plays for the stage. **Tragedy, comedy**, and a lesser known form called the **satyr play** became the chief fare of the Greek stage; what we know of them is based on the extant plays of Aeschylus, Sophocles, Euripides, Aristophanes, and Menander.

**FIGURE 10.7**

All Greek plays were a part of a great choral drama that, many would argue, is underappreciated as such in more contemporary times. Playwrights wrote the chorus, whether tragic or comic, as an integral part of the action in their dramas. Within the play, the chorus served a variety of functions: as a group "character," setting the mood or tone; as a narrator; and/or as an "ideal spectator," suggesting how the playwright wanted the audience to think about the events unfolding before them. Today, directors sometimes overlook the importance of the chorus, relegating it to the background or cutting it altogether.

In a way, this is what Roman playwrights did. As great assimilators of aspects of other cultures, the Romans borrowed much from Greek theatre, including the structures and plots of plays; however, they did not value the chorus as an integral part of that drama, eliminating it altogether in their comedies. But in most ways, the dramas were quite "Greek." In fact, the first plays in Rome were written by a Greek import, Livius Andronicus, whose first play was produced in 240 BCE. Our knowledge of Roman drama, though, is based on only three writers whose plays have survived to us: Plautus and Terence (who wrote comedies), and Seneca (who wrote tragedies probably not intended for production). The Roman taste for variety entertainment (see Chapter 14), as seen in such **paratheatricals** as the mimes, chariot racing, and gladiator combats, drove tragedies and comedies from the stage. Roman drama would become influential during the Renaissance, but except for occasional adaptations such as the musical *A Funny Thing Happened on the Way to the Forum* (adapted from Plautus's Pseudolus), they rarely are studied or produced today.

**FIGURE 10.8**

The same largely holds true for the religious dramas of the European Middle Ages. A culture steeped in Catholicism, which permeated all aspects of life, from government to entertainment, Europe of the Middle Ages was homogenous in many ways, no matter where you traveled on the continent or British Isles. A kind of international Western religious drama developed during this period, unchanged significantly until altered by the effects of a growing Protestant Reformation. Particularly in Spain, Catholicism maintained an iron grip after the rulers of other countries had pursued autonomy from the church. But under the umbrella of religious drama, a number of forms arose, most of which were by anonymous authors, because writing for the glory of God precluded taking individual credit for work.

It is quite possible that this age of great religious drama began in the churches with **liturgical dramas**, performances of biblical stories, in Latin, separate from the very performative workings of the mass itself. The earliest is thought to be the *Quem Quaeritis Trope*, about the visit of the three Marys to the empty tomb of Jesus and their encounter with an angel announcing that Jesus had risen from the dead. These adaptations of stories from the Bible, however, are not necessarily plays; more elaborately written texts would wait until, at some point, these stories were moved out of doors for elaborate performances in the streets and town squares. Known as **cycle or mystery plays**, the latter perhaps from "maestri," a Latin term for the members of the trade guilds that produced them, these mostly anonymous dramas, written in the vernacular (the common language of the people), tended to be didactic (reinforcing Church teachings), in rhyme (easier for illiterate actors to memorize), episodic, and far reaching in scope.

**FIGURE 10.9**

Other categories of plays during this time included **morality plays** (such as *Everyman*) and miracle plays, about the lives of the saints, some of which were written by Hrosvitha, the first known female dramatist—and the first known playwright of the postclassical era—a tenth-century canoness of a nunnery in what is present-day Germany. This great age of religious drama died a rather unnatural death in many locations throughout Europe during the sixteenth century when many rulers, such as Elizabeth I in England, created laws to restrict or forbid the plays altogether in an attempt to avoid religious conflict during the Reformation, paving the way, some would argue, for the Golden Age of drama to come.

Beginning in the same age as the Western Middle Ages, non-Western classical theatrical forms were developing. Although plays *were* written for many of these forms, more often than not the text was a brief outline for a much more elaborate performance. The language of performance in these forms—still performed today—is considered much broader than words, often including movement, music, and dance. Dramatic structure is essentially non-Aristotelian and often episodic in nature. As mentioned before, Sanskrit drama, such as *Sakuntala*, by Kalidasa, was unified not by action, but by rasa. During the height of Sanskrit theatre, from 200–800 CE, over 1,000 plays were written.

In Japan during the fourteenth century, **Noh** theatre grew out of the minimalism of Zen Buddhism as well as support from the shogunate. Each Noh play has a three-part structure—jo, ha, and kyu—that includes two characters interacting with a chorus. Plays are classified into five types—god, man, woman, insanity, and demon—that traditionally would be performed together. Extensive exposition reveals the emphasis on the effects of past events, and rationality is abandoned for intuition and understanding. Some 200 years later, between Noh dramas, **Kyogen** appeared, comic plays depicting more common people and themes. The more spectacle-based **Kabuki** appeared later in the seventeenth century and was centered on plays based more on heroism or romance.

**FIGURE 10.10**

In China, the primary classical form, Beijing Opera, developed from a period considered the Golden Age of Chinese drama, the fourteenth-century Yuan dynasty. Created from classical novels and stories, the multi-act plays included songs, and characters were divided into four types: man, woman, and two different kinds of clowns. By the nineteenth century, **Beijing Opera** had arisen as the primary form, and its name indicates the increased prominence of music in the performances of the plays. The form focused on the actor, who specialized in one of four character types: male, female, painted face, and clown.

Indigenous African performance has traditionally extended the de-emphasis of written plays that is a hallmark of most of these non-Western forms; the performance "text" is often improvised and transmitted orally. However, more and more theatre in postcolonial Africa is a hybrid of indigenous traditions and more Westernized forms that include a reliance on a written text.

## GOLDEN AGES

During the period of the Western Renaissance, dramas became increasingly secularized—except for many written and performed in Spain, where the Catholic Church maintained an iron grip of control, thanks in part to such events as the Spanish Inquisition. For some playwrights, the Golden Age of Spain, usually dated 1580–1680, was a period of amazing creative output; for example, Lope de Vega may have written as many as 1,800 plays! (Compare this with the fairly prolific American playwright Arthur Miller, who wrote 22 plays in his lifetime.)

However, some would argue that the emphasis during this Golden Age was more on quantity than quality. Playwrights wrote in several different genres, such as *autos sacramentales*, religious/morality plays, perfected by Calderon de la Barca (see Figure 10.11); *comedias*, any full-length secular drama, either serious or comic; *capa y espadas*, or cloak-and-sword plays; and short pieces such as *loas*, performed as prologues, and *entremeses*, brief plays performed between the acts of comedias.

**FIGURE 10.11**

Reformation was rocking the foundations of the Catholic Church; for both sides of the contest, the religious dramas were troublesome because of their potential to foment disquiet in society. Therefore, the religious plays of the Middle Ages died a fairly quick, unnatural death in most places; for example, they were outlawed in Paris in 1548, by the Council of Trent by 1563, and in England in 1558. In the latter country, this early demise of religious plays, as well as other forces, paved the way for a new drama and a Golden Age in theatre that was to outshine even that of Spain. The philosophical and artistic developments of the Renaissance, begun in Italy, were finally making their way north; the development of the printing press promoted a freer exchange and availability of ideas; theatre, having lost its church support and communal functions that allowed it to flourish in the Middle Ages, became professionalized; and Queen Elizabeth I, who reigned from 1558 to 1603, brought stability and greatness to England. All of these events paved the way for the plays of William Shakespeare and his contemporaries.

Drawing on classical ideals disseminated throughout Europe during the Renaissance, Shakespeare's predecessors began to lay the groundwork for the Golden Age to come. A group of educated men, known as University Wits, began to apply these ideals to the English public stage. Playwrights such as Thomas Kyd and Christopher Marlowe wrote innovative new tragedies that borrowed from the Roman playwright Seneca. Kyd authored *The Spanish Tragedy*, initiating the popular "revenge" tragedy of which the most famous example would become *Hamlet*. Marlowe perfected **blank verse** and created complex characters and episodic plots in such plays as *Doctor Faustus, The Jew of Malta*, and *Edward II*. The University Wits blended classical and medieval playwriting that served as a bridge to the age of Shakespeare.

**FIGURE 10.12**

The fact that Elizabethan England—also known as the English Renaissance—was a Golden Age of theatre and drama is, of course, attributed in no small part to the work of William Shakespeare (although he was by no means the only playwright of the period). Often called the greatest playwright of all time, at least in the Western world, Shakespeare transformed drama in England, perhaps because he was involved in more aspects of the creation of theatre than any of his contemporaries were, including acting and producing. He was a true "man of the theatre." He began writing sometime around 1590, authoring or coauthoring some 40 plays, although the exact authorship of some—or even all—of the plays attributed to him is contested by some historians.

**FIGURE 10.13**

Shakespeare's complex dramaturgy includes a number of key characteristics. He utilized large casts of often-complex characters, revealing a deep understanding of human nature, and his sometimes epic, multiple plots were frequently borrowed from other sources. His brilliant language is extraordinarily varied and in one single play may include lofty poetry, blank verse written in **iambic pentameter**, elegant speeches, slang, prose, and bawdy wit, showing his insightful knowledge of the diverse audience for which he wrote. He also coined many words still used in the English language, such as "dawn," "bedroom," and "advertising"! Although his plays are often divided into three categories—histories, comedies, and tragedies—in truth they are not so clearly delineated within the texts. Plays such as *Romeo and Juliet, A Midsummer Night's Dream, Othello*, and *Henry IV, Parts I and II*, in many ways defy typical **genre** distinctions.

Although Shakespeare was not the only dramatist of his era, he has proven to be the most influential, with his plays performed more than those of any other playwright in the world today. One notable example of Shakespeare's contemporaries is Ben Jonson, who wrote pieces for the public theatres as well as the court **masques**, allegorical spectacles that showcased the power of the rulers who followed Elizabeth, James I, and Charles I. Jonson was named "Poet Laureate" of England for his authorship of such plays as *Every Man in His Humour* and *Bartholomew Fair*, but they are rarely produced today.

## DRAMA AND THE ADVENT OF ILLUSIONISTIC STAGES

Before the Renaissance, theatre artists were not attempting to replicate real life on their stages; theatre was viewed as quite separate from life. One set for plays, often with simultaneous staging, was the norm in the theatre of Classical Greece, Rome, and the Middle Ages. But beginning with this period of rebirth in the Western world, theatre shifted to a path toward illusionism: performance that gives the illusion of real life. As a result, the way that plays were written shifted to suit these stages, culminating in the birth of modern drama in realism and naturalism. (See Figures 10.14, 10.15, and 10.16.)

**FIGURES 10.14, 10.15, AND 10.16**

As mentioned, the Renaissance began in Italy, and its artists and philosophers borrowed heavily from the classical cultures of ancient Greece and Rome. This **neoclassicism**, or "new classicism," had effects on much Western European drama that were to last for over 200 years. As first developed by the Italians, neoclassical drama was based on verisimilitude and decorum, three genres, three unities, a five-act form, and a twofold purpose.

Verisimilitude involved reality, universality, and morality, dictating that plays should show only the "truth," an admittedly complex and relative concept, but one that, to the Renaissance mind, meant arriving at fundamental, essential, universal qualities in life that could be applied to most humans. This involved a fairly strict code of morality, with good rewarded and evil punished. A related concept was decorum, or the idea that characters should behave in ways appropriate to their class, rank, age, gender, and so on. Those who did not were subject to punishment or, at the least, ridicule. This emphasis on order was carried out through restrictions in genres; neoclassical plays were divided into three types: tragedy, comedy, and pastoral. The former two were the primary forms. Tragedy had to have an unhappy ending; lofty, poetic language; and characters of high birth involved in weighty moral issues. Comedy had to have a happy ending, use everyday language, and depict the middle and lower classes involved in more domestic concerns.

Although Aristotle discussed only unified action in his *Poetics*, neoclassicists advocated three unities: time, place, and action. In order to promote verisimilitude, many playwrights limited the passing of time in their plays to either "real time" or, at the most, 24 hours. They believed that only locations that could be reached in that period should be used; multiple plots or actions that would strain verisimilitude were avoided as well. By the late sixteenth century, playwrights divided their plays into five acts, after Roman tragedian Seneca's practice of dividing his plays into five sections.

Finally, during this period, theorists and playwrights delineated a twofold purpose for drama and theatre: to teach—from the emphasis on morality—and to please, recognizing that theatre can entertain as well. However, according to the neoclassicist, it should do both. By 1600, these precepts had been widely adopted among institutionalized state and court theatres. Their emphasis on control and order suited the needs of those in power. However, no sooner did they become the "norm" than resistance to them began to develop, such as the rise of the demand for spectacle, as well as such popular entertainments as **commedia dell'arte**—not to mention resistance from playwrights such as Shakespeare, who displayed little concern for adopting the neoclassical ideal.

**FIGURE 10.17**

The period in England after Shakespeare is known as the Restoration, so called from the restoration of the line of King Charles to the throne after 20 years of Puritan control. After 1660, **Italianate staging** was brought to the English theatre, and in an even greater shift from the period before, women were allowed on the stage. Plays shifted accordingly; for example (and unfortunately), rape scenes became more frequent, as did **"breeches" roles**, in which actresses played female characters who dressed up as men at some point in the play, allowing for the titillation of women's legs seen out from under skirts. Although the plays of Shakespeare and his contemporaries continued to be produced, new plays were written more closely along the lines of neoclassicism. The most long lasting of these forms was the **comedy of manners**, written by such playwrights as William Wycherly and William Congreve. However, these deviated from neoclassicism in that they depicted aristocratic society, although lower-class characters often were included. Through the eighteenth century, other forms, such as opera and pantomime, satisfied the growing taste for spectacle.

In France, neoclassicism took a firm hold, the government recognizing its usefulness to control culture there. During the early seventeenth century, King Louis XIII and his second in command, Cardinal Richelieu, formed the French Academy to serve as the arbiters of French culture, and the group of eminent literary figures became aggressive advocates of the Neoclassical Ideal. When the play *The Cid*, which deviated somewhat from the rules, became extremely popular in 1636, the Academy censored it and its author, Pierre Corneille, setting a precedent for conformity to the neoclassicism in France for nearly two hundred years. Racine's tragedy *Phèdre*, a model of neoclassicism, would solidify the Ideal in that country in a way that never occurred across the channel.

Jean-Baptiste Poquelin, who combined neoclassicism, *commedia,* and farce into enormously popular plays that ridiculed such things as social and religious hypocrisy, depicting characters whose downfalls come from deviating from proper decorum. Yet, in spite of generally following the neoclassical ideal, Molière became embroiled in controversies, particularly surrounding his play *Tartuffe* (see Figure 10.18), resulting in the denial of last rites by the Catholic Church, until the intervention of King Louis XIV granted him a Christian burial.

**FIGURE 10.18**

Neoclassicism's grip on theatre loosened gradually throughout Europe during the eighteenth century, and its dominance over French theatre was finally challenged with the enormously popular production of Victor Hugo's nonneoclassical romantic tragedy,

*Hernani*. The 1830 play caused a cultural battle between the neoclassicists and the Romantics, and the latter won. Romanticism was a diverse movement that, nonetheless, involved some general tenets, including the rejection of "universal rules," embracement of the natural world, and the idealization of the artist as genius. It grew out of the numerous revolutions that fomented in European and American society during the late eighteenth century and was a reaction against the restrictions of neoclassicism as well. Whereas Shakespeare—hardly a follower of the neoclassical ideal—had fallen out of favor, his plays became popular again through **romanticism**. This movement paved the way for the most popular theatrical form of the nineteenth century: melodrama.

**Melodrama**, meaning "music drama," developed as a form of escapism from the social ills that grew out of the Industrial Revolution, including poor working and living conditions. The plays presented two-dimensional stock characters including a villain, hero, and heroine, with strict poetic justice—the evil were punished and the good rewarded. The episodic plots involved suspense, narrow escapes, abductions, reversals, hidden documents and identities, special effects (the melodrama of *Ben Hur* included real horses in a chariot race on a treadmill), comic relief via a servant or ally to the hero, and exotic locales. The plays always ended happily. Music underscored it all, as it does in today's films, heightening the emotions and clearly indicating to the audience how to feel about one character or another. Guilbert de Pixérécourt in France and Dion Boucicault in Ireland and then America were two of the most prominent writers of melodrama during the nineteenth century. Melodramas are not so popular in theatre today; they are more common in the media of television and film (See Chapter 14).

## MODERN DRAMA

The same societal conditions that gave rise to melodrama also contributed to the development of modern drama, beginning with **realism** and its more extreme form, **naturalism**. Whereas some artists responded to the social ills that developed from the Industrial Revolution by creating escapes from those ills, other artists chose to confront them. It was out of this impulse that realism arose to become the dominant form of nonmusical drama in the twentieth century.

During the latter half of the nineteenth century, various social movements, theories, and philosophies contributed to realism's development. Charles Darwin's theories on evolution, survival of the fittest, and heredity versus environmental influences on humans; Sigmund Freud's exploration of psychological motivation; and Auguste Comte's advocation of the scientific study of human social relations—sociology—all influenced realistic drama. Playwrights began to apply the scientific method to their art, searching for truths about humanity in order to improve societal conditions. They believed that truth could be discovered through the careful, objective observation of the material world around them, using the five senses: touch, taste, sight, smell, and sound. Therefore, the subjects of their plays tended to be themes of the contemporary world, which they could observe firsthand by using these methods.

Realistic drama was in part a reaction against what was viewed as unrealistic, unmotivated action in melodramas. (However, in actuality, the work of such early realists as Henrik Ibsen was not a *complete* break from melodrama.) In order to create linear, cause-to-effect plots through which to communicate their serious themes regarding social ills, realist playwrights looked to the classics, shaping the ancient climactic structure of plays such as *Oedipus Rex* into what would become known as the "well-made play," perfected by Ibsen. Setting became crucial, as many plays highlighted the conflict between the effect of environment versus heredity on characters' actions. Previously popular aspects of plays—such as supernatural characters or epic spans of time—were abandoned as unrealistic, as was the simplicity of "poetic justice." In realism, there tended to be few clear-cut heroes, villains, or happy endings. Ibsen brought these trends into focus with his work, much of it controversial for its shocking (for the time) subject matter; for example,

*Ghosts* and *A Doll's House* both treat the subject of syphilis, and the latter play depicts a Victorian woman leaving her family, unheard of for the period.

**FIGURE 10.19**

Anton Chekhov and George Bernard Shaw also wrote realistic plays, still performed with some frequency today. Less influential have been the plays of the naturalists, often referred to as "slice of life" for their authors' attempts to re-create real life on stage. A more extreme form of realism, naturalism includes the work of August Strindberg, such as his play *Miss Julie*, as well as that of American playwright and director David Belasco, who, in his New York production of *The Governor's Lady*, replicated Childs restaurant down to the smell of bacon cooking.

**FIGURE 10.20**

Modified forms of realism (allowing for devices such as flashbacks or ghosts not accepted by the early realists) continue to dominate nonmusical stages in the Western world and increasingly in the non-Western world; however, no sooner had realism entered the mainstream than there appeared reactions against it. These alternatives appeared through a variety of movements from the late nineteenth century, beginning primarily with symbolism and continuing up to absurdism and its heir, postmodernism.

Drawing in part on some of the same influences from which realism drew—for example, Freud's theories on the unconscious mind and the importance of dreams—these movements questioned the very concept of a knowable, perceivable truth. Instead of foregrounding the material world perceived through the five senses, many artists in these movements looked inward for meaning in dreams, emotions, and the subconscious mind; they emphasized subjectivity over objectivity. **Symbolism**, begun in 1885, emphasized the use of symbols to approximate some semblance of truth; symbolist playwrights set their plays in the past or in the world of fantasy. But the vague nature of their work baffled audiences, and although it is significant for its challenge to realism, symbolism proved less influential than such later movements as **expressionism**, which emerged around 1910 in Germany.

The expressionists rebelled against the materialism of the machine age, seeking to reshape the human spirit, which they perceived to have been distorted by external forces. Their dramas often focused on this distortion. Instead of cause-to-effect, linear narratives, these plays were message centered, with generic, stereotyped characters and telegraphic dialogue. Fantasy and magic were embraced, and the overall effect was that of "allegory clothed in nightmare." This movement has been longer lasting than many of the antirealistic movements, due to its emphasis on text, as well as to the contributions of some significant playwrights such as Georg Kaiser, Ernst Toller, Eugene O'Neill, Elmer Rice, and Sophie Treadwell.

**FIGURE 10.21**

Other movements of the early twentieth century, including **Dadaism** and **futurism**, though radical in some of their ideas, proved less immediately influential. This was due partly to the rather unspecific nature of their ideas and forms, some of which seemed designed merely to flout authority and institutions, and partly to their de-emphasis of the play text. (The futurists wrote short plays, called syntesi, which often compressed full-length plays into a few lines.)

Perhaps the most influential of all of these reactions against realism grew out of German expressionism. Bertolt Brecht deplored the passive spectator which he believed that realistic drama engendered. He wanted intellectually active audiences that were spurred on to change the world via the theatre they saw. Therefore, his dramas employed what he called *verfremdungseffekt*, or the **alienation effect** (or A-effect), alternately distancing the audience and then drawing it back in again. Plays such as *Mother Courage and Her Children* and *The Caucasian Chalk Circle* are structured in a series of episodes separated by songs, signs, or narratives, often relating the events about to unfold and thereby eliminating audience involvement through suspense. Instead, the audience can think critically about the actions of the play, leave the theatre, and reshape life for the better. (For Brecht, that would mean reshaping life along Marxist lines.) Brecht also advocated a variety of means in production by which to achieve the A-effect, including not hiding theatrical devices such as lighting instruments.

**FIGURE 10.22**

In the mid-twentieth century, a movement developed in France out of earlier avant-garde movements, such as Dadaism and surrealism. The new movement was labeled "**absurdism**" by scholar Martin Esslin. After such events as World War II, the Holocaust, and the development of weapons of mass destruction, the group of artists forming this movement questioned the very rationality of a chaotic world in which such events could occur and concluded that there was no way out of the chaos. Therefore, bereft of governments that could provide social and moral order, each individual would have to create his or her own value system by which to live. To the absurdists, the world was an illogical, meaningless, sometimes even hostile place. In their dramas, they abandoned narrative for exploring a condition; instead of using linear structures, theirs were circular or spiraling, often ending where they began. Characters were archetypal, not specific, and the themes often involved humans trapped in an illogical, chaotic, meaningless, hostile—dare we say it?—absurd world. Nobel Prize winner Samuel Beckett's *Waiting for Godot* epitomizes these characteristics. Other absurdist playwrights include Jean Genet, Eugene Ionesco, Edward Albee, and Harold Pinter.

**FIGURE 10.23**

Beckett's work could be viewed as having one foot in absurdism and another in postmodernism; certainly, the postmodernists have been influenced by the many antirealistic movements that preceded them. Besides absurdism and Epic Theatre, there are few antirealistic movements which left plays that are still staged. In fact, one hallmark of most **postmodern plays** *is* a de-emphasis on the text. Plays that exist are often reworkings of existing texts, or they serve as mere outlines for much more elaborate, imagistic work. Heiner Muller's *Hamletmachine* fits both characteristics; loosely based on *Hamlet*, it bears little resemblance to Shakespeare's work. Verbal language is devalued and fragmented; in fact, the words, not unlike many in the plays of the absurdists, often make little logical sense. Incongruous ideas and images are juxtaposed. However, postmodern works are far from meaningless; instead, they often open up multiple meanings through their rejection of the more mainstream, traditional form of realism.

Challenges to realism occurred with greater frequency as the twenty-first century approached. By the late 1960s and early 1970s, many marginalized groups, such as feminists, Latinos, blacks, gays, lesbians, and others were experimenting with various modes of theatre, to both challenge the status quo and empower their own members. Other artists not focused on a particular political or ethnic identity also rose to prominence, experimenting with the form of theatre itself. Together, these many groups formed an eclectic **avant-garde** movement that shattered the rigid expectations of the past. Some scholars label this period as postmodern, a term meant to encompass the radical shifts in politics, science, culture, and the arts that followed. Most importantly, postmodernism marked the remarkable shift away from widely shared cultural and intellectual assumptions about objectivity, truth, meaning, progress, and identity.

Despite its many notable successes and innovations, **postmodernism** has yet to produce the radical revolutions in mainstream theatre that many of those artists and activists envisioned. All these groups, both in theatre and in the larger culture, have made significant gains, but for some, such as GLBT (the gay lesbian bisexual and transgender community), a significant struggle remains. Furthermore, while neither Broadway nor Hollywood has been unaffected by these shifts, the fundamental structures and expectations of dramatic storytelling that have been dominant for thousands of years have remained the standard fare. Indeed, all of the postmodern groups can be (and have been) studied and critiqued using the basic structures of drama first set out by Aristotle and explained in Chapter 2.

## A SCRIPT: TWO CHARACTER PLAY

The history of modern and postmodern drama could easily fill whole books; indeed, several are listed at the end of this chapter. However, readers (and instructors) can exploit the hands-on opportunity created by the postmodern script commissioned for and included in this textbook. Note that classroom exercises and in-class performances of this script are covered under "fair use"; however, the rights for any production before a ticketed audience must be secured through the author of the play (information provided on the next page).

Chris White, introduced in Chapter 5, is the author of *Two Character Play*, a work commissioned for this textbook. Her work straddles several of the genres and styles previously outlined, offering readers multiple points of entry into the issues and ideas that lie at the very heart of play scripts and playwriting. In Chapter 11, we chart the development of this script from its conceptual stage to its final presentation as a live, theatrical event. In this chapter, however, we include the PDF version of the actual prompt book that was used in production and the final version of the script that Ms. White wrote after the production had closed. As you read the first version of the script, try to imagine all of the work of the artists whom you have learned about in the previous chapters. Many of the notations in the margins of the script give clues as to how those artists tried to accomplish the vision that the words on the page suggest.

Because this play was a work in progress all the way up to (and even beyond) opening night, the prompt book has dialogue that was eventually cut or changed in the live version recorded for Chapter 11. We hope that readers will be able to not only spot the points at which the director and producer made cuts to the script only days before we opened, but also to begin to puzzle out how and why Ms. White made the rather significant changes found in the final version of the script.

## STUDY AND DISCUSSION QUESTIONS

The script which you just read was the "blueprint" for a production that you will see in a mediated format in the next chapter. This particular version, however, is only one of countless versions that are possible from this script. The link that follows will launch a PDF of the "final" version of the script. As you compare the changes that Ms. White made to her original script, take a few moments to go over the following questions to try to imagine how you might begin to create your own version of *Two Character Play*:

1. What are the different stories that are woven together in the script?
2. How do these stories seem to intersect (or not)?
3. What characters were dropped from the second version of the script?
4. Why where those characters dropped?
5. What would be the major challenges that you might face in mounting this production?
6. Whom would you cast in these roles, and why?

Go to www.pearsonexploretheatre.com for a PDF of the complete *Two Character Play* script.

*If you would like secure the rights to produce a version of this play, please contact:

Christine White
English Department
DePauw University
100 East Seminary Street
Greencastle, IN 46135-0037
E-mail: chriswhite@depauw.edu

## For Further Information

Anderson, Lisa M. *Black Feminism in Contemporary Drama.* 2008.
Bentley, Eric. *The Life of the Drama.* 1964.
——. *The Theory of the Modern Stage.* 1968.

Esslin, Martin. *An Anatomy of Drama.* 1976.
——. *The Field of Drama.* 1987.
Saddik, Annette J. *Contemporary American Drama.* 2007.

## Suggested Films

*A Life in the Theatre* (1993): David Mamet play, filmed. Young actor befriends an older actor.
*Miss Julie* (1999): Good filmed example of one of modern drama's most important works.

*Wit* (2001): Good example of an adapted modern play.

## Glossary

**absurdism**   A mid-twentieth-century dramatic movement that emphasized the confused, illogical, meaningless, unknowable condition of humans; began in postwar France.

**alienation effect**   An aspect of Bertold Brecht's epic theatre in which the audience is alternately distanced from, and then drawn into, the world of the play, in order to combat passivity and cultivate a more critical spectator.

***autos sacramentales***   Religious/morality plays in Golden Age Spain.

***avant-garde***   Literally, the "advance guard" of a movement, usually in art, characterized primarily by a radical change in that art.

**Beijing Opera**   A classical traditional Chinese form that combines music, dance, and speech with elaborate, codified costumes, makeup, and movement.

**blank verse**   Unrhymed verse.

**"breeches" roles**   Historical term for roles in which actresses play female characters who dress up as men.

***capa y espadas***   Spanish cloak-and-sword plays.

**characters**   The fictional people who perform the actions in the play and are the primary element from which plots are created.

**closet dramas**   Plays written to be read, not produced or performed.

***comedias***   Any full-length secular drama, either serious or comic, in Golden Age Spain.

**comedy**   A play that deals with ordinary life in a predominantly funny way and that ends happily.

**comedy of manners**   Comedy, originating in the seventeenth and eighteenth centuries, that focuses on the proper social behaviors of members of certain classes.

**commedia dell'arte**   A comedic form, influenced by Roman comedy, that developed as popular street performances in Renaissance Italy and later influenced the writing of such playwrights as Moliére.

**cycle or mystery plays**   Medieval plays based on stories from the Bible that were elaborately staged, often performed during Christian festivals.

**Dadaism**   An artistic reaction to World War I that celebrated randomness, disharmony, and disorder. It became more influential to later artists.

**diction (or language)**   The qualities of the language within the play.

***entremeses***   Short plays performed between the acts of comedias.

**episodic play**   As an alternative to the well-made play, emphasizes organization around an idea or theme, with various parts—scenes and/or acts—standing on their own instead of relying on progressing from cause to effect.

**expressionism**   An offshoot of symbolism that exaggerates reality in order to reflect inner truths and meanings; most prominent in Germany.

**futurism**   An aesthetic movement found primarily in Italy and Russia that rebelled against harmony and good taste and celebrated youth, the technological triumph of humanity over nature, and a passionate nationalism.

**genre**   A kind or type of something.

**iambic pentameter**   A line of verse commonly used during the English Renaissance and consisting of five iambic "feet," in which an iamb refers to an unstressed syllable followed by a stressed syllable.

**Italianate staging**   The use of perspective to create the illusion of depth in stage design in the late Renaissance. Features included mechanized, changeable sets with wings, drops, and boarders on a raked stage.

**Kabuki**   A classical Japanese form of music theatre developed in the eighteenth century and emphasizing spectacle.

**Kyogen**   Brief comic plays depicting common people and inserted between Noh dramas.

**liturgical dramas**   Performances developed during the Middle Ages by and within the Catholic Church to communicate Christian teachings.

***loas***   Short dramatic pieces performed as prologues to full-length dramas during the Golden Age of Spain.

***masques***   Elaborate court performances of the Renaissance that highlighted the power of the monarchy and featured great spectacle.

**melodrama** "Music drama" that grew out of the social ills of the Industrial Revolution to become the most popular Western form during the nineteenth century. It is marked by a strict adherence to poetic justice, stock characters, and escapism, as well as accompanying music that underscores the action.

**morality plays** Allegorical medieval drama that featured ordinary humans in struggles between good and evil.

**music** The use of music before, during, or after a play, or the musicality of the dialogue itself.

**naturalism** An extreme form of realism that attempted to duplicate a "slice of life" onstage.

**neoclassicism** A period in Europe during and after the Renaissance that grew out of a renewed interest in the classics of Greece and Rome, such as the philosophies of Aristotle and the plays of Seneca. During this period, many in positions of power urged artists and writers to follow the "neoclassical ideals," a sometimes-distorted interpretation of classical culture.

**Noh** A classical Japanese form created in the fourteenth century; emphasizes minimalism as a reflection of the influences of Zen Buddhism.

**paratheatricals** Ancient Roman entertainments performed outside of the theatre structures that housed tragedies and comedies. During the time of the empire, they became increasingly common, replacing theatre as the primary form of entertainment. Common types were gladiatorial combats, chariot racing, venationes (animal fights), and naumachiae (re-created sea battles).

**play** A (two-dimensional) plan, blueprint, or outline for a production, consisting of stage directions, dialogue, and dramatic action (the question, problem, or theme that forms the central focus of the play).

**plot** Both the story told in the play or the collected events that occur in a play, *and* the meaningful arrangement, or structure, of those events.

**postmodern plays** Plays that abandon a linear narrative and cause-to-effect events for pastiche and fragmented language; they avoid "closure of meaning" for open-ended interpretations and often embrace nostalgia, parody, and technology.

**postmodernism** An umbrella term for a philosophy, a condition, or a movement, depending on one's perspective, in the contemporary world that reflects such characteristics as pastiche, fragmentation, disunity, and suspicion of any one explanation for things, or "grand narratives," as outlined by such philosophers as Fredric Jameson and Jean-François Lyotard.

*rasa* Translated as "mood," "tone," or "flavor"; the goal of Sanskrit drama.

**realism** A movement that developed as a reaction against the escapism of melodrama, seeking to confront the social ills of nineteenth-century industrialized society; has outlived melodrama to become the most prevalent form of nonmusical theatre during the twentieth and twenty-first centuries in the Western world.

**romanticism** Developed in part as a reaction against the restrictions of neoclassicism and the intellectualism of the Enlightenment, this late-eighteenth–early-nineteenth-century movement influenced literature, music, visual art, philosophy, and theatre and emphasized subjectivity and emotions; brought Shakespeare back into favor.

**Sanskrit drama** Plays of classical India (circa 200–600 CE) written in the language of Sanskrit.

**satyr play** Brief Ancient Greek drama that featured a chorus of half-men, half-goat characters called satyrs.

**spectacle** The visual elements suggested in the script that might constitute the setting and costumes for the play when performed.

**symbolism** Late-nineteenth-century movement, reacting against realism, in which playwrights utilized abstract symbols to communicate meaning.

**theme** The intellectual issues expressed by the play.

**tragedy** A serious play with an unhappy ending brought about by a leading character with a tragic flaw, as defined by Aristotle in his ancient text *The Poetics*.

**well-made play** Term for the climactic play structure codified by Eugene Scribe and marked by cause-to-effect action, with heavy reliance on exposition, discoveries, complications, and reversals. The term is now sometimes used derisively.

## Key Concepts

- The play as a "dramatic composition or piece" has served as the basis of theatre since its beginnings, although in some cultures and periods it has served as a mere outline for a much more elaborate performance and is considered relatively insignificant as an object apart from a production context.
- Playwrights may emphasize different elements and goals in their plays, utilizing different structures, from climactic to episodic to postmodern.
- The increasing secularization of drama has been linked to several historical Golden Ages in the Western world, except in Spain, where the Spanish Golden Age was closely linked to the Catholic Church.
- The way that plays were written shifted to suit the development of illusionistic stages.
- No sooner did realism become the dominant dramatic mode in the late nineteenth century in the West than a number of anti-realistic movements sprang up.
- A script is a blueprint for performance, and any given set of artists may come up with radically different staged versions of a script.

# 11

# Backstage at *Two Character Play*

**Chapter Outline**

Introduction

Learning Objectives

Rehearsals

Technical and Dress Rehearsals

Preshow and Preparation

The Performance
   The Program

Part One
Part Two
Part Three

**The Run of the Show**
   A Backstage Pass

Glossary

Key Concepts

*To view the figures in this chapter, log on to www.pearsonexploretheatre.com.*

## INTRODUCTION

Audiences' experience of live theatre is always different not only for each person, but also for each performance. As explained in Chapter 3, multiple forces affect both artists and audiences each time the performance is given, so that a repeat performance is nearly impossible to achieve. Even when we watch **mediatized** performances (film, TV, video, or recorded live performances), each individual audience member brings a unique set of expectations, experiences, and expertise to his or her own viewing. And even when we view the same film a second time, our expectations, experiences, and level of expertise will have changed, and the experience of that film will be a different one from the first viewing. These same, variable forces affect theatre artists as well, and some knowledge of how theatre artists experience the work of "doing theatre" can help you become a better audience member.

**FIGURE 11.1**

In the previous chapters, you have been introduced to the various members of the artistic team that creates theatre. Most of these types of artist were involved in the creation of *Two Character Play*, a work that was commissioned for this textbook. The play explores the intersections of live and mediatized performance, with the hope of prompting discussion and debate among both the audience members—who experienced the live theatrical event—and the readers of this text, who experience a mediatized version of the play. This play was, and is, a work in progress. Our intent is not to provide a "perfect" example of live theatre; indeed, that goal would be impossible in this "mediatized" format. We do hope, however, that readers will grow to appreciate the extraordinary effort and complexity live theatre requires. Although the authors believe that the live experience is always preferable, this mediatized one offers viewers and readers a "backstage pass," an intimate look at some of the dynamics of performance that audience members rarely see.

## LEARNING OBJECTIVES

### After reading and watching Chapter 11, you will be able to:

* Identify and discuss the major factors that affect the rehearsal process.
* Use the vocabulary from the preceding chapters of this textbook to identify and describe the major artistic elements of *Two Character Play*.
* Identify and discuss the factors that affect live performances and distinguish live theatre from mediatized performance.
* Identify ways in which the playwright, Chris White, changed her script after this production and discuss what those changes might mean for future productions of *Two Character Play*.
* Discuss what the nature and purpose of live theatre have been and speculate on what they might be in the future.

## REHEARSALS

Once a show has been cast, rehearsals can begin at any time from the next day to several years in the future, depending on the availability of talent and resources. Most professional productions are cast well in advance of the actual performance, sometimes more than a year in advance. Broadway shows often use a major-name actor to help sell tickets and generate publicity, and then other, less-well-known, but usually just-as-good (if not better), actors fill in if the show runs for a long time. Educational theatres often cast shows the semester prior to the performance, dividing up the talent available to them for all shows in a given semester. *Two Character Play* was cast in November and started rehearsals in February for an April run of two weeks. Amateur theatres often cast shows just prior to the beginning of rehearsals, hoping to harness the attention and commitment of nonprofessional actors and participants for a set period.

**FIGURE 11.2**

The amount of rehearsal for a show is also related to the level of skill and availability of the participants. Some film directors have only a single rehearsal, if they have one at all. Professional productions usually have a two-week rehearsal period. This short time frame is possible because professional theatre artists do not also work a day job and can be in rehearsal for a full eight hours a day. Most educational and amateur shows rehearse at night to allow participants to attend classes or work, and these rehearsals generally last from four to six weeks, depending on the complexity of the production and the skill of the participants. *Two Character Play* had 31 rehearsals over a six-week period.

One of the major goals of the rehearsal process in educational and amateur theatre is to create an ensemble capable of artistically, physically, and emotionally sustaining its members through the prolonged effort necessary for both rehearsals and performances. For eight or nine weeks, a group of individuals comes together to practice and then perform theatre before a live audience. For some, the community formed during rehearsals helps them deal with the inevitable stage fright that is part of public performances. For others, the most important benefits are the connections to other people who feel similarly compelled to tell stories, to practice at being human. Performance is a physical, intellectual, and emotional exercise, so rehearsals also prepare actors to engage in physical, intellectual, and emotional activities.

**FIGURE 11.3**

No two rehearsal processes are alike. Different directors, actors, scripts, and genres each contribute to the factors that affect the length and complexity of rehearsals. (See *The Rehearsal* in Chapter 9.) A musical will usually require more time than a nonmusical because actors will have to learn and practice the music, choreography, and scene work. A longer work will require more rehearsal time than a shorter one, and new work will usually require more time than a well-known script. What is common to all rehearsal processes is the work. When we account for all of the hours put into the process by actors, designers, directors, authors, and technicians, we can begin to see that even a brief show requires an enormous amount of time. Most theatre artists offer up this time joyfully, and many do it for free. Few actors actually make their living by acting, but both amateurs and professionals share many of the same processes and challenges. Each actor will find his or her own journey toward the performance that the artists finally offer.

**FIGURE 11.4**

There are several characteristics of *Two Character Play* that distinguish its rehearsal process from many others. First, the script was original, commissioned for this textbook. The playwright, Chris White (see *Training and the Profession* in Chapter 5), had written several drafts prior to auditions and then continued to refine her play during the rehearsal process. In fact, significant changes were made to the script (by the executive producer and director) a few days before opening. Second, other than the faculty director, all of the other artistic team members were students, a feature that significantly affected technical rehearsals (see the next section). Finally, because the entire process was filmed, both actors and artistic team members were conscious of the camera, and how much that affected the process is unknowable. Be alert to these factors as you watch the documentary in Figure 11.5.

**FIGURE 11.5**

## TECHNICAL AND DRESS REHEARSALS

While the actors and director(s) rehearse the show, the rest of the artistic team has already been at work developing the physical and technical aspects of the production (see Chapters 7 and 8). Sets, costumes, lights, sound, and other elements must be added to the rehearsal process prior to opening. In professional productions, where theatres are expensive to rent, the show may **put in** at the last possible moment, with only a single day of technical rehearsals and one or two dress rehearsals.

Professional crew members are expected to perform intricate and difficult cues, perfectly, with very little practice. In educational theatres, technical rehearsals are important labs in which theatre students learn how to perform those difficult cues or operate complex equipment. These technical rehearsals may take several days, and there are generally three: **paper tech**, dry tech, and wet tech. In paper tech, the designers for sets, lights, and sound meet with the director and stage manager to write the cues into the **prompt book**, which you read in Chapter 10. These cues will often get changed during both the dry and wet techs; they are usually written in pencil or other changeable media. In the **dry tech**, the technical crew (all of the people needed to operate the lights, sound, set changes, costume changes, **fly rail**, and props) goes through each cue without the actors on stage. This technical rehearsal gives the director and designers a chance to see how the lights, sound effects, and sets look from moment to moment so that they can be changed, modified, or perfected before the actors arrive. In the **wet tech**, the entire show is run with the actors on stage in a cue-to-cue, a rehearsal that allows the technical crew to practice their cues with the actual lines from the show, skipping over any large sections of text where there is no cue.

**FIGURE 11.6**

After the technical rehearsals, the cast and crew undertake one or more **dress rehearsals**, which will usually be the first time that costumes are seen with all of the other elements in place. Dress rehearsals are also the only rehearsals in which the show is not stopped for problems to be fixed or for actors to go back to pick up dropped lines. In professional productions, a single dress rehearsal is usually followed by several "preview performances," sometimes lasting several weeks, to which audience members can purchase reduced-rate tickets, with the knowledge that the show may be stopped during the evening or that the show might be changed prior to opening night. Many famous Broadway shows were significantly changed in previews, so some audiences saw a version of the show that was not as good as the final one. In educational theatres, there might be several dress rehearsals, but shows are rarely changed or modified, primarily because copyright prevents any unauthorized changes to most scripts performed in these venues.

The technical rehearsals for *Two Character Play* were very challenging. Some of the students were in their very first position of responsibility as a designer or technician, and thus some mistakes were made. The paper tech took place on a Thursday afternoon (not filmed, because the camera operator was in class), and the dry tech started at 10 a.m. Saturday morning. Notice how the different students handled their particular responsibilities and how they affected one another during the process.

**FIGURE 11.7**

## PRESHOW AND PREPARATION

Cast and crew are usually called to the theatre one or two hours before the audience arrives. Depending on the demands of the show, some crew and cast members can be called several hours prior to "curtain"—the term derived from the twentieth-century practice of drawing up the main curtain to signify the start of the show. Cast members in the long-running Broadway musical *Cats*, with their extensive makeup, wigs, and costumes, were called to the theatre two or three hours before curtain. On days when there was both an afternoon matinee and an evening performance, cast members had to spend the entire day in their makeup and wigs, eating dinner looking like cats, because there wasn't enough time to change in between shows. In shows that involve complex or dangerous technical effects, like flying people (*Mary Poppins*) or set pieces (*Chitty Chitty Bang Bang*), technicians are called several hours before curtain to perform safety checks. In many plays, especially Shakespearean, actors must also arrive early enough for **fight call**, a special time set aside to rehearse physical combat, contemporary violence, or staged falls. Any action onstage that might cause injury is usually practiced each night before the performance.

**FIGURE 11.8**

As the cast begins to get into makeup and costumes, the crew performs checks on all of the sets, lights, and sound equipment used in the performance. Notes from the previous night's rehearsal or performance are first checked to see whether any problems were noted. After any needed repairs or replacements are made, the crews check their equipment for readiness. The master electrician and light board operator check each circuit, dimmer, and lighting instrument to make sure that there are no burned-out lamps or gels and that all lights are working correctly. Follow spot operators check their instruments; the sound operator checks all effects, speakers, microphones, and circuits; and the props master checks all props for readiness. The costume crew readies each costume for the actors and prepares for any quick changes or other special costume effects. There are often up to three backstage technicians or crew members for each actor that the audience sees onstage.

For *Two Character Play*, the preshow routine included a fight call, a flight call (to practice the flying effect), and equipment checks on sound, microphones, video projection, cameras, lights, follow spots, and props. Because the show was technically demanding, there were 27 crew members backstage supporting the 10 performers on stage. The clip presented in Figure 11.9 documents the preshow routine for this production. Notice how the sound technicians protect the body mics from the actor's sweat and how the sound-board operator sets the levels for each microphone.

**FIGURE 11.9**

## THE PERFORMANCE

One of the most powerful lures of live theatre is the wonderful—and terrible—tension that is shared among the cast, the crew, and the audience gathered to see their work, and nowhere is this crackling energy more powerful than on opening night. When the house lights dim and the audience hushes, there is a collective deep breath taken backstage, a shared hope that on this night the show will be perfect! No one will miss lines, no one will miss cues, and the gun won't misfire! The punch line will create a tsunami of laughter, or the hero's sacrifice will bring a torrent of tears! The same tension is often present before sporting events, but in film and television the tension is not the same. The audience understands that the film or a recorded show is complete and nothing they can do will change it. Only in live theatre does this creative tension exist.

For the audience members, the opening lines to *The Drowsy Chaperone* perhaps best capture the tension that they often feel. The audience sits in complete darkness for several moments before the narrator, who is known only as the "Man in Chair," starts speaking into the darkness, saying "I hate theater." The dates and spouses who had been dragged to the theatre tend to laugh the loudest here, but the Man in Chair continues, "You know what I do when I'm sitting in a darkened theater waiting for the curtain to rise? I pray. 'Dear God, please let it be a good show. And let it be short, oh Lord in heaven, please!'" There is another pause, usually filled with more surprised and supportive laughter, and then he continues, "You know there was a time when people sat in darkened theaters and thought to themselves, 'What have George and Ira got for me tonight?' or 'Can Cole Porter pull it off again?' Can you imagine? Now it's 'Please, Elton John, must we continue this charade?'" The audience usually erupts into laughter for several minutes, and the stage lights come up slowly to reveal a man sitting in a chair on stage right.

**FIGURE 11.10**

Almost everyone who goes to live theatre wants the show to be good. Audiences generally want to get their money's worth, to be diverted and entertained, or sometimes to be challenged or provoked. *Two Character Play* was written and produced to challenge audiences, to provoke them into thought and action. The mediatized version of that play shown here is imperfect; the script was/is a work in progress, designed and performed by students who were still learning their craft, and the play was recorded rather than experienced live. Yet the production is worthy of attention because the script is, in part, about live theatre itself, and it was performed by artists who knew that their audience would include you, the readers of this text. We are conscious of the production's flaws, but we hope that the opportunity to follow its process to the end will outweigh those flaws, provoking thought and discussion on what the nature and purpose of live theatre has been—and what it might be in the future.

The original performance of *Two Character Play* ran for 60 minutes, and the following version has been divided into three parts. Each "act" contains its own study questions and prompts to help viewers think about key issues in the play. This play is not a comedy, but it does have moments of humor. This play is not a tragedy, but it does have moments of pathos. This play is a question, of sorts—one that only audience members can answer for themselves. The answers that you develop, through self-reflection, talking with friends or classmates, or talking with your instructor, will hopefully allow you to enrich the theatrical experiences you have on your own at the theatres in and beyond your community.

## The Program

As with most performances, a program accompanied this performance and was meant to help audiences prepare for this experience. The link that follows will launch a PDF version of the original program for *Two Character Play*. The program not only documents the people who contributed to this effort, but also includes a Director's Note, which you should read before proceeding with the videos that are presented next.

**FIGURE 11.11**

### Part One
**FIGURE 11.12**

### Part Two
**FIGURE 11.13**

### Part Three
**FIGURE 11.14**

## THE RUN OF THE SHOW

Although both actors and audiences hope for the perfect show each and every night, such perfection is usually far beyond our reach. In shows that enjoy a long run, especially on Broadway, where a hit show can run for several years, the cast and crew must work diligently to make sure that the show is nearly perfect every night, as fresh and lively on the 2,452nd night as it was on the first. *Phantom of the Opera* opened on Broadway on January 26, 1988, and performed its 8,947th show on August 2, 2009. Hundreds of actors have worked their way through that show, and some were with the show for many years. Some crew members have been with the show from its very beginning.

The cast and crew of *Two Character Play* had a run of only eight performances, but in those eight performances they underwent the full range of good and bad experiences. In fact, they experienced that dreaded moment in a show in which an actor loses his or her place and everyone scrambles to adjust.

**FIGURE 11.15**

## A Backstage Pass

The final video in this chapter is uninterrupted by any breaks or text slides, but it does include shots from various angles and activities backstage. The main frame is slightly smaller, and the backstage shots appear around the periphery. This version starts with the same preshow routine that was shown earlier, in part to help create a mood and context for the uninterrupted version. This final version may be helpful for review or discussion. (This section features a video. To view it, log on to www.pearsonexploretheatre.com)

**FIGURE 11.16**

Finally, the playwright, Chris White, made significant changes to the script after the play premiered. The full text of the revised play can be found in Chapter 10. Your instructor may ask you to discuss some ways in which this final version of the play has changed from the original, filmed version that you have just watched. New scripts are often changed in this way, especially before the script receives a major premiere, such as on Broadway or London's West End. Some of the changes that Ms. White made are significant (such as eliminating a character and reassigning some of those lines to other characters), and others were minor. How do these changes affect your understanding of this play? Is the final version better? Why or why not?

## Glossary

**dress rehearsal**   A technical rehearsal during which the costumes are added and the show is not stopped for any reason.

**dry tech**   A technical rehearsal without the actors on stage.

**fight call**   A nightly rehearsal in which cast and crew members practice dangerous stunts or technical effects prior to each performance.

**fly rail**   A control area in a theatre, usually off stage right, with ropes or cables, levers, counterweights, and pulleys that allows technicians to move set pieces, lights, and other equipment on and off the stage by flying them in or out, from above.

**mediatized**   Presented through, or including a significant component of, a medium like film, video, or new media (e.g., Internet, Web 2.0).

**paper tech**   A technical rehearsal with only the director, stage manager, and designers during which the cues for the show are written into the prompt book.

**prompt book**   A book that is a copy of the script which the stage manager creates that has all of the blocking and rehearsal notes, technical cues, and other instructions written into it so that the stage manager can "call the show."

**put-in**   Also known as a "load-in," a work call for which crew members install all the sets, lights, and other technical equipment for a show into a theatre or performance venue (such as a stadium for a big concert).

**wet tech**   Also known as a "cue-to-cue," a technical rehearsal with the actors on stage, but one during which only the actual cue changes are practiced, not all the lines or songs in the show.

## Key Concepts

- The rehearsal process is varied, idiosyncratic, and arduous.
- An enormous number of person-hours are put into even the simplest of productions.
- Theatre artists must always be prepared to adapt to changes, even ones that occur at the very last minute.
- The backstage crew usually is two or three times the number of people on stage.
- Preparing a show goes far beyond learning lines and blocking.
- The preshow routine is complex and demanding.
- Individual audience members, who exist within a specific social–political–economic context, reflect on the production and determine a play's meaning or significance.

# Musical Theatre

## Chapter Outline

*To view the figures in this chapter, log on to www.pearsonexploretheatre.com.*

## INTRODUCTION

Musical theatre is distinctive for a number of reasons: It is the most popular form of theatre; in its manifestation as the Broadway musical, it is America's primary contribution to world theatre; and it is, arguably, the most complex form of theatre, combining music, the spoken and sung word, and, often, dance, with all of the other elements of theatrical production. The combination of music and theatre, however, is not new; as will be discussed, musical theatre is as old as theatre itself and has, in actuality, been the dominant mode of theatrical expression throughout history. Furthermore, although this chapter will focus on the American Broadway musical, it will also include considerations of ways in which music and drama have been combined in other cultures, both Western and non-Western.

**FIGURE 12.1**

## LEARNING OBJECTIVES

### After reading Chapter 12, you will be able to:

- Understand the complexities involved in defining "musical theatre."

- Identify the four primary elements of a musical: music, lyrics, libretto, and dance.

* Trace the development of the modern musical from its antecedents to its birth, through its Golden Age, and beyond, to the present.
* Identify key composers, lyricists, directors, and other creators of the musical.
* Describe the four traditional Asian music theatre forms: Sanskrit theatre, Beijing Opera, Noh, and Kabuki.

## PART ONE: THE BROADWAY MUSICAL: ELEMENTS OF THE MUSICAL

Musical theatre is difficult to define. In its most basic form, it is the combination of music and theatre. But opera is a theatrical event with music; so are **melodrama** and **Kabuki**. In its twentieth-century manifestation, the musical has most commonly involved performers who both speak and sing, and, often, who dance, usually accompanied by an orchestra. But then how does the 2000 **Tony Award** winner for best musical, *Contact,* fit within this definition? In *Contact,* none of the performers sing and there is no orchestra; all of the music is prerecorded. Or what about Andrew Lloyd Webber's *Cats,* which includes very little dialogue? (Many critics and historians label Lloyd Webber's musicals "popera.") Recognizing the slippery slope on which trying to define the musical places us, we might find it most useful to identify several of the most common elements that come together to create the contemporary Broadway musical.

**FIGURES 12.2 AND 12.3**

### Music

The music in a musical, created by an artist called a composer, is presented in two general ways: alone—as the overture, to provide background, or to accompany dance—or combined with lyrics, or words. The music consists of the *melody*, a sequence of musical notes; *harmony*, the juxtaposition of notes together; *rhythm*, the pattern of musical movement through time; and *tempo*, which dictates the pace of the melody. Music is implicit, not explicit; in other words, it suggests and evokes meanings, moods, and emotions—some say, more powerfully than mere words. In the best musicals, the music is specific to the setting.

**FIGURE 12.4**

### Lyrics

The lyrics are words set in a pattern to the music that tell a story or convey a theme, written by the lyricist, who frequently is different from the composer (although not always, as in the case of Cole Porter or Stephen Sondheim). Lyrics most commonly rhyme, both at the end of a phrase and internally, but there are exceptions. Like the dialogue in a play or in the libretto of a musical (the dialogue between songs), lyrics must compress often grand, sweeping ideas into as few words as possible, relying on the music to complete their meaning through implication. The best lyrics give the singer something to act. The music combines with the lyrics to make songs, and all of the songs in a musical are called, collectively, the *score*.

Although there are exceptions, most musicals follow a formula for the types of songs included. Such a formula might comprise the following:

* *Opening number:* Sets up the mood of the show and the kind of world the characters inhabit.
* *Character song:* Develops character information through lyrics and music. This type of song includes what is termed the "I want" song, in which a main character expresses his or her desires and motivations.
* *Love song:* Focuses on love relationships and is often a ballad (simple melody, slow tempo).

- *Dance number:* Written primarily to showcase dance and movement.
- *Eleven o'clock song:* A rousing, sometimes full-cast number designed to "wake" the audience before the finale. (Musicals used to begin at 8:30 p.m. and last approximately three hours; this song usually began around eleven o'clock—hence, its name).
- *Finale:* The last song, which reinforces the world of the show set up by the opening number (sometimes reprising it).

**FIGURE 12.5**

## Libretto

The **libretto**, or book, is the outline of dramatic development, which includes the dialogue and actions that occur between songs. Some musicals, often referred to as "book musicals," have long librettos, such as those written by Richard Rodgers and Oscar Hammerstein II; others have little or none, as in the shows of Andrew Lloyd Webber or the recent rock opera *American Idiot.* Alan Jay Lerner, writing during a time when book musicals reigned supreme, called the libretto "the fountain from which all waters spring" in his preface to the Tony Award-winning *My Fair Lady.*

**FIGURES 12.6 AND 12.7**

Like any nonmusical play, a libretto will have well-crafted characters, plot, dialog, and themes. Unlike a playwright, the librettist has less time to communicate her meanings, which are completed through the music and lyrics and, often, dance. However, although this outline of dramatic action may be, on the whole, briefer than most plays, it can be no less of an artistic achievement; indeed, a number of libretti have been awarded the Pulitzer Prize for Drama, beginning with *Of Thee I Sing* (1932) and, most recently, *Next to Normal* (2010). Recent scholarship even focuses on analyzing libretti as literature.

The resource Musical Theatre Online contains the complete libretto for the Broadway musical *Glory Days* (2008), and plans are underway to archive other libretti here.

## Dance

Although musicals do not always include dance, many do, and it is one of the most popular elements. Most of the antecedents to the musical, described in the next section, included dance, so it is not surprising that many musicals that grew out of them do as well. Common forms of dance in the musical are tap, jazz, and ballet, although the dance forms in musicals have ranged from ballroom dancing to hip-hop.

**FIGURES 12.8 AND 12.9**

Dance serves a variety of functions in the musical: It advances the plot, establishes mood and atmosphere, generates comedy, provides spectacle, and transcends spoken language. It is the latter that is perhaps the primary reason for its popularity, and its increased importance in communicating significant meanings in the musical is best exemplified by the rise of director/choreographers, such as Jerome Robbins, Bob Fosse, Tommy Tune, Susan Stroman, and Graciela Daniele, in recent years.

## PART ONE: THE BROADWAY MUSICAL

### Antecedents

As mentioned, combining music with drama is hardly new. According to Aristotle, Classic Greek tragedy grew out of the ***dithyramb***, a chorus of men who sang hymns in honor of Dionysus, the Greek god of wine and fertility. At some point, improvisations by the leaders of the *dithyrambs* led to more formalized spoken drama. But Greek theatre continued to maintain the close connection between music and theatre suggested by these origins. All Greek tragedies—by Aeschylus, Sophocles, Euripides, and those whose works are not extant—were sung and danced in parts, accompanied by the *Aulis* (flute) and other instruments, such as the stringed lyre. The music evoked emotions or ideas; the dances were closely related to the words through symbolic gestures. Roman dramatists utilized music in a similar fashion, although they did not value it as highly as the Greeks did.

The religious drama of the Middle Ages grew out of passages sung by priests in the churches, and music was prominent as well in most medieval productions that occurred outside of the church. This trend contributed to the importance of music to Renaissance dramatists, including Shakespeare. Of Shakespeare's 38 plays, 25 include singing; the comedies usually end in a dance. A trumpet flourish signaled important moments in performances of the English Renaissance, from the beginning of the play to the entrances of kings. That most adult actors were required to sing attests to the importance of music in the theatre of this period.

**FIGURE 12.10**

During the Renaissance and beyond, several theatrical forms arose at court that relied heavily on music and dance to enhance the spectacle—a spectacle intended to awe the subjects of the ruler in whose honor the event was performed, who sometimes even participated as a performer. In Italy, a combination of elaborate scenery, costumes, lights, special effects, music, and dance came to be known as *intermezzi*, which were performed between acts of dramas at court. Eventually, the *intermezzi* became absorbed into the form known as opera. In France, a similar form, *the ballet de cour*, developed and eventually became the popular *comédie ballets* for which such playwrights as Molière wrote. In England, this form manifested itself as the masque, for which dramatist Ben Jonson wrote and Inigo Jones designed.

**FIGURE 12.11**

During the eighteenth and nineteenth centuries in both Europe and America, a number of popular entertainments developed that eventually contributed to musical theatre as a specific form. **Ballad opera** interpolated lyrics set to tunes of popular songs or ballads into otherwise spoken drama; the most celebrated example is John Gay's *The Beggar's Opera* (1728), which Bertolt Brecht, Elisabeth Hauptmann, and Kurt Weill popularized during the twentieth century as the musical *The Threepenny Opera* (1928). The term "**burlesque**" has come to be synonymous with "striptease," but before, it referred to parodies of well-known plays and events that included songs and dances. In America, a white performer named T. D. Rice observed an old, black slave named Jim Crow (after whom segregation laws a century later were named) and created a performance impersonating Crow. That performance grew into the immensely popular, but problematic, form known as **minstrelsy**, in which white performers in blackface performed their impressions of slave music, dances, and culture. Eventually, black performers co-opted the form, also, ironically, utilizing blackface paint made from burnt cork.

**FIGURE 12.12**

**Melodrama**, which means "music drama," emerged as the most popular form during the nineteenth century in parts of Europe and in America. Melodrama grew out of the Industrial Revolution, as an escapist entertainment for the working class oppressed by difficult working and living conditions. The plots are simple, with a hero or heroine triumphing over an evil villain (leading to a happy ending) and devices such as disguises, abductions, concealed identities, and odd coincidences. A servant or ally of the hero provides comic relief, and spectacle is infused into the production through exotic locales, local color, and special effects. The music was most often used for mood and effect, and to manipulate audiences' emotions, not unlike film music. In fact, the genre of live melodrama has been largely subsumed into film. (Think of such movies as *Raiders of the Lost Ark* and *Enchanted*.)

The beginnings of musical theatre, apart from these antecedents, are often said to lie in a rather quirky story about a rather ordinary melodrama, *The Black Crook*. In

1866, scheduled to open the play at Niblo's Garden in New York City, producer William Wheatley insightfully interpolated a French ballet company, stranded when the theatre in which they were to perform burned down, into the play. The resulting mixture of song, dance, story, spectacle, and scantily clad dancers became one of the most popular productions of nineteenth-century America. From there, the musical gradually developed into what is commonly known as the Broadway musical.

### The Birth of the Modern Musical

During the late nineteenth century and into the early decades of the twentieth century, music took precedence over the book in musicals. The plot was often loose, a mere excuse to tie together songs that sometimes had little to do with one another. (This characteristic was taken to its extreme in the revue, in which songs are strung together without concern for a story.) As in *The Black Crook*, the practice continued of adding dances that were hardly connected to the story. And romance, comedy, and the happy ending reigned supreme, remnants of the escapism of melodrama. But although the stories sometimes came across as silly and barely there, the music was often enchanting and set a precedent for musical theatre songs becoming popular standards.

**FIGURE 12.13**

But even while musical comedy dominated this period, several shows deviated from this norm to herald the coming of a more serious musical drama. The complex plot of *Showboat* (1927) includes themes of race relations, as does *Porgy and Bess* (1935). The first musical to win a Pulitzer Prize in drama, *Of Thee I Sing* (1932), is a strident political satire. *The Cradle Will Rock* (1938) depicts the struggle of steelworkers to unionize against the evil capitalist, Mr. Mister. Government officials shut down *The Cradle Will Rock* due to its perceived left-wing propaganda, but its creators defied the officials later that day with a scaled-down production which brought the audience to its feet.

**FIGURE 12.14**

During the 1920s and 1930s, a number of composers and lyricists contributed to the birth of the modern Broadway musical, both comedic and dramatic, on which the foundations of the later Golden Age of musical theatre were laid. These artists included Irving Berlin; Richard Rodgers and Lorenz Hart; Jerome Kern and Oscar Hammerstein; Vincent Youmans; the Gershwin brothers, George and Ira; and Cole Porter.

Often overlooked, until recently, were the important, early contributions of women and African Americans to the birth of this form. For example, lyricist Rida Johnson Young wrote over 30 plays and musicals, and the lyrics for more than 500 songs, before her death in 1926. Albertina Rasch choreographed some of the most promising young dancers, including Fred Astaire, in numerous Broadway productions from 1926 to 1941. The influence of black dance and music, beyond the influence of minstrelsy, on the musical cannot be overestimated. Bert Williams and George Walker created the first all-black musical to play a major Broadway theatre, *In Dahomey* (1903). And Noble Sissle and Eubie Blake's *Shuffle Along* (1921) was a huge Broadway success, spawning a series of imitators and breaking the rigid barriers of segregation in the audience. The Gershwin brothers readily admitted the influence of black music, particularly jazz, on their work.

**FIGURE 12.15**

### The Golden Age of Musical Theatre

Although some historians include the '20s and '30s in what has been termed the **Golden Age** of the Broadway musical, most date to this era, when musicals reached their zenith, from the 1943 opening of Richard Rodgers and Oscar Hammerstein's *Oklahoma!* The characteristics of the Golden Age musical, which can still be seen in most musicals dominating Broadway to the present, had been seen in musicals before 1943; however, never before had they come together so completely and with such brilliance as they did in *Oklahoma!* which set a standard for musicals to come. Richard Rodgers and Oscar Hammerstein II were hardly new to the Broadway stage; Rodgers, a composer, had collaborated most regularly with Hart, and Hammerstein, a lyricist, with Kern. Their first production together, *Oklahoma!* marked the beginning of a fruitful, if sometimes conflicted, collaboration that resulted in such musicals as *Carousel, South Pacific, The King and I,* and *The Sound of Music.*

**FIGURE 12.16**

Golden Age musicals display the shift from the primacy of song over story to the dominance of the book over the score. All songs and dances exist in service to the plot; creators of these musicals worked to integrate every element into the story, ensuring that each song or dance helped to further that story. The libretto, as a result, tends to be fairly substantial. Other hallmarks of the musicals of this era include an optimistic view of the world, manifested in the opening number and punctuated by a happy ending; a romance or two, with an emphasis on love between heterosexual couples; and stock, rather simple, characters.

Besides Rodgers and Hammerstein, two of the best-known creators of these musicals are Alan Jay Lerner and Frederick Loewe. Lerner wrote the book and lyrics, based on George Bernard Shaw's *Pygmalion,* and Loewe the music, for one of the most beloved Broadway and film musicals, *My Fair Lady.* Other writers during this era include Frank Loesser, with his joyous depiction of lovable gangsters and their girls, *Guys and Dolls*; Jerry Herman; Betty Comden and Adolph Green; Dorothy Fields; Jule Styne; and Meredith

**FIGURES 12.17 AND 12.18**

Willson, who wrote the Tony Award–winning The Music Man. Cole Porter continued to write hits, including *Kiss Me, Kate*, an adaptation of Shakespeare's *Taming of the Shrew.*
This era also saw the rise of numerous great directors and choreographers, as well as artists whose careers combined both roles. Agnes de Mille revolutionized musical theatre dance when she created a "dream ballet" for *Oklahoma!* in which future events in the show are foreshadowed, starting a vogue for this type of dance number. Bob Fosse began his career as a dancer, but moved into direction and choreography, placing his unique stamp on Broadway musical dance with such characteristics as tiny, tight moves; erotic "bump and grind"; a slouching, angular, pigeon-toed posture; and the extensive use of hats and props, such as a cane. *Pajama Game, Damn Yankees,* and *Chicago* are all stamped with this style. And George Abbott wrote the libretto, directed, and/or produced no less than 45 different musicals in a career that spanned more than 75 years.

This era also saw the rise in popularity of the movie musical. Most of the early movie musicals were adaptations of stage musicals, although a handful, such as the one considered the greatest film musical of all time, *Singin' in the Rain* (1952), were written for film. Many Broadway performers, such as Fred Astaire and Julie Andrews, found that their stage talents translated well onto film, and in spite of the increasing number of tours of stage musicals throughout the United States, film versions, along with **cast albums**, enabled a much larger percentage of the population to experience the shows. Nevertheless, from the 1970s up the present, the popularity of movie musicals has waned, and in spite of the popularity of such film musicals as *Evita, Moulin Rouge,* and

**FIGURES 12.19 AND 12.20**

*Chicago,* more recent ones such as *Phantom of the Opera, Rent,* and *The Producers*—all flops as films—suggest that a movie musical renaissance is not in progress.

In spite of the prevalence of comedy, romance, optimism, and the happy ending, some creators began to sow the seeds of rebellion against the Golden Age musical formula during this period; two examples of musicals on the vanguard of these changes are *West Side Story* and *Gypsy*. It is interesting that young composer–lyricist Stephen Sondheim was involved as a lyricist in the creation of both of these shows, although his own rebellion against the Golden Age would not completely foment until later.

*West Side Story* (1957) is a musical retelling of Shakespeare's *Romeo and Juliet*, set amidst gang wars in 1950s Hell's Kitchen in New York City. Tony, a member of the Anglo gang the Jets, falls in love with Maria, whose brother is a member of the Puerto Rican Sharks. As in Shakespeare's play, prejudice conspires to keep the lovers apart until they are separated, permanently, by death. The show largely follows the Golden Age formula, and the original production integrated its elements even more fully than did *Oklahoma!* or any other musical that had come before. However, *West Side Story* deviates from what had become the norm in one significant way: It does not end happily. Although the musicals mentioned previously often include serious themes (*Carousel*, spousal abuse; *South Pacific*, war and prejudice), they usually end on a high note. *West Side Story* ends quite darkly, although the efforts of members of both gangs to carry off Tony and console Maria add a small note of hope at the end.

*Gypsy* (1959), in a way, perfected the Golden Age musical comedy format, with a tight book (by Arthur Laurents) flawlessly integrating the musical numbers, a score by Jule Styne and Sondheim, and brilliant direction by Jerome Robbins. But the show also went beyond the format, eschewing the primary focus on romance and presenting characters more complex than had been seen on the musical stage before. Although, superficially, *Gypsy* relates the career of real-life burlesque star Gypsy Rose Lee, the plot actually pivots around her mother, Rose, played by Ethel Merman in what perhaps was the performance of her lifetime. Merman's portrayal of the stereotypical stage mom, determined to make stars of her daughters and forsaking all, including love, to do it, ends somewhat ambiguously, with Rose's realization that what she did was for herself and not for her daughters.

**FIGURES 12.21 AND 12.22**

Although both *West Side Story* and *Gypsy* are now heralded as masterpieces of the musical stage, neither won the Tony Award for Best Musical, losing, respectively, to *The Music Man* and *The Sound of Music*.

## Beyond the Golden Age

Although many Broadway musicals up to the present exhibit characteristics of the Golden Age, such as *Thoroughly Modern Millie* and *The Producers*, and many musicals produced on Broadway today are revivals of the great musicals of mid-century America, most historians mark the end of this era, when musicals were at their height in popularity, at the appearance of a show that broke the rules, *Hair* (1968). Supported by a series of songs connected by a thread of a story about hippies protesting the Vietnam War draft, the themes included rebelling against all institutions and societal restrictions, a rebellion represented by the long hair that hippies often sported. *Hair* broke ground for a number of reasons: Its loose plot seemed to break away from the emphasis on the libretto; the cre-

**FIGURE 12.23**

ators utilized profanity, nudity, and rock music; and it depicted what was known as the "counterculture." None of these characteristics was typical on the commercial, Broadway stage; and even though *Hair* was not the first Broadway show to exhibit those characteristics, it was the first to combine them into such a phenomenally popular product.

The most influential leader of this rebellion during the past 40 years has been Stephen Sondheim, who, as mentioned earlier, wrote the lyrics for *West Side Story* and *Gypsy*.

Sondheim found that he had a talent for composing as well, as in the uproariously funny *A Funny Thing Happened On the Way to the Forum* (which had an extremely successful revival in 1996 with a cast led first by Nathan Lane and then by Whoopi Goldberg). But it was after 1970 that the composer–lyricist began to hone the style for which he made his mark on musical theatre history, a style characterized by disturbing plots without happy endings; intellectual, sometimes didactic themes; an ironic, cynical tone; unconventional

**FIGURE 12.24**

relationships; skepticism about traditional morality; highly sophisticated lyrics; less reliance on dance; and sometimes dissonant music combined with unusual rhythms. Sondheim believes that content should dictate the form of the musical and that "people beat scenery," meaning that the focus should be on the actors and not on what surrounds them. Sondheim's first shows post-1970—*Company, Follies, A Little Night Music*, and *Pacific Overtures*—set the cynical, antiromantic, and anti-idealistic tone that he would perfect in later works such as *Sweeney Todd, Into the Woods*, and *Assassins. Sweeney Todd,* subtitled *The Demon Barber of Fleet Street* (1979), is based on a nineteenth-century melodrama about a barber bent on revenge against a judge who unjustly imprisoned him for years in order to steal his wife and child. As the judge eludes him, and as his thirst for revenge rages out of control, Todd begins to murder his customers while shaving them. He is aided in the disposal of the bodies by Mrs. Lovett (played brilliantly in the original production by Angela Lansbury), who, as the purveyor of a failing pie shop situated below the "tonsorial parlor" (the barber shop) discovers that customers flock to the shop when she begins "popping" the flesh of Todd's victims into the pies. One of the more hilarious, but disturbing songs in the show, "A Little Priest," comes at the moment when Mrs. Lovett dreams up her nefarious plan:

| | |
|---|---|
| MRS. LOVETT: | Seems a downright shame… |
| TODD: | Shame? |
| LOVETT: | Seems an awful waste… |
| | Such a nice, plump frame |
| | Wot's 'is name has… |
| | Had… |
| | Has! |
| | Nor it can't be traced… |
| | Bus'ness needs a lift, |
| | Debts to be erased… |
| | Think of it as thrift, |
| | As a gift, |
| | If you get my drift! |
| | No? |
| | Seems an awful waste… |
| | I mean, with the price of meat |
| | What it is, |
| | When you get it, |
| | If you get it… |

**FIGURE 12.25**

| | |
|---|---|
| TODD: | HAH! |
| LOVETT: | Good, you got it! |

At the show's end, the stage is riddled with bloody bodies, including Todd's. *Sweeney Todd* won a total of eight Tony Awards, including Best Musical.

In spite of such critical acclaim for Sondheim's works post-1970, these works have been less than successful at the box office. The one exception is *Into the Woods*, originally produced in 1987 and revived on Broadway 10 years later. Based on a variety of fairy tales, the show follows the traditional stories of such characters as *Little Red Riding Hood, Cinderella, Jack and the Beanstalk*, and *Rapunzel* as they each strive for "happily ever after." The stories are linked by an original tale of a baker and his wife

**FIGURE 12.26**

and their attempts to have a child. At the end of Act One, all of the characters seem to have found their happy ending. But, in his typically cynical fashion, Sondheim reveals in Act Two the reality of what happens after "happily ever after," and the characters come to their various understandings of that sometimes harsh reality.

*Assassins* takes as its unlikely subject the men and women who have killed or attempted to kill U.S. presidents. Through a series of songs performed by such portrayed assassins as John Wilkes Booth and John Hinckley, the show examines the themes of the American Dream and the marginalization of outsiders. The controversial, original production in 1991 never made it to Broadway, and a planned Broadway production a decade later was cancelled in the wake of 9/11; the show finally made it to Broadway in 2003 and won the Tony Award for Best Revival of a Musical.

Broadway audiences have not seen a Sondheim musical since *Passion* (1993). His most recent show, *Bounce,* has failed to find an audience for productions in Chicago and Washington, D.C. Fortunately, heavily influenced by Sondheim, some young composers, such as Jason Robert Brown, Tina Landau, Adam Guettel, and Michael John LaChiusa, are following in his footsteps by experimenting with form. But in spite of the fact that audiences and some critics have labeled Sondheim's work too intellectual, cold, and depressing, most historians recognize that Sondheim's pushing at the margins—of taste, conventions, form, and morality—represents the most significant subversion of the traditional Golden Age musical formula in modern times.

## The British Invasion

Throughout the twentieth century, the musical has been identified as a largely American product. However, for the past 30 or so years, shows originating in London seem to have overtaken those coming out of New York City. In fact, as of this writing, all but one of the top five longest-running Broadway musicals did not originate in America. Critic Frank Rich wrote of the phenomenon in a *New York Times* article entitled, "The Empire Strikes Back." Not everyone has been happy with this development in musical theatre history, explained further shortly, but no one can deny the huge numbers of audience members that these commercial blockbusters have attracted to Broadway.

The British Invasion musicals, also termed "European megamusicals," share a number of characteristics: They tend to be **sung through**, with little dialogue, sometimes earning the label "opera" (or "popera"); many utilize pop or rock music, as well

**FIGURE 12.27**

as amplification of the performers; they incorporate a great deal of scenic spectacle; and they tend to be extremely melodramatic. Most of these s hows originated in the West End (London's commercial theatre district, equivalent to Broadway), the creators are not necessarily British, and many can be connected to producer Cameron Mackintosh. The most successful creator of these shows has been Lord Andrew Lloyd Webber, a composer who began his work in the 1970s by collaborating with lyricist Tim Rice on

**FIGURE 12.28**

*Jesus Christ Superstar, Joseph and the Amazing Technicolor Dreamcoat*, and *Evita*. During the next decade, Lloyd Webber struck out on his own, creating, with a variety of collaborators, some of the most popular musicals of all time, including *Starlight Express, Cats, Phantom of the Opera*, and *Sunset Boulevard*.

The second longest-running musical in Broadway history (7,485 performances; see Appendix), *Cats* (1982) is based on poems by T. S. Eliot and is a series of character songs sung by a group called "Jellicle cats" as they prepare for the Jellicle Ball, when one of them will be chosen to achieve immortality in the mystical Heavyside Layer. At the climax, an old cat named Grizabella is chosen, and she ascends on a large, junk spare-tire elevator amidst smoke and soaring music. Her song, "Memory," is one of the most popular of contemporary musical theatre.

*The Phantom of the Opera* (1988), as of this writing, is the longest-running Broadway show in history—over 8,000 performances and still counting. The story is about a disfigured, masked inhabitant of the sewers beneath the Paris Opera who is obsessed with a young opera singer, Christine. With sets that include the grand staircase of the Opera House, a cloud-swept view of nighttime Paris, the candlelit sewers under the streets of Paris, and a chandelier that nearly crashes onto the audience, the spectacle is often credited for the show's popularity, as is the soaring, dramatic music.

Three other figures are closely associated with this British movement and with creating some of the world's most popular musicals. Although Claude-Michel Schonberg and Alain Boublil are from France, their shows *Les Miserables* and *Miss Saigon*, the third and ninth longest-running Broadway musicals, respectively, originated in London in the West End. And the influence of the producer of their musicals, Cameron Mackintosh, cannot be overestimated. Mackintosh has been the marketing mastermind behind Boublil and Schonberg's hits, as well as some of Lloyd Webber's, including *Cats* and *Phantom*, perfect-

**FIGURE 12.29**

ing the concepts of advanced ticket sales and releasing the cast album before the show is open.

However, the British Invasion in musical theatre may be nearing its end; Lloyd Webber's last two shows, *Whistle Down the Wind* and *The Beautiful Game*, never made it to Broadway, nor did Boublil and Schonberg's collaboration, *Martin Guerre*. Their newest Broadway musical, *The Pirate Queen*, has not gotten the best reviews.

## The Broadway Musical Today

Economics has, in many ways, shaped the Broadway musical landscape today. Escalating costs have made the Broadway musical a risky endeavor for producers; five out of six new shows lose money. Therefore, producers look for security in revivals of proven

**FIGURE 12.30**

shows, such as *Oklahoma!* or in shows that utilize film stars, such as *The Boy From Oz,* which featured a mesmerizing, Tony Award–winning performance by Hugh Jackman. The "movical," a term coined by Martin Kohn of the *Detroit Free Press* for stage musicals adapted from films, has become increasingly common, partly because of the brand-name phenomenon, or the belief that audiences will buy tickets because of their familiarity with the original film version. Examples of these branded hits are *The Producers, The Full Monty, The Wedding Singer, Legally Blonde*, and the upcoming *Fight Club*.

One response to this economic situation has been the rise of corporate, as opposed to individual, producers of musicals. The most successful during the past decade has been the Walt Disney Company. There, executives saw an opportunity to expand the company's audiences beyond film and theme parks; at the same time, it insightfully began to take part in the renovation of the New York City theatre district on and around Broadway and 42nd Street. Since the 1970s, this area had become increasingly unsafe and seedy, with dilapidated theatres turned into adult-film houses and with prostitutes and homeless people wandering the streets. The company bankrolled the renovation of the New Amsterdam Theatre and built a Disney Store in Times Square. Its first theatrical adaptation, that of the animated film *Beauty and the Beast*, has been enormously popular, but critically panned as a mere live copy of the film. The company's next production, *The Lion King*, has been both critically acclaimed and a box-office success, partly because of the contributions of its formerly avant-garde director and designer, Julie Taymor. *The Lion King*, *Beauty and the Beast*, and the corporation's third theatrical offering, *Aida*, have been credited with attracting a new family audience to Broadway, and Disney has been lauded for its efforts to renovate and rejuvenate Times Square. Notwithstanding these benefits, critics of what has been termed the "Disneyfication" of Broadway fear the commercialization and corporate control that they see inherent in the process.

A number of musicals over the past decade have succeeded in attracting to Broadway a diverse audience, which, historically, has been largely white and over 40. *Bring in 'Da Noise, Bring in 'Da Funk* (1996), conceived and directed by George C. Wolfe, showcased the talents of dancer and choreographer Savion Glover in a passionate, often rousing history of African American culture, as told through music and dance. Jonathan Larson's Pulitzer Prize–winning *Rent* (1996), with its contemporary pop–rock sound and the retelling of the rebellious, bohemian story from Puccini's nineteenth-century opera *La Bohème,* has attracted young audiences, partly because its relatively young producers insightfully set aside $20 seats for each performance to ensure that such audiences could afford tickets. But the show's popularity is also due to its talented creator's ability to communicate the angst of a society faced with AIDS, prejudice, crime, and homelessness, as well as the temporality of relationships and of life itself. In a tragic mirroring of art and life, Larson died of an aneurysm just prior to

**FIGURE 12.31**

the show's opening on Broadway. A rarely seen Latino audience flocked to see *Capeman*, by pop music legend Paul Simon and Pulitzer Prize–winning playwright Derek Walcott. Although the true story of a gang member of Puerto Rican descent imprisoned for murder was panned by critics, this production proved that the most rapidly growing minority group in the United States was interested in seeing representations of their culture, beyond the stereotypes that had dominated, on the musical stage. The new hip-hop show *In the Heights* has affirmed this phenomenon.

Bringing in audience members who would not normally attend musical theatre is one of the self-professed goals of the young creators of *Avenue Q* (2003): Jeff Marx, Robert Lopez, and Jeff Whitty. Raunchy and irreverent, the show is named after the fictional "outerborough" New York City street on which it is set (a parody of *Sesame Street*). The show chronicles the lives of twenty-somethings, depicted by hand puppets, their visible human manipulators, and actors without puppets, making their insecure way in the world after college. Its departure from the happily-ever-after optimism of Golden Age musicals is perhaps most evident in such song titles as "It Sucks to Be Me," "Everyone's a Little Bit Racist," "The Internet Is for Porn," and "You Can Be as Loud as the Hell You Want [When You're Makin' Love]." *Avenue Q*, and shows like *Urinetown* (2001), a musical about a rebellion by citizens who are suffering from a drought in a town that has banned private toilets and instigated corporate control of public ones and that ends with the death of the hero, could well signal a renewed interest in the irony, sarcasm, pessimism, and unhappy ending embraced by Stephen Sondheim. Duncan Sheik and Steve Sater's pop–rock musical *Spring Awakening* (2006) is the latest offering in this vein, featuring masturbation, incest, S&M, and other explicit themes (and language) in its retelling of the German play about the angst of repressed late-nineteenth-century teens.

**FIGURE 12.32**

Interestingly, a mid-twentieth century connection between television and musicals—when stars of the musical stage frequently appeared on primetime television to perform numbers from their shows—is currently being revisited. Reality television personalities like Fantasia Barrino (*The Color Purple*), Jordin Sparks (*In the Heights*), and Constantine Maroulis (*Rock of Ages*) appear in musicals; reality shows are created specifically to cast revivals like *Grease (You're the One That I Want)*; and in a reflection the other way, television shows like *Glee* consistently draw from stage performers and musicals for stars and material.

## PART TWO: ASIAN MUSIC THEATRE

The combination of music and theatre is hardly unique to the Western world; in fact, non-Western cultures in Africa and the Near East likely developed ritualized forms of music theatre that predate the *dithyrambs* of the Greeks. But just as the integration of music into theatre has been ubiquitous in much of Western theatre, so various non-Western cultures have valued, and continue to value, the ability of music to raise the listener to a higher emotional plane in theatre. Dance is also a prominent element, so much so that some of the forms that will be examined here are often referred to as dance theatre or dance drama. Admittedly, some of the music and dance might barely be recognizable as such to the

**FIGURE 12.33**

Western ear and eye. And as globalization establishes the influence of Western culture on the rest of the world (an influence that remains relatively unreciprocated), these forms are in danger of becoming extinct; fortunately, they remain vital contributors to world theatre. Although music, theatre, and dance are combined in myriad performative traditions throughout the world, from South African township musicals, to indigenous African, Australian, or American Indian rituals, to Asian classical theatre, this section will focus on the latter in order to convey the fact that the combination of theatre and music can be conceived in radically different ways from the way the Broadway musical is conceived.

### Sanskrit Theatre

Classical **Sanskrit theatre** in India, named after the ancient language in which the tradition developed, was more sophisticated and highly developed than that being written or produced anywhere in the world between the second and seventh centuries CE. Like most of the forms discussed here, Sanskrit performance is closely tied to its religious roots—in this case, Hinduism—and its "rules" are dictated in the Indian equivalent to Aristotle's *Poetics*, the *Natyasastra*, attributed to Bharata Muni and dated somewhere between 200 BCE and 200 CE.

**Sanskrit** theatre avoided what we would term "realistic" production practices; the emphasis is on the actor, with no scenery, and elaborate makeup and costume. Furthermore, the makeup and costume, as well as the movement, dance, and gesture per-

**FIGURE 12.34**

formed by the actor, are all highly codified into a system of signs. For example, red makeup signaled to audiences that the character was of a high caste, or class. An elaborate system of intricate gestures, or *mudras*, conveyed everything from emotions and objects to actions and locations. The actors, who were both men and women, would speak and sing in elaborate patterns of intonation, pitch, and tempo. Instruments varied, depending on the play, from stringed and woodwind instruments to flutes, cymbals, and, most important, drums. Sanskrit theatre was traditionally performed on a small rectangular stage within a roofed building that seated from 200 to 500 spectators. At the back of the stage, two doors provided access to the dressing area behind, and the orchestra sat between the two doors.

Sanskrit performance was based on a written text. The length of the plays varied, but they could be quite long; however, even if they presented 10 acts, they served as a mere outline for a much longer, more elaborate performance than the words on the page suggest, similar to a musical theatre libretto. Unlike most Western theatre, the goal of Sanskrit drama was not to reach a climax, develop character, or raise philosophical issues. Instead, the central goal was to communicate the appropriate *rasa*—a term that has been translated as mood, tone, or overall taste—and thus induce a sense of harmony. To achieve one predominant rasa from among eight (erotic, comic, pathetic, furious, heroic, terrible, odious, and marvelous), the performers communicated eight basic human emotions, or *bhavas* (pleasure, mirth, sorrow, wrath, vigor, fear, disgust, and wonder). This notion of inducing a sense of harmony is related to the Hindu goal of reaching nirvana.

Sanskrit plays are still produced in India today, although Sanskrit performance has been mostly subsumed by other, more recent (relatively speaking) forms that developed from Sanskrit, such as Kutiyattum and Kathakali.

### Beijing Opera

China's rich cultural heritage goes back some 6,000 years. **Beijing Opera**, the most widely known form of Chinese classical theatre, developed fairly recently; most date it to 1790. But it draws on a variety of earlier theatrical traditions in China, combining music, speech, dance, and even acrobatics. Beijing Opera is still performed, although it experienced a variety of changes under communism.

The bare stage of this form is furnished with only a few props, and although drably attired stage attendants and musicians people that stage, the heart of Beijing Opera, like Sanskrit theatre, is the actor, who also relies on an elaborate system of codified dance, movement, gesture, makeup, and costume to communicate to the audience. For example, if the script calls for a long journey, the performer walks around in a circle to signify that journey. The amount of training required to become a performer in the Beijing Opera

**FIGURE 12.35**

might astound the Western actor, who may value training, but is ever aware that many actors walk onto a stage or a film or television set with none. This would be impossible in Beijing Opera, as it would with all of the Asian forms discussed here. Traditionally, most actors are apprenticed into a training company from a very young age, concentrating on learning and perfecting a single role, and they are not considered proficient in that role for many years. One of the most distinctive roles has been the *dan*, or female impersonator. For some period, only men were allowed on stage, and some actors specialized in *dan* roles; indeed, many patrons and audiences believed that no actress could so beautifully depict a female ideal on the stage as the *dan* could.

Music is such an integral part of the performance that the musicians remain on stage throughout the performance. Most of the onstage action is performed to music; although the actors are accompanied by only strings and flute, thunderous percussion accents entrances, exits, and other important moments. That all classical Chinese theatre is referred to as *xiqu*, or "tuneful theatre," attests to its reliance on music to communicate its meanings.

**FIGURE 12.36**

### Noh

The long history of **Noh theatre** (or *No* theatre) is wrapped up in Japan's complex history of religion and government, having been influenced first by Shintoism, then by Buddhism, as well as by the emperors of Japan and the shogunate. Noh developed out of various Shinto rituals, and began to take its classical form in the fifteenth century with the work of perhaps the greatest Japanese playwright of all time, Zeami Motokiyo.

Under the patronage of a powerful shogun with a love of the arts, Zeami refined Noh into the dominant form of its time.

Noh, the oldest continuously performed theatrical tradition in the world, is still performed today in much the same way as it was over 600 years ago, the traditions handed down by families of (mostly male) actors whose legacy goes back as far as 56 generations. Described as a "musical dance–drama," Noh makes great demands on its audience. Out of its relationship to Zen Buddhism, with its attendant bßeliefs in serenity, acceptance, and abandonment of desire, grows its often glacially slow pacing and reverence for the explo ration of seeming minutiae. For example, great emphasis is placed on the mere act of walk-ing, highlighted by the sometimes slow, shuffling walk of the actor. This walk, as well as all aspects of Noh, requires years of disciplined training to perfect. The actors wear elegant silk costumes, symbolic, but less rigidly codified—and less gaudy—than those of the Beijing Opera performer, and approximately half of the actors wear painted, wooden masks.

The distinctive Noh stage, basically unchanged since Zeami, consists of a square wooden platform surrounded on only two sides by audience members: at the front of the stage and at stage right. The roofed stage is connected to the backstage dressing room by the hashigakari, or bridge, on which the actors make the distinctively solemn entrances and exits characteristic of Noh. At the rear of the stage, a painted pine tree provides the only scenery, save for a few occasional small props and set pieces. An orchestra of four sits at the back, and at stage left sits a chorus that, along with the orchestra, provides continuous musical accom-paniment. The performers combine dance and movement with singing, speech, and chanting to create a look and sound that is spiritual, reverent, and ritualistic in tone and feeling.

**FIGURE 12.37**

Although Noh hardly attracts mass audiences and is often thought to be in danger of extinction, it has been declared a national treasure and has a devoted following in Japan. More recently, tours and the work of international scholars have brought atten-tion to the form.

## Kabuki

Whereas Noh is considered a more elitist form and is often equated with the Western form of opera, Kabuki, a much more popular Japanese form—and a form that relies more on spectacle—is often equated with the Broadway musical.

Kabuki began in the time of Shakespeare, and although women associated with prostitution originally performed it, by 1652 it had become the all-male form that it is today. Like most of the Asian classical theatrical forms, Kabuki is not a literary form; the text, drawn from plays written for the Noh and **Bunraku** (Japanese puppet performance) theatres, is a mere outline for a much more elaborate visual perform-ance. And although the actor is at the heart of each of the Asian traditions examined here so far, the spectacle of Kabuki sometimes overshadows the individual per-former. Sondheim's belief that "people beat scenery" is anathema to this form.

The Kabuki stage has undergone some changes throughout its history, but key elements have been in use for over 100 years: a long stage with a low proscenium, in front of which sits a typically large audience; a revolving stage, used in Japan before anywhere else; and the hanamichi, a raised, narrow runway that connects the stage to the back of the auditorium, and that is used by actors for entrances, exits, and short scenes, providing both a physical and an emotional connection between performer and spectator. Today, elaborate scenic effects put a distinctive stamp on plays per-formed for hundreds of years; for example, black lights are used for underwater scenes in which stage attendants in black support actors and props, dressed and painted in colors that glow under the lights, so that the actors and props look as if they are swimming in water.

Still, the actors, who are trained from childhood, provide much of the pleasure of watching Kabuki—particularly the equivalent of the dan of Beijing Opera, the *onnagata*, a female impersonator who, in his white makeup and delicate silk costume, is highly skilled at capturing the essence of femininity through stylized gesture and movement. One hallmark of Kabuki acting is the *mie*, or poses that are struck at cli-

## For Further Information

Arnott, Peter. *The Theatres of Japan*. 1969.

Banfield, Stephen. *Sondheim's Broadway Musicals*. 1993.

Bean, Annemarie, ed. *Inside the Minstrel Mask: Readings in Nineteenth Century Blackface Minstrelsy*. 1996.

Bowers, Faubion. *Theatre in the East: A Survey of Asian Dance and Drama*. 1969.

Citron, Stephen. *Sondheim and Lloyd Webber: The New Musical*. 2001.

——. *The Musical Theatre from the Inside Out*. 1992.

Clum, John M. *Something for the Boys: Musical Theatre and Gay Culture*. 1999.

Flinn, Denny Martin. *Musical: A Grand Tour*. 1997.

Kislan, Richard. *The Musical*. rev. ed. 1995.

Leiter, Samuel L. *The Art of Kabuki: Famous Plays in Performance*. 1979.

Macherras, Colin, ed. *Chinese Theatre: From Its Origins to the Present Day*. 1983.

McConachie, Bruce A. *Melodramatic Formations: American Theatre and Society, 1820–1870*. 1992.

Richmond, Farley P., Darius L. Swann, and Phillip B. Zarilli, eds. *Indian Theatre: Traditions of Performance*. 1990.

*The Tradition of Performing Arts in Japan*. Videocassette. 1989.

Walsh, Michael. *Andrew Lloyd Webber: His life and works: A critical biography*. 1997.

Woll, Allen L. *Black Musical Theatre: From Coontown to Dreamgirls*. 1989.

Yan, Haiping, ed. *Theatre and Society: An Anthology of Contemporary China*. 1998.

Zadan, Craig. *Sondheim & Co*. 2nd ed. 1986.

## Suggested Films and Resources

Minstrelsy: *Bamboozled* (2000)

Melodrama: *Raiders of the Lost Ark* (1981)

Beijing Opera: *Farewell My Concubine* (1993)

1930s "Serious" Musical Drama: *Cradle Will Rock* (1999)

Cole Porter: *Kiss Me Kate* (1953), *De-Lovely* (2004)

Golden Age Musicals: *Oklahoma!* (1955), *The Sound of Music* (1965), *My Fair Lady* (1964), *Chicago* (2002)

Rebellions against the Golden Age: *West Side Story* (1961), *Sweeney Todd* (2007), *Sunday in the Park with George* (1986), *Into the Woods* (1991)

British Invasion: *Phantom of the Opera* (2004)

Noh, Bunraku, and Kabuki: *The Tradition of Performing Arts in Japan*

The History of the Musical: *Broadway: The American Musical* (2004)

Archive of Musical Theatre Performances on Video: http://bluegobo.com/

## Glossary

**ballad opera**   A form popular beginning in the eighteenth century in which songs with interpolated lyrics set to popular tunes are interspersed within the dominant dialogue.

**Beijing Opera**   A classical, traditional Chinese form that combines music, dance, and speech with elaborate codified costumes, makeup, and movement.

**British Invasion**   A wave of musicals, primarily during the 1970s and 1980s, that transferred to New York City from the West End of London and topped the lists of longest-running Broadway musicals into the 1990s.

**Bunraku**   Intensely lifelike classical Japanese puppetry form in which each puppet is manipulated by three puppeteers.

**burlesque**   Parodies of well-known plays and events that included songs and dances, popular during the nineteenth century. Eventually came to refer more to "girly shows" with striptease.

**cast album**   A sound recording of all the songs in a musical made by the opening-night cast of shows produced in New York or London.

*dan*   The female impersonator in Beijing Opera.

*dithyramb*   In ancient Greece, a chorus of men who sang hymns in honor of Dionysus; may have been the precursor to tragedy.

**Golden Age**   Term used by some historians to refer to a period in the twentieth century when the integrated American musical was at its height, roughly from 1942 to 1968.

*intermezzi*   A combination of elaborate scenery, costumes, lights, special effects, music, and dance that was performed between acts of dramas at the courts of the Italian Renaissance. In France, a similar form was the *ballet de cour*; in England, *the masque*.

**Kabuki**   A classical Japanese form of music theatre developed in the eighteenth century that emphasizes spectacle.

**libretto**   The book of a musical, which includes the dialogue that is spoken between the songs.

**melodrama**   "Music drama" that grew out of the social ills of the Industrial Revolution to become the most popular Western form during the nineteenth century. It is marked by a strict adherence to poetic justice, stock characters, and escapism, as well as accompanying music that underscores the action.

*mie*   Poses that are struck at climactic moments in the action of Kabuki, punctuated by furious claps of wooden blocks and appreciative cheers and clapping from the audience.

**minstrelsy**   Controversial form, popular during the nineteenth century, in which white performers in blackface performed their impressions of slave music, dances, and culture. Eventually, black performers in blackface performed as well.

**Noh theatre**   A classical Japanese form created in the fourteenth century; emphasizes minimalism as a reflection of the influences of Zen Buddhism.

*onnagata*   The female impersonator in Kabuki.

**Sanskrit theatre**   An ancient Indian theatre form, in the language of Sanskrit, that avoided realistic practices and involved codified performance, including elaborate costumes, makeup, and a complex set of movements and gestures known as *mudras*.

**sung-through**   A musical with little or no dialogue between the songs.

## Key Concepts

- Musical theatre is as old as theatre itself and has been the dominant mode of theatrical expression throughout history.
- Musical theatre is difficult to define, but usually includes some combination of music, lyrics, libretto, and dance.
- The Broadway musical developed out of such forms as opera and ballad opera, burlesque, minstrelsy, and melodrama.
- The increasing primacy of story over song, with the integration of all elements, led to a "Golden Age" of musicals during the mid-twentieth century.

- The work of Stephen Sondheim represents one of the most significant "rebellions" against the Golden Age.
- British Invasion musicals challenged the "Americanness" of the Broadway musical.
- Numerous classical non-Western forms rely heavily on music to communicate meaning and to entertain.

## Appendix

### Longest Running Shows in Broadway History (as of September 19, 2010)
*Denotes show still running

| Show | Performances |
| --- | --- |
| 1. The Phantom of the Opera* | 9,419 |
| 2. Cats | 7,485 |
| 3. Les Miserables | 6,680 |
| 4. A Chorus Line | 6,137 |
| 5. Oh! Calcutta | 5,959 |
| 6. Chicago* | 5,748 |
| 7. Beauty and the Beast | 5,461 |
| 8. The Lion King* | 5,333 |
| 9. Rent | 4,609 |
| 10. Miss Saigon | 4,092 |

# The Film, or Mediated Performance

**Chapter Outline**

*To view the figures in this chapter, log on to www.pearsonexploretheatre.com.*

## INTRODUCTION

For thousands of years, theatre has been an ephemeral art—saved only in memory or in pictures and mementoes associated with the live performance. Although many scripts have survived and some theatre structures still exist, we have few records of the ways by which the Egyptians, Greeks, Romans, medieval monks and nuns, Elizabethans, Spaniards, or many others actually performed their shows. None of the **ephemera** from those historic productions survive, such as costumes, sets, programs (if they had them), actors' **sides**, and so on. Scholars attempting to reconstruct and describe those historic productions must use evidence gathered from other sources, such as paintings, diaries, legal records, and other artifacts that have survived, which offer clues of the methods by which artists may have created those performances.

**FIGURES 13.1, 13.2, 13.3, 13.4, AND 13.5**

When technology that was developed in the late nineteenth century allowed for mediated forms of performance, those artifacts (on celluloid film, videotape, and now digital forms of storage, such as DVDs and DVRs) could be saved, copied, and distributed to a wider audience than could be gathered into a single theatre on a single evening. Live theatre endured even as mediated forms proliferated; indeed, no mediated performance can ever replace live performance. Nevertheless, the genie had been released from the bottle, and theatre artists discovered that mediated performances offered some advantages over live ones. Not only could a larger audience be reached, but also the work of performance artists could be directly viewed many years after the original performance. In this way, theatrical works of art gained a kind of permanence that they had never before enjoyed. Scholars can now visit the Billy Rose Theatre Collection of the New York Public Library to view video recordings of Broadway shows, and famous actors can be seen performing in such online collections as The Blue Gobo (www.bluegobo.com).

As mediated forms of performance matured, they developed particular strengths and characteristics that differentiated the cinema from live theatre. Live theatre both gave birth to and continues to cross-pollinate with mediated performances, and this chapter briefly charts the history of mediated performances and then explores the similarities and differences between the two in the example of *Finale*, a full-length film adapted from *Two Character Play* (presented and discussed in Chapter 11). This chapter also follows the same organizational pattern that we have used throughout *Explore Theatre*, integrating historical information as we move from author and adaptor to directors, designers, and actors. We finish with the film itself and a documentary on the differences between film and theatre, but first we begin with some history.

## LEARNING OBJECTIVES

### After reading and watching Chapter 13, you should be able to:

- Identify several important differences and similarities between film and theatre.
- Explain how those differences and similarities are likely to affect your viewing.
- Use appropriate vocabulary when analyzing mediated performances.
- Discuss the contributions that each of the major artists in a film makes (author, producer, director, production team, actor, postproduction team).
- Develop a critical analysis of a mediated performance which identifies the major factors that shaped your response to it.

## BACKGROUND

The earliest forms of mediated performance—namely, the cinema—borrowed wholesale from the theatre of the day. Scripts, actors, directors, designers, and technicians are common to both live theatre and mediated performances. Indeed, many of the early "talkies" were play scripts that were only modestly adapted for the camera.

As the art form matured, new texts created for mediated performance were developed from original stories or adapted from other material, including play scripts. **Screenplays**— the name itself a symbol of the genealogy of film—still mirror scripts for live performance (plays) in their use of character, dialogue, plot, and structure. One primary difference has been that, so far, scripts for mediated performance are rarely viewed as "products" in and of themselves and are clearly written to be produced via mediation, with fairly proscriptive directions in the script as to how they should be produced.

Although most plays throughout history have been written to be performed, many tend to be open to interpretation, and the work of playwrights often has been appreciated as literature disconnected from its place in a performance context. Playwright and screenwriter José Rivera provides one perspective on the difference between writing for the stage and writing for the screen when he states, "You write a play with your ears and a film with your eyes." August Wilson agreed: "The way I see it, the stage tells the story for the ear, and the screen for the eye."

Screenplays are written most often in what is termed "studio format," using standard headings and terms, fonts, and spacing. A traditional rule of thumb is that each page of a screenplay will translate into one minute of screen time, and screenplays are often 90–130 pages long. Whereas a single author typically writes the script for a stage play, films often have many contributors to the final script.

**FIGURE 13.6**

In addition, other collaborators, such as the **storyboard artist** and director of photography, can make significant contributions to the screenplay. When all of those contributions are complete, a **shooting script** is a final draft from which the movie is shot and includes such information as camera angles. **Teleplays** have a similar, albeit often briefer, format, with some changes, such as including "act breaks" to allow for commercials.

**FIGURE 13.7**

The **pinhole camera** and the **camera obscura** had been used for centuries, but modern photography did not emerge until the early nineteenth century, and "moving pictures" followed at the end of that century. These early films were silent and were more akin to the work of a photographer, a recorder of visual images, than that of a theatre artist, who created the artistic representation of human drama. These moving picture shows were often presented as part of vaudeville entertainments (see Chapter 14) and regularly focused on news of the day. Other popular subjects included magicians' tricks, everyday scenes, and travelogues. The camera rarely moved, imitating the experience of a seated theatergoer.

When so-called narrative, or story films, emerged at the beginning of the twentieth century, most notably in *The Great Train Robbery* (1903; see Figures 13.8 and 13.9), they were, according to film historian Robert Sklar, "in no sense original: certainly not in relationship to similar works of popular literature and theater, or even to earlier films." Nevertheless, these early narrative films lay the groundwork for later developments in cinema storytelling, including camera movement, jump cuts, and other effects that are impossible on a live stage.

**FIGURES 13.8 AND 13.9**

Early silent films quickly subsumed melodrama, eclipsing theatrical melodramas by their ability to capture or create more and better spectacle. Because these films were silent, dialogue had limited importance. When sound was added, realism became a common genre for film, with documentaries taking the place of naturalism. However, as in theatre, film artists quickly took up alternative modes, such as expressionism and surrealism; today's independent films often explore alternatives to the mostly melodramatic and realistic filmmaking that occurs in Hollywood and beyond. Filmmakers such as Quentin Tarantino and Christopher Nolan explore more postmodern, fragmented structures, abandoning linear narratives, in movies such as *Pulp Fiction* and *Memento*.

The use of new technologies has inevitably shifted the focus in performance from narrative to spectacle, and this is certainly common in live performances that are combined with virtual reality (VR), a new trend in theatre. The goal of some VR performance is to enhance the interactivity of the audience, which may appear as **interactors** in the performance via digital technology or may manipulate virtual actors working on stage with live actors. Other virtual reality performances involve little audience interaction. Many combinations are possible and have been experimented with, such as those shown in the Institute for the Exploration of Virtual Reality's 2003 production of *The Magic Flute*, in which, for example, actors performed with such CGI (computer-generated imagery) characters as "Wolfi" the dragon, who even appears to be stabbed by live actors with swords.

**FIGURES 13.10 AND 13.11**

*The Magic Flute* is a good example, however, of how text becomes de-emphasized in favor of spectacle; the creators, calling the dialog "boring," cut it considerably. Most

VR theatre, like postmodern performance (of which it is a part), either adapts and reinterprets original texts, or works from a minimal blueprint or none at all. It remains to be seen whether or not new technologies will extend what will constitute a play in the future.

## ORGANIZATION

The organizational structure and chronological engagement of the artistic personnel for a film are somewhat different than those for live theatre. In the latter, playwrights write scripts to be selected by producers and/or directors, who then coordinate and collaborate with the other theatrical artists as the show is being developed and rehearsed, working with everyone to create the final product, which will be performed each night by the actors and technicians. In film, the process often starts with producers, who hire writers to develop screenplays, sometimes in collaboration with a director. The producer and director then assemble a large team of artists to plan how the film will be shot, edited, and produced. Although live shows cost money to produce and develop, their primary costs are in the continuous running of the show over time. Problems can be fixed or changes to the live show can be added after the actors have rehearsed and even after the show has already opened. Films, on the other hand, are relatively cheap to show in movie theatres each night, but the cost of bringing back the cast and crew to fix a problem after the film has been shot is too great for most films. A film director must have a very clear idea of what the finished product will look like long before he starts to shoot.

**FIGURE 13.12**

There are several processes fundamental to filmmaking: development, preproduction, production, postproduction, and distribution. Unlike stage directors, film directors are usually involved in each of these processes. Stage directors are usually hired long after the script has been finalized, and their work is done once the show is open, regardless of how long the show runs. Film directors can spend up to three years or more working on a single movie as it moves from conception to production.

Once a film project has been finalized for shooting in **development** and a shooting script has been completed, the **preproduction** process identifies all the material and personnel needs for the film (locations, casting, costs, sets, second units, special effects, camera types, sound needs, lighting, composer for the music, craft services, technicians, etc.). With an overall plan in place, the actual **production** shooting (photography and sound) can begin. Filming can last anywhere from a few days to a few months or, in the case of an epic film such as *Lord of the Rings*, several years.

The **postproduction** process often begins as shooting continues. Each morning, the director, producer, and others will watch the dailies, a rough assembly of the previous day's shots. If no acceptable shots can make the final cut, a reshoot is scheduled. Once "the film is in the can," or shooting is completed, the postproduction process begins in earnest. The editor, sometimes in collaboration with the director and/or producer, assembles, arranges, and cuts the film into a narrative sequence.

After many weeks or months, the film reaches the point of "picture lock," a cut of the film that everyone agrees is the final, visual arrangement of the shots. Now the sound engineers and Foley editors add their contributions, rerecording dialog to match the final cut, and adding sound effects or "sweetening" the sounds that the on-location microphones picked up. The composer or music supervisor adds original or adapted music, and everything is blended together in a final cut of the film. Now, sometimes years after the project was begun, the film is ready for sales and **distribution**.

**FIGURE 13.13**

## STAGE TO SCREEN

Because most students likely to read this textbook have far more experience viewing mediated performances (film and television, and increasingly, Internet video) than live theatre, we felt that it was important to explore ways in which each medium affected the story being told. After the stage version of *Two Character Play* had been performed and documented for this textbook, we asked one of our theatre students, Maggie Kubley, to adapt the script into a screenplay. Maggie was a senior performance major who had written several short scripts for class and other projects, who writes her own music and lyrics for her own band, and who had developed a one-woman show.

**Adaptation** has been a common feature of film since the early days of Hollywood, and indeed, many famous films have come from works of journalism, autobiography, comic books, Holy Scripture, plays, and even other films. Few stories, however, are literally transferred from one medium to another; they must undergo **elision** or **interpolation**. J.R.R. Tolkein's novel *The Lord of the Rings* initially proved to be very difficult to adapt to performance, with several earlier versions ending up both financial and critical flops. Peter Jackson was able to elide (cut) some parts of the story while interpolating (combining and changing) other parts in order to make his film version a worldwide smash hit.

Other stories seem as though they should make good movies, but prove nearly impossible to adapt. *Adaptation* (2002) depicts the struggles that Hollywood film writer Charlie Kaufman faced in trying to adapt the best-selling novel *The Orchid Thief* into a screenplay. Susan Orlean's popular novel proved so difficult to adapt that Kaufman eventually wrote a screenplay about the process of adaptation rather than simply one about the plot of the novel. Some stories are more easily adapted into film; a notable example is Bernard Shaw's *Pygmalion*, which was also adapted into a famous musical, *My Fair Lady*, both of which were made into successful Hollywood films.

When Chris White was commissioned to write the script for *Two Character Play* (see Chapter 11), she knew that we intended to have another writer adapt her stage play into a screenplay. Her play explored the "liveness" of live theatre, challenging the audience to think about the nature, purpose, and possibilities of the live theatrical event. Few movies successfully bridge the divide between the screen, with its unchanging and unalterable presentation, and the live audience gathered to watch the film. Woody Allen's *Annie Hall* is a notable example of an exception to this general rule.

Although Maggie Kubley faced significant challenges in adapting Chris White's play, she did not have the same horrific experiences as Charlie Kaufman's character in *Adaptation*. Her working title for the screenplay was *Interviews*, which was replaced with *Finale* about halfway through the shooting of the film. The video in Figure 13.14 documents Kubley's process as she adapted White's original play into a screenplay.*

**FIGURE 13.14**

## PREPRODUCTION

Shakespeare's *Hamlet* is, arguably, one of the most famous plays in the world. The total number of unique productions of this play probably numbers in the hundreds of thousands; indeed, the play has been produced on Broadway alone at least 66 times. Dozens of adaptations and original plays have followed in *Hamlet*'s extraordinary wake, including *I Hate Hamlet* by Paul Rudnick, *Dogg's Hamlet* and *Rosencrantz and Guildenstern Are Dead* by Tom Stoppard, and *The Mask of Hamlet* by Ario Flamma.

*Hamlet* has also proven to be popular in Hollywood, and audiences can watch recent versions with Kenneth Branagh, Mel Gibson, or Ethan Hawke in the title role.

---

* **Note:** Students interested in adapting materials for the screen should be aware that they must secure permission to do so from the original author or the current rights holder (such as a studio), unless the original source is in the public domain. Maggie Kubley had both permission and advice from Chris White, the author of the original play.

Each of these actors brought a very different look and energy to the role, and each of these film versions of the same play is different from the others. Although different stage versions can be equally remarkable, the actors are usually only one factor in the different audiences' experiences. Because the camera gets so close to the actors, and because a significant portion of the film experience is dominated by close-ups on their faces, the actors themselves are much more important to a film than to a stage play, relative to the other elements, such as location (sets), lighting, and costumes.

Casting, therefore, is one of the most important aspects of filmmaking. The actors' faces and bodies are the primary visual elements in most films, and audiences get most of their information visually. Sound, lights, sets, and costumes are still important, but actors carry the primary burden of communicating mood and meaning. In major Hollywood films, a specific individual, the casting director, works for the film director to find the ideal cast for each film. Casting directors may go though thousands of headshots and casting calls to find the right actor for a specific role. For smaller films, the film director often functions as her own casting director. For *Finale*, director Steve Marra functioned as his own casting director; the video in Figure 13.15 focuses on the casting process for this film.

**FIGURE 13.15**

Several Hollywood legends exist of a relatively unknown actor who is "discovered" by a director or producer and becomes a major star. These stories typically involve young people who are doing something other than acting when they are discovered. Nick Mitchell started out as the storyboard artist for the film, but after the casting process had begun, Steve Marra decided that Nick was the person he needed for the male lead. The documentary in Figure 13.16 depicts Nick's journey from preproduction collaborator to lead actor.

**FIGURE 13.16**

## PRODUCERS

Because actors serve as both the characters whom they are portraying and the major visual elements in a film, the actors must be age appropriate for their characters. In the stage version of *Two Character Play*, the actor who played the dual role of Actor/Father was able to play both a 22-year-old boy and a 37-year-old father. The film, however, did not allow for this kind of artistic flexibility. The film required an actor who both looked like and acted as a real father, so the executive producer of the film, Rodger Smith, was asked to act in the role of the father. The documentary in Figure 13.17 explores both the need for the older actors and how Dr. Smith functioned as both an actor and executive producer.

**FIGURE 13.17**

Although professionals served as executive producer and director for this film, an undergraduate student, Jessica Keffaber, performed most of the day-to-day responsibilities of the producer. The documentary in Figure 13.18 shows many of the jobs that Jessica undertook as she worked to keep a very complex and difficult process on track and within budget.

**FIGURE 13.18**

## DIRECTORS

Although the role of stage director had already emerged prior to the advent of filmmaking, stage directors and actor–managers did not become commonplace until after World War II (see Chapter 6). Film directors, on the other hand, dominated the early film industry, often performing many of the duties that are now shared by many individuals, including the casting director, director of photography, storyboard artist, line producer, script supervisor, stunt coordinator, and location manager. In the early days of filmmaking, directors were more likely to achieve widespread fame than the actors whom they filmed.

Film directors continue to be well known, although actors have eclipsed them in terms of fame (but not fortune). Stage directors tend to be well known to knowledgeable theatre audiences, but with so many Hollywood stars performing on Broadway, audience members are far more likely to know and remember the actors' names than their director's. A rare few individuals are famous as both actors and directors; notable among them are Charlie Chaplin, Buster Keaton, Orson Wells, Clint Eastwood, and Woody Allen.

Most film directors do not enjoy the rarified reputations of the stars whom they direct, and many more still, such as Steve Marra, the director for *Finale*, labor in relative obscurity along with the majority of artists in theatre and film. Whether the budget is large or small, or the cast is famous or unknown, the work of directing a film remains much the same. The documentary in Figure 13.19 explores the major issues faced by Steve and his assistant directors, director of photography, and other crew members.

**FIGURE 13.19**

The relationship between a director and his director of photography (DP) varies; some partnerships are very collaborative, whereas some DPs serve, more or less, as a technician for the director. The DP, or **cinematographer**, is responsible for achieving the artistic visions of the director through careful selection and use of camera type, lens, aperture, shutter speed, placement, angle, and movement. He also supervises all of the camera operators, dolly grips, and other technicians associated with the camera, usually the single most expensive item on a film set. The camera is treated separately from other areas in production, such as sets, locations, props, lights, and costumes, because it is an expensive, highly complex, and sometimes fragile instrument. Excellent cinematographers are worth their weight in gold, and many famous directors work with a favorite DP because these artists can have a significant impact on the overall look and feel of a film. The documentary in Figure 13.20 charts the journey of Sam Day, the DP for *Finale*, and several of his crew members.

**FIGURE 13.20**

## DESIGNERS AND TECHNICIANS

On a big-budget film, hundreds of people might report to the **production designer** (also called the art director), who is responsible for the overall look and style of a film. Production designers hire the storyboard artist, set decorators, costume designer, property master, graphic designer, model maker, and special-effects supervisor. On ultra-low-budget or "no-budget" films, like *Finale*, the director and her assistants might serve in many of those functions. In fact, many of the students on the crew of *Finale* rotated through many of the jobs on the shoot in order to gain valuable experience and skills.

The art department, as this area is sometimes called, is responsible for set construction and painting, as well as for modifications to existing locations, such as changing road signs, trimming shrubs, mowing the grass, and installing temporary walls or making other physical modifications. Carpenters, painters, plasterers, riggers, propmakers, greensmen (landscapers), sign painters, and scenic artists can all be found in the art department.

The **set decorator**, often an interior decorator, finds appropriate furniture, wallpaper, lighting fixtures, and bric-a-brac. He or she also supervises a crew of buyers and set dressers who arrange furniture, hang curtains, and dress the set. As in live theatre, a **props master** works closely with the director and actors to provide the items handled directly by the actors, such as newspapers, weapons, musical instruments, and food. These crew members also work with the **script supervisor** (or continuity supervisor) during the shoot to make sure that various items and props are in the same positions for each shot.

For *Finale*, most of the students on the artistic team served more than one function, and several of their stories have already been partially told. One of the few who filled the same role in both the stage play and the film version was the costume designer, Jenn Turley. Because the costumes for the film were all found or bought, as opposed to being designed or built, Jenn was given the title of **wardrobe supervisor** for the film, and her experiences are documented in the video in Figure 13.21.

**FIGURE 13.21**

In film, the person who functions as a lighting designer is called a **gaffer**, a term that originally referred to a respected elderly person, but was adopted by Hollywood for the person who used a gaff (a long pole) to move overhead lights in the studio. The gaffer works for and reports to the DP, and depending on the complexity of the shoot, the gaffer can have many assistants. The first assistant is called the **best boy**, and the crew members supervised by the gaffer are the **grips**, electricians, and sparks. There is little agreement as to the origins of the name *grip*. Some argue that the term was imported from vaudeville, where workmen carried their tools in a "grip" or bag. Others argue that the term originates from the days of hand-cranked cameras, during which several strong men had to keep a good grip on the tripod in order to keep it from shaking. *Sparks* came to use because the crew members also managed the power cords for lights and other equipment, so the name is a humorous reference to what can happen when a crew member makes an error. On a complex shoot, 20 to 50 grips or sparks might be needed, whereas on simpler shoots only a gaffer and his best boy are used. (Few gaffers are women because crews are drawn largely from the male-dominated construction industry.) The gaffer for *Finale*, Derek Hammer, is a professional artist who taught and supervised a large crew of grips and sparks for the film. In the video in Figure 13.22, he explains what the fundamentals of light do for a film.

**FIGURE 13.22**

The large student crew learned a great deal from Derek. In the video in Figure 13.23, they explain what their experiences taught them about how films are made and what each of these jobs entailed.

**FIGURE 13.23**

The visual elements are made visible (or not) by the lighting effects used in a film. As with live theatre, if you are supposed to see the action and you cannot, then nothing else matters much. In the video in Figure 13.24, the artists and technicians who created the special effects for *Finale* explain how they achieved some of the more important moments in the film.

**FIGURE 13.24**

## ACTORS

Actors did not become the big stars in films until studios began to employ stock companies of actors who appeared frequently in several one-reel releases. The unusual intimacy that the camera created between the screen and the audience made these early film actors recognizable to an enormous viewing public. When serials emerged a short time later, audiences began to associate certain actors in favorite roles, such as Charlie Chaplin as "the Tramp," Clara Bow as the "'It' Girl," and Mary Pickford as "America's Sweetheart."

Because films with well-known stars could make more money, seemingly without regard to the quality of the screenplay, studios began to promote their actors in an industrial manner, creating and distributing "facts" about their stars' private lives or professional aspirations that bore little resemblence to the truth. Some of the more powerful artists in Hollywood—the director D. W. Griffith and the actors Charlie Chaplin, Mary Pickford, and Douglas Fairbanks—resented the control that studios exerted over both their public work and their private lives. Therefore, they formed United Artists in 1919. Strong-willed actors and powerful studios have continued to struggle for artistic and financial control in the years since.

**FIGURE 13.25**

Nearly all film actors during the Golden Age of Hollywood worked for one of eight major studios. The studio system allowed a few large studios to control a significant percentage of all film production and distribution in Hollywood from the early 1920s through the 1950s. Studios produced movies on their own lots with their own "stable" of actors, directors, and technicians, and then distributed these movies to their own network of movie theatres. These eight major studios—RKO Radio Pictures, Warner Bros., Fox, Paramount, Loew's/MGM, Universal, Columbia, and United Artists— dominated the landscape of American film, and many actors and directors chafed under the studios' restrictive contracts.

Actors working for a movie studio found that life was more similar to working in a factory than in a theatre. Everyone but the biggest stars entered through a main gate, went to their assigned stations, worked long hours, ate in a communal cafeteria, and left at the same time. Some actors might work on more than one film set in a day, as the studios shot hundreds of films a year.

One advantage of the studio system was that, because so many films were made, not every film had to be a smash hit for its studio to do good business. Many significant films, such as *Citizen Kane*, were made with only modest budgets and casts of relatively unknown actors. Other films, such as *Gone with the Wind*, matched the biggest names with the biggest budgets to create epic films, which have remained a staple of Hollywood.

In 1948, the U.S. Supreme Court issued an antitrust ruling against the eight major studios, signaling the end of the Golden Age of Hollywood. Actors in Hollywood today must rely on a network of agents, personal managers, and casting directors to find work, rather than be subject to the paternalistic control of one studio or another.

In both film and theatre, actors are cast, given a script, handed props, blocked and rehearsed by a director, put into a costume, and asked to give a professional performance of a fully realized character. But the process for film acting differs greatly from that for stage acting. Plays are usually rehearsed in sequence, starting with the first page of the script and working through to the last page. Movies are usually filmed out of sequence, with the very last scene of the film sometimes being the very first thing that is shot. Some actors find this process confusing and disconcerting and enjoy stage acting over film, whereas others find the daily grind of eight shows a week and acting the same show over and over again to be intolerable and prefer film acting. In films, an actor has to act the scene perfectly only once, whereas a Broadway actor must perform, more or less perfectly, night after night for hundreds or even thousands of performances.

In the videos offered next, four of the actors who appeared in both *Two Character Play* and *Finale* share their experiences, lessons learned, and accomplishments as they moved from the stage to the screen.

**FIGURES 13.26, 13.27, 13.28 AND 13.29**

Most of the actors working in Hollywood and on Broadway do so under a veil of relative anonymity. For every major star, there are hundreds of actors who spend their entire lives acting, making a living, raising families, and living somewhat normal lives. The general public never learns their names or notices much of their work, even when they see those actors in countless shows, films, or commercials. Many young actors, waiting for fame and fortune, spend much of their careers as extras, the other people in the shot who are not the main or supporting stars. The video in Figure 13.30 provides a glimpse into the trials and tribulations of the extras, as told from the perspective of *Finale*'s Second Assistant Director Josh Carver, who was also the "extras wrangler."

**FIGURE 13.30**

## EDITORS AND POSTPRODUCTION

Once the film or mediated performance has been shot, the footage is given over to a team of artists who create the final product. Both mediated and live performances share actors, directors, and designers, but only recorded performances have editors, a characteristic that distinguishes filmmaking and television from the other performance forms that preceded it. Editors not only assemble recorded footage, but also integrate the many layers of images, sounds, shots, dialog, and music into a cohesive whole that has pace, emotional resonance, and a clearly told story. Some stage actors have resisted film acting because the editors exert enormous power over their performance.

In some cases, editing turns the film into something quite different from what it was originally envisioned to be. For example, for *The Night They Raided Minsky's*, the editor, Ralph Rosenblum (who wrote a book based on this experience; see Further Information), took footage that was too predictably structured, with a major star (Bert Lahr) who had died before filming was finished, and created a groundbreaking film that won great acclaim for its director, William Friedkin.

Editors historically have worked on only one part of a film, such as the picture, sound, music, or effects. Today, with the advent of digital editing software, a single editor might edit the entire work, especially on short films without many special effects. Most editors seek to create and maintain the emotional continuity of a story, which, if done successfully, will cause audiences to overlook errors in the physical continuity of the shots.

For *Finale*, the same team of students that shot the film also participated in the editing process. In the video in Figure 13.31, the team of students who worked on the audio for the film documents the demands that mediated performances put on sound designers and technicians. In the video in Figure 13.32, the team of students who collaborated on the editing process talks about the many challenges that they faced as they worked to put together the final cut of the film.

**FIGURES 13.31 AND 13.32**

## THE FILM: *FINALE*

Like *Two Character Play*, the film *Finale* (Figure 13.33) was created and documented to help students learn about the nature of dramatic storytelling and the similarities and differences between live and mediated performances. Unlike *Two Character Play*, the medium upon which you will watch the performance, namely, this screen, is the format for which *Finale* was intended. In other words, rather than watching a film recording of a live performance, you will be watching a film created and designed to be watched as a film. As you watch, be alert to the major differences both in the story and in the storytelling (the ways in which the cameras were used, how shots add to or detract from your emotional involvement in the story, how the film creates intimacy, etc.).

**FIGURE 13.33**

## THEATRE AND FILM

Audience members at any dramatic performance—live or mediated—are likely to have some awareness of the other forms of performance. A few audience members may lack direct experience in other forms—for instance, some people have never seen a live play, whereas others have never watched a webisode on the Internet—but almost everyone is familiar with the general idea of performance itself. Almost everyone understands what an actor is, even if they do not understand how actors act or what it takes to be a great actor.

The documentary in Figure 13.34 explores some of the major differences and similarities between theatre and film, the two most dominant forms of dramatic storytelling of the last 100 years. Notice how even the artists themselves disagree about what is the same and what is different. Be aware that this documentary is meant to raise questions rather than to provide answers.

**FIGURE 13.34**

## For Further Information

Burton, Graeme. *More Than Meets the Eye: An Introduction to Media Studies*. 3rd ed. 2002.

Carver, Gavin, and Colin Beardon, Eds. *New Visions in Performance: The Impact of Digital Technologies*. 2004.

Haag, Judith H., and Hillis R. Cole. *The Complete Guide to Standard Script Formats: The Screenplay*. 1980.

Hudson-Mairet, Stephen, Mark Reaney, and Delbert Unruh. "The Edge of Illusion: A Virtual Reality Production of 'The Magic Flute.'" *TD&T* 40.4 (Fall 2004): 10–19.

Rivera, José. "Split Personality: Random Thoughts on Writing for Theater and Film." *Cinema Journal* 45.2 (2006): 89–92.

Rosenblum, Ralph, and Robert Karen. *When the Shooting Stops ... The Cutting Begins: A Film Editor's Story*. 1979.

Sklar, Robert. *Film: An International History of the Medium*. 2nd ed. 2002.

Tibbetts, John C. "August Wilson Interview." *Literature Film Quarterly* 30.4 (2002): 238–242.

Trottier, David. *The Screenwriter's Bible: A Complete Guide to Writing, Formatting, and Selling Your Script*. Rev. ed. 1995.

## Suggested Films

*Sunset Boulevard* (1950): An Academy Award–winning film noir directed and cowritten by Billy Wilder, and produced and cowritten by Charles Brackett. It was nominated for eleven Academy Awards and won three, and is often cited as one of the most noteworthy films of American cinema.

*Singin' in the Rain* (1952): Tops the American Film Institute's list of the 25 best American musicals of all time and humorously documents the shift from silent films to "talkies" in Hollywood.

*A Star Is Born* (1954): An American musical film directed by George Cukor and written by Moss Hart that marked Judy Garland's comeback as a major Hollywood star. (See the restored 1983 version, rather than the slash-edited original release.)

*Cinema Paradiso* (1988): Won the Special Jury Selection at the Cannes Film Festival and the Best Foreign Language Film Oscar in 1989.

*Chaplin* (1992): A 1992 British biographical film about the life of English comedian Charlie Chaplin that documents filmmaking from its early days through the Golden Age of Hollywood. It was produced and directed by Richard Attenborough and stars Robert Downey, Jr., Dan Aykroyd, Kevin Kline, and Anthony Hopkins.

*Ed Wood* (1994): An Academy Award-winning comedy–drama biopic directed by Tim Burton and starring Johnny Depp as cult filmmaker Edward D. Wood, Jr.

*Adaptation* (2002): A comedy–drama directed by Spike Jonze and written by Charlie Kaufman; tells the story of Charlie Kaufman's difficult struggle to adapt a popular novel, *The Orchid Thief*, into a film.

## Glossary

**adaptation**  The transfer of written works—usually novels, short stories, or plays—to feature films.

**best boy**  The first assistant to the gaffer.

**camera obscura**  A box or a room with a small hole in one side which is focused on a mirror that projects the image onto a screen or wall from which a highly accurate tracing can be made.

**cinematographer**    Also called the director of photography (DP), this artist selects the camera type, film stock (digital stock), lens, and filters for each shot in order to capture or record the director's artistic vision.

**development**    The stage of a film in which a script is developed and a "dream team" of actors and artists is proposed to studios or financial backers in order to make a major motion picture.

**distribution**    The stage of a film production during which the finished film is sold to distributors, video stores, or other outlets in order to share the film with the public.

**elision**    The omission or cutting of parts of a story, including subplots, characters, and major plot points.

**ephemera**    The costumes, designs, sketches, sides, prompt books, and other materials not usually saved or preserved; from the Greek "lasting no more than a day."

**gaffer**    The person who serves as the lighting designer and supervisor on a film shoot.

**grip**    Named for the grip this person needed to keep on unsteady cameras, grips are responsible for setting up, operating, and taking down electrical and mechanical equipment on a film shoot.

**interactors**    A term for participants in virtual reality (VR) performances.

**interpolation**    The addition of new material (characters, subplots, etc.) or the combining of two old characters into a new character in an adapted story.

**pinhole camera**    A lightproof box with a single small hole in one side. Any image will be captured, upside down and in reverse, on the opposite side of the box.

**postproduction**    The stage in the making of a film in which all the shots, sounds, and special effects are cut, ordered, sequenced, and blended together into a finished film.

**preproduction**    The stage in the making of a film in which all film locations, props, cast members, costumes, crews, technicians, special effects, visual effects, logistics, and costs are identified and a detailed shooting schedule is made.

**production**    The stage in the making of a film in which all the raw materials for a film are captured and recorded (video, sound, special effects, etc.).

**production designer**    Also called the art director, is responsible for the overall look and style of a film and supervises set decorators, costume designers, property masters, graphic designers, model makers, and special-effects artists.

**props master**    Provides items handled directly by actors, such as newspapers, weapons, musical instruments, and food.

**screenplays**    Written dramatic texts meant to be mediated (filmed) with a camera and to be shown in an uninterrupted format.

**script supervisor**    Also called the continuity supervisor, watches all filming in order to make sure that actors and props are in the same positions for each shot.

**set decorator**    Finds appropriate furniture, wallpaper, lighting fixtures, and bric-a-brac, and supervises a crew of buyers and set dressers who arrange furniture, hang curtains, and dress the set.

**shooting script**    A final draft of a screenplay that includes all of the dialog, locations, and camera angles and shots to be used in the film.

**sides**    Sections from a play text used by an actor that include only his or her dialogue.

**storyboard artist**    A collaborator who develops a comic-book-like drawing or plan for each camera shot in a screenplay.

**teleplays**    Written dramatic texts meant to be mediated (filmed) with a camera and to be shown in an interrupted (or commercialized) format.

**wardrobe supervisor**    The person who coordinates the wardrobe needs on a film shoot, organizing which costumes correspond with each location and each shot.

## Key Concepts

- Texts created for mediated performance have been influenced by those created for the stage.
- The use of new technologies has shifted the focus in dramatic performance from narrative to spectacle.
- Both live and mediated performances must adapt the story to the strengths and weaknesses of each medium.
- Although film and theatre share important characteristics and artistic processes, there are several significant differences, each of which points to key strengths of recorded and live performances.
- Film artists share many similar jobs, but have their own culture and vocabulary that guide what they do to create their art.

# Popular Entertainments

## Chapter Outline

*To view the figures in this chapter, log on to www.pearsonexploretheatre.com.*

## INTRODUCTION

Director, theorist, teacher, and writer Richard Schechner argues that performance genres, behaviors, and activities exist on a continuum between play and ritual, represented as a line on the printed page but more accurately thought of as an "overlapping and interlacing spheroid network."

**FIGURE 14.1**

The majority of this text is concerned with what society calls "theatre"—a concept that lies primarily between and around "popular (or pop) entertainments" and "performing arts" on the continuum. This chapter explores some boundaries of the concept of theatre, looking at selected forms that many historians and theorists would place under the category of popular entertainments. You will likely have experienced many of these forms and might be curious regarding their connections with theatre. Musical theatre, in its many manifestations, has and can continue to be considered popular entertainment, depending on the musical, context, period, and so on (see Chapter 12). But there are many other forms of entertainment that can be as well.

As outlined in Chapter 1, all performances share a number of characteristics, with live performances having even more in common. But what differentiates popular entertainment from Schechner's next category on the continuum, performing arts, or from the category of theatre that lies between the two? Although it is difficult to make generalizations about the diverse forms included within this chapter, many share common characteristics: as the name implies, popular entertainment tends to attract audiences in greater numbers; historically it has cost less to attend in order to attract those larger audiences, although notable contemporary exceptions will be discussed. The performing arts tend to be associated with "high" culture, the elite, the upper classes, while popular entertainment aims at the "masses," the middle and lower classes, a lower common denominator.

**FIGURE 14.2**

Also, what we think of as theatre as well as the performing arts tends to be scripted; many forms of popular entertainment do not rely on a script or written text. Historically, theatre and the performing arts have been valued more by those in power, and thus records of these forms have been better preserved, although this is also likely due to the fact that it is easier to record a form that has a script attached to it when the form is as ephemeral as performance. But even if records may not exist, popular entertainment has been around since the beginning of time.

**FIGURES 14.3, AND 14.4**

## LEARNING OBJECTIVES

### After reading Chapter 14, you will be able to:

- Identify and discuss the major differences between popular entertainments and other forms of entertainment.
- Make connections between forms of popular entertainments and the various cultures in which they were created and thrive, as well as connections between historical forms and their modern-day counterparts.
- Identify the main forms of live popular entertainment in both Western and non-Western societies and those which have enjoyed popularity as mediatized entertainments.

## MIME AND PANTOMINE

While the great dramas of Aeschylus, Sophocles, Euripides, and Aristophanes were being presented on the state-supported, institutional theatres of Greece, many types of popular entertainment, known collectively as **mime**, flourished on the streets of Athens, Sparta, and other city–states of the ancient culture. Greek mime was not silent, but a form of variety entertainment that could include brief plays, dance, singing, juggling, acrobatics, and more. The first form to include women performers, mimes were also likely the first professional entertainers, and unlike the performers of tragedies and comedies, they did not wear masks.

This form continued and flourished during both the Roman Republic and Empire, eventually eclipsing the popularity of regular drama. Evidence suggests that much of the material performed by mimes was bawdy and/or violent; one emperor even ordered sex acts to be performed realistically! During the Roman Empire, the mimes sometimes ridiculed Christian teachings and beliefs, making them unpopular with the nascent religion. Under the Empire, **pantomine**, a storytelling dance that began in Greece and could be considered the precursor to ballet, also flourished.

After the fall of the Roman Empire, organized theatre disintegrated, for a variety of reasons. However, entertainment continued in a number of forms, including mime, in spite of a number of church edicts against the performers. But as the Catholic Church gained power and reinstated theatre as an institutional, state/church-supported form, mime fell out of favor.

One could argue that it influenced the development of **commedia** (see *Commedia Dell'arte* later in this chapter) or that it resurfaced primarily as a hybrid form with pantomime in eighteenth-century England. British pantomime combined elements of commedia and farce with dance, spectacle, topical satire, and stories drawn from mythology. Pantomime became the most popular entertainment form in England by 1723, although until the nineteenth century it was largely a short form used between acts of regular plays. During the nineteenth century, pantomime developed into a longer form, but its popularity was eclipsed by melodrama and survives to the present mainly as a Christmas entertainment.

**FIGURES 14.5, 14.6, AND 14.7**

## ROMAN PARATHEATRICALS

During the Roman Empire, in order to appease a restless population, the government offered more and more **paratheatricals**, often increasingly violent. Perhaps most popular were the gladiatorial combats, hand-to-hand combats involving well-trained fighters, many slaves but some free men—and women—as well. Fighting in such arenas as the Coliseum in Rome, the gladiators often were considered precious commodities and not as dispensable as current films make them seem. They could rise to superstar status, their sweat used for women's beauty creams and wealthy men and women even requesting their "services" out of the arena.

**FIGURE 14.8**

Another popular—and violent—form was the *venationes*, or animal fights, which could involve fights exclusively between animals or animal versus human contests. As the Roman Empire spread, so did the exoticism of the animals in the arenas; thousands of animals could die in one event, as could people in another entertainment, the *naumachiae*. These were re-created naval battles, presented on lakes or in flooded arenas.

A fourth form was the chariot race, in which charioteers competed in races in two-wheeled carts, each usually pulled by four horses. These events occurred in structures known as circuses, which could hold as many as 300,000 spectators, and they could be as bloody as the other entertainments.

As these "blood sports" increased in popularity, the "regular" comedies and tragedies could no longer compete, falling out of favor later in the Empire. In contemporary Western society, it is easy to be critical of the Romans' appetite for such violent entertainments, until we remember that we have the ability to produce mediatized versions of violent entertainment—such as films, television, and video games—to appease our own appetites for violence; if we did not, would we crowd into arenas and circuses to watch thousands die? As it is, many enjoy such live sports as boxing, NASCAR racing, and hockey, forms that often involve *real* violence and even death.

**FIGURE 14.9**

## TOURNAMENTS

Although generally not quite as violent as the paratheatricals, the tournament could be considered the medieval heir to the Roman entertainments and could be equally categorized as sport as much as performance. Begun in the tenth century as a means to train knights in the arts of war, these often elaborate contests involved primarily feats on horseback. Initially the knights merely attempted to unseat each other, but eventually tournaments became much more elaborate, with the knight fighting to capture a mock castle—inhabited by costumed ladies—or other structures representing such allegorical concepts as love or piety. Although often a part of the general tournament, jousting—combat between two knights—was never the central feature of the event.

**FIGURE 14.10**

Tournaments enjoyed massive popularity for a time but were denounced by the Church, leading to their waning in the fourteenth century; the last known tournament was reportedly held in Bruges, Belgium in 1379. O f course, related forms have flourished, and one could argue that some popular contemporary descendents of tournaments, albeit forms that are more about entertainment than efficacy, are reenactments of jousting at Renaissance Faires and at the combination restaurant/sports arena franchise known as "Medieval Times." Found in various cities across the United States, Medieval Times features actors posing as knights and their ladies, participating in a tournament that begins in the lobby of the complex as spectators wait to be seated and are sold drinks, souvenirs, and photos with the ladies. In the arena, spectators are served roast chicken and other supposed fare of the Middle Ages while watching exhibition riding by knights and, finally, jousting tournaments, rooting for a certain knight based on costume color. Lights, fog, and costumes add to the spectacle, and although prices can top $50 per spectator, Medieval Times has proven an enormously popular concept.

**FIGURES 14.11 AND 14.12**

## COMMEDIA DELL'ARTE

Commedia Dell'arte was the most popular form of entertainment in Europe for over 200 years. It originated in Italy during the 1560s but was influenced in part by mimes; Atellan farce, a southern Italian improvised entertainment with stock characters; and the Roman comedies of Plautus and Terence. Commedia was largely an unscripted, improvised form, although later texts were written on the basis of the performances.

One of the keys to the success of commedia was adaptability, for since the actor was the heart of the form, it could be played virtually anywhere: the street, town squares, at court, on platforms, in permanent theatres. Troupes of professional actors would improvise performances based on scenarios, or rough plot outlines; *lazzi*, or comic bits; and the stock characters in which they specialized.

There were two main types of stock characters: the unmasked and the masked. The unmasked characters consisted of a pair of young lovers, the handsome *inamorato* and the beautiful *inamorata*, the former male and the latter female. The masked characters consisted of the Masters, or blocking characters, and the servants, or *zanni*. Three primary Masters appeared on the commedia stages: the Capitano, a braggart but coward who often wore a cape and carried a sword; the Pantalone, a middle-aged or elderly merchant, often represented by a person with a large, hooked nose; and the Dottore, a lawyer or doctor who loved to show off his frequently incorrect knowledge and was often the friend or rival of the Pantalone.

A common scenario made the Pantalone the father of the *inamorata*; he wished for his daughter to marry the Capitano or Dottore, hence blocking her from marrying her true love, the *inamorato*. Usually aiding the young lovers' attempts to get together were the *zanni*, although they might be just as prone to trick the young lovers as their masters. Some of the most popular *zanni* included the Harlequin, an acrobatic mixture of cunning and stupidity, usually represented by a person with diamond-shaped patches on his costume and carrying a slapstick; and Scapino, cruel, cynically witty, and sometimes the companion to Harlequin.

**FIGURES 14.13 AND 14.14**

Commedia was most popular in Italy but found a second home in France and then spread throughout Europe. The influences of the stock characters and *lazzi* popularized in commedia can still be felt today, particularly in sitcoms on television.

**FIGURE 14.15**

## VAUDEVILLE

**Vaudeville**, a precursor to modern-day musical theatre, was an enormously popular form in its own right during the late nineteenth and early twentieth centuries, and it has had a rebirth of sorts at the turn of the twenty-first century. Diversity was the hallmark of vaudeville; an evening's bill consisted of many unrelated acts strung together, such as animal acts, short plays, juggling, revues, acrobats, and so on, most to musical accompaniment.

**FIGURES 14.16, 14.17, AND 14.18**

Originally known as "variety theatre," the form developed out of saloons that wanted to offer some entertainment with their drink. Eventually, the form moved into theatres, but it took with it the rather disreputable reputation it had gained as an amusement form attached to taverns. (In England, a related form was known as "music hall" entertainment.)

In spite of the form's spotty reputation, some of theatre's and, later, film's most outstanding performers and personalities of the early to mid-twentieth century got their start in vaudeville: George M. Cohan, W.C. Fields, Mae West, Will Rogers, Fanny Brice, Ethel Waters, and many more. Much of the popular music of the day, sold as sheet music or phonograph records or heard on the radio, was written for vaudeville.

Popular with all classes in America for fifty years, vaudeville declined during the Depression and with the advent of film. Still, a new type of variety entertainment, often labeled "New Vaudeville," has sprung up during the past twenty-five years. Such performers as Bill Irwin, the Flying Karamazov Brothers, Avner ("the Eccentric") Eisenberg, De la Guarda, the Blue Man Group, and Penn and Teller incorporate music, clowning, juggling, acrobatics, dance, and magic into their acts.

## CIRCUS

Bill Irwin's performances as a clown could also be classified under the entertainment known as "circus." Circus-like entertainment has existed in many cultures throughout history, but the beginnings of the modern concept of the circus are credited to Philip Astley, who, in 1770, used a circular space for exhibiting trick riding and other feats of horsemanship. The round space enabled the feats to be viewed on all sides, and the horse could never gallop out of sight. The size of his ring, forty-two feet in diameter, is still the circus standard.

**FIGURE 14.19**

Astley took his concept, begun in London, to Paris, and it soon spread throughout Europe and America, expanding in the nineteenth century to include other animal acts, a sideshow with "freaks" or "oddities"—some real and some not—from throughout the world, clowns, singers, jugglers, acrobats, and so on (until, in many ways, it closely resembled vaudeville).

Perhaps the most famous creators of circus have been the Ringling Brothers and the partners P.T. Barnum and James Bailey, who, in 1919, all combined to create "The Greatest Show on Earth," a show that continues today. American circus practices influenced the character of the modern circus, bringing about an increased spectacle and lessening the prior focus on such characters as the clown. Internationally, circus troupes gained prominence during the twentieth century, often touring around the world, from the Moscow State Circus, to the Chinese State Circus, to the Vazquez Hermanos Circus in Mexico.

But rivaling the circus in popularity is the revisionist circus troupe, Cirque du Soleil. Founded in Canada in 1984, the company began touring three years later and now has resident companies in both Orlando and Las Vegas. People, not animals, are their only performers, and their shows consist of stunning visuals and acrobatics organized around a loose plot. Among their most successful shows have been *Mystére*, *La Nouba*, *O*, and *Dralion*, as well as their more "adult" production in Las Vegas, *Zumanity*. Cirque has become a notable exception to the general rule of popular entertainments as economically accessible; single tickets can run into the hundreds of dollars depending on the show. Still, high ticket prices have not inhibited Cirque's huge popularity.

The success of Cirque du Soleil has spawned a number of imitators, including Neil Goldberg's *Cirque*. In Australia, *Circa*, which was founded in Brisbane in 1987 as the

Rock'n'Roll Circus, uses music, multimedia, improvisation, and acrobatics to deconstruct the traditional notion of circus. Their self-professed mission is "to create a highly expressive new art form out of the traditional languages of circus." In their piece "This Text Has Legs," the troupe invites audience members to send text messages, which are then projected behind the performers, who create a collaborative work based on the messages.

**FIGURES 14.20 AND 14.21**

## PUPPETRY

Using puppets to entertain may date back thousands of years; one of the first forms to develop may have been shadow puppetry. Popular in Turkey, India, Indonesia, China, and other largely Asian countries for centuries, shadow puppets are two-dimensional cutouts, usually fashioned out of translucent leather and manipulated with sticks. Their shadows are projected onto a cloth by candlelight, with the manipulators of the puppets, behind the cloth, providing the dialogue and musicians providing accompaniment.

The puppet, or doll, theatre of Japan known as **Bunraku** developed in the seventeenth century as a part of the desire of the shoguns to promote distinctive Japanese art forms; at the same time, the increased prosperity of lower classes led to a demand for more popular forms. Using a long, narrow stage, Bunraku involves the manipulation of a three-dimensional, often exquisitely detailed and lifelike puppet by three handlers, all in full view: one who operates the feet, another who controls the left hand, and the most experienced, who manipulates the right hand and the head. Training to master the latter can take as much as thirty years. Accompanied by a samisen player (the samisen is similar to the Western guitar) and a narrator, the approximately three-feet-tall puppets perform such detailed and lifelike actions that the puppeteers seem invisible. Bunraku reached the height of its popularity in the eighteenth century.

**FIGURES 14.22 AND 14.23**

In the West, three-dimensional puppets may have grown out of commedia dell'arte; one popular British puppet character, "Punch," developed from the antics of the servant character in commedia, Pulcinella. In France, this character developed as "Guignol," in Germany, "Hanswurst." All over Europe, puppet shows, developed in the seventeenth century, were centered on similar insolent, witty characters. Although in recent history puppets have been associated largely with children's entertainment, the humor communicated by some puppets has historically been quite "adult," since the puppet provides some distance between the performer and spectator and such material can seem more digestible when communicated by an inhuman figure.

But whether for children or adults or both, puppet performances are likely appealing, as they allow humans to make inanimate objects animate; half the fun is seeing how the puppeteer brings his or her puppet, whether on strings or a hand puppet or a marionette, to "life."

Puppets have enjoyed an upsurge in popularity in the West through the largely mediatized muppets of Jim Henson; however, the work of the Bread and Puppet Theatre and musicals such as *The Lion King* and *Avenue Q* show the continuing appeal of puppets on stage. Founded in 1961 by Peter Schumann, the Bread and Puppet Theatre uses puppets of various sizes (some as tall as twenty feet) combined with live actors and well-known stories to promote messages of love and charity in an effort to combat materialism. Based in Vermont, the troupe still performs today.

Combining actors and puppets on stage has become a trend, as evidenced by *The Lion King* and *Avenue Q*. Disney's stage version of their animated film, designed and directed by Julie Taymor, employed more than fifty performers and a hundred puppets to represent various species on the African plain setting. A mixture of Javanese puppetry, Balinese headdresses, and African masks, the design combined with the music, much of it written by Elton John, contributed to a show that has become enormously popular, both on Broadway and on tour. Many of the characters in *Avenue Q* are an ingenious combination of puppet and actor; the audience sees both meld into the character. (For more on *Avenue Q*, see Chapter 12.) *Avenue Q*, which closed on Broadway after a run of over five years, has enjoyed a post-Broadway life with a brief run in Las Vegas and, at this writing, an ongoing run off-Broadway.

**FIGURES 14.24 AND 14.25**

## CONCERTS

The tradition of the concert—a gathering of people for the sole purpose of listening to music played live—goes back some four hundred years. Before then, music was enjoyed primarily in sacred contexts—that is, as a part of ritualistic/religious ceremonies and services. Although exceptions exist, such as the troubadour and minstrel of the Middle Ages, the concert developed as a form during the Renaissance. For most of its history, the concert has been associated primarily with instrumental music and has been thought of as an entertainment for the elite, until well into the nineteenth century. The music of Mozart, Handel, Haydn, Bach, Beethoven, and many others could be enjoyed in various halls and "pleasure gardens." As with other entertainment forms, the growing working class began to assert its tastes in the mid-nineteenth century, and more and more venues for concerts began to appear to accommodate their numbers, with classical music stepping aside somewhat to make way for "band music" like that of John Phillip Sousa.

**FIGURE 14.26**

In the twentieth century up to the present, the concert form has become incredibly diverse, offering something for everyone, from classical to New Age to rock music. But, particularly with the latter, there has been an increasing tendency toward an emphasis on providing not only aural spectacle, but *visual* spectacle as well. Perhaps concerts have shifted to accommodate the advent of recording technologies from the phonograph, to eight-track and cassette tapes, to CD and digital formats, formats that have enabled anyone to *listen* to music anytime and anywhere. In order to compete, concerts must also provide something to see. The Irish rock band U2 is a perfect example of musicians who have come to not only recognize this fact but embrace it as well. Their concerts regularly incorporate a variety of technologies, including elaborate lights, multimedia displays on enormous screens, and large set pieces (one of their favorites is a ramp that thrusts out into the audience space, bringing them closer to their fans) to entertain fans. The increasingly high cost of tickets leaves concertgoers demanding more than simply live music.

**FIGURE 14.27**

## STAND-UP COMEDY

Comic entertainments have been part of both popular culture and the dramatic arts since antiquity, including some forms already covered in this chapter (e.g., mime, commedia dell'arte, and vaudeville). Although many scholars and critics have treated comedy as a lesser form than tragedy or "serious drama," comedy continues to be widely popular in film, television, and nightclubs as well as theatre, in happy disregard of those like the elderly blind monk Jorge in *The Name of the Rose* (1986), who believed that laughter was the sound of the devil. As a popular entertainment, comedy in general—and stand-up comedy specifically—deserves special attention because it has become such a significant force within contemporary political and cultural life.

**Stand-up comedy** has its roots in vaudeville, clowning, Yiddish theatre, and other sources. Primarily a one-person, partly improvised show, the form is performed informally, often with the use of a microphone and, like many forms of popular entertainment, involves direct interaction with audience members. Although it can be relatively easy for new talent to enter the field, with the proliferation of "open mic" nights in the United States and beyond, many consider it to be one of the most difficult entertainment forms to master, since historically the focus is completely on the performer, not set, costume, technology, or other forms of "spectacle." Will Ferrell has called stand-up "hard, lonely, and vicious."

**FIGURE 14.28**

The legitimacy of stand-up comedy as a career has often been called into question. It has been viewed as a mere stepping-stone to careers in other forms of entertainment, and those who opted to perform more vulgar or obscene jokes, known as "blue" humor, had an even more difficult time breaking into the mainstream until the 1960s and 1970s, when comedians like Lenny Bruce, Richard Pryor, and George Carlin came to prominence; Chris Rock, Eddie Murphy, Robin Williams, Whoopi Goldberg, and Andrew Dice Clay are performers who have proven the effectiveness of "blue" material on the stages of stand-up. Comedy Central's Celebrity Roasts specialize in this type of "blue" humor, and some public figures, such as Pamela Anderson, agree to be roasted to raise money and public awareness for charitable causes. Bill Cosby, Steve Martin, Ellen DeGeneres, Jerry Seinfeld, and others have gone on to great success with more "gentle" humor.

**FIGURE 14.29**

What all these comics share is a keen insight into the ridiculous within everyday life and a willingness to make fun of our worst or most foolish traits in front of a live audience. For the past 70 years, comedians have moved back and forth from television to nightclubs, from the old Borscht Belt comedy circuit to Hollywood films, from prime-time sitcoms to *Saturday Night Live*. Well-known comedians return to the "wellspring" of stand-up to develop new material, challenge new assumptions, and test their comic mettle against a live audience. Shakespearean actor Ian McKellen, perhaps better known to younger audiences as Gandalf or Magneto, famously said, "I don't make much distinction between being a stand-up comic and acting Shakespeare—in fact, unless you're a good comedian, you're never going to be able to play Hamlet properly."

## MAGICIANS AND THE ART OF ILLUSION

Performances that contemporary audiences would recognize as a *magic show* have occurred throughout history. In his controversial *History of Magic* (1913), Eliphas Levi said that magic can be broadly understood as "the art of producing effects in the absence of causes," but Arthur C. Clarke more famously explained, "any sufficiently advanced technology is indistinguishable from magic" (*Profiles of the Future*, 1961). The ability to fool or trick the audience is at the heart of both the actor's and the magician's trade. Large-scale tricks, like the Greeks' Trojan Horse, would likely have seen similar manifestations that were civic entertainments, and those same skills of deception were likely used in gambling and games of skill. Ancient religious leaders likely used such techniques as well to frighten the uneducated into belief, a practice that continued in the modern world (e.g., *Elmer Gantry*). However, the emergence of the professional illusionist, the modern magician, began in the eighteenth century.

In 1584, Reginald Scot published The *Discoverie of Witchcraft*, a work that tried to show that witches did not exist by exposing how the "magic" they allegedly did was actually accomplished. The book is considered the first textbook on "how to" do magic tricks ever published, as opposed to a *grimoire*, which was a book that purported to teach readers how to do "real" magic, spells, and the like. Despite Scot's rationalist approach, many copies of his book were burned on the accession of James I in 1603 and few original copies remain.

Modern magicians owe much to Jean Eugène Robert-Houdin (1805–1871), originally a clockmaker, who opened a magic theatre in Paris in the 1840s. His specialty was the construction of mechanical automata that appeared to move and act as if they were alive. Robert-Houdin developed many of the famous illusions that magicians still use today, like mind reading, levitation, and teleportation.

**FIGURE 14.30**

Robert-Houdin also popularized a style for magicians that lasted into the late twentieth century. Since he performed in the parlors of the Parisian aristocracy, he adopted a formal style of dress and presentation. That style reached its apex in Alexander Herrmann (1844–1896), known as Herrmann the Great. Herrmann was also French and was part of the Herrmann family, the so-called first-family of magic. Herrmann's primary innovations were in sleight-of-hand tricks, rather than Robert-Houdin's complex mechanical wonders. He is credited as the first performer to include card throwing as a part of a magic act. Herrmann could place a card in the lap of any spectator who raised his or her hand and could easily reach the back wall of large theatres. Later in his career, he became an American citizen and published a famous book on magic.

The most famous American magician of the Golden Age of Magic was the escapologist and magician Harry Houdini, who took his stage name from Robert-Houdin. Houdini developed a wide range of stage magic tricks, many of them based on escapology, a word not used until after his death. Houdini began his career with card tricks, but after he met his soon-to-be wife, Bess, he gained great fame as an escape artist. He developed extraordinary skills in lock picking and physical control over his body, but he also developed original conjuring techniques, including magical equipment and strategies for collusion with individuals in the audience. Perhaps Houdini's greatest skill was his sense of showmanship. The "Handcuff King," as he was sometimes known, could keep an audience on edge for hours, while he read a newspaper behind a curtain, having escaped from whatever contraption he had been confined to long ago. For many years, he was the highest-paid performer in American vaudeville.

**FIGURE 14.31**

Late in his career, after the death of his beloved mother, he became equally famous as debunker of supernatural frauds who had successfully fooled scientists. He was a member of a Scientific American committee that offered a cash prize to any medium or spiritualist who could successfully demonstrate supernatural abilities. None were able to do so, and the prize was never collected. Houdini chronicled his debunking efforts in a book, *A Magician Among the Spirits* (1924). He knew that all magical effects are accomplished by sleight of hand, misdirection, deception, collusion with a member of the audience, an apparatus with hidden mechanisms, mirrors, or other forms of trickery. The magician creates an effect that the audience thinks is otherwise impossible, and the audience agrees to be entertained by something they know to be an illusion. Houdini gained great fame by using his knowledge of these tricks to debunk charlatans, a tradition continued by magicians such as James Randi, Arthur Ellison, P.C. Sorcar, and Penn and Teller.

**FIGURE 14.32**

David Blaine's street-savvy performances are a combination of Houdini-style escapology and physical endurance displays rather than feats of illusion. The mid-twentieth century saw magic transform in many different aspects. Some performers preferred to renovate the craft on stage (such as The Mentalizer Show in Times Square, which mixed themes of spirituality and kabbalah with the art of magic). Others successfully made the transition to TV, which opens up new opportunities for deceptions and brings the performer to huge audiences. Most TV magicians perform before a live audience, which provides the remote viewer with a reassurance that the illusions are not obtained with post-production visual effects.

## For Further Information

Bailey, Michael. *Magic and Superstition in Europe: A Concise History from Antiquity to the Present.* 2007.

Baird, Bil. *The Art of the Puppet.* 1973.

Barber, Richard W. *Tournaments: Jousts, Chivalry, and Regents in the Middle Ages.* 1989.

Beacham, Richard C. *Spectacle Entertainments of Early Imperial Rome.* 1999.

Culhane, John. *The American Circus: An Illustrated History.* 1990.

Davis, Janet. *The Circus Age: Culture and Society Under the American Big Top.* 2002.

Gordon, Mel. *Lazzi: The Comic Routines of the Commedia dell'arte.* 1983.

Keene, Donald. *Bunraku: The Art of the Japanese Puppet Theatre.* 1965.

Mangan, Michael. *Performing Dark Arts: A Cultural History of Conjuring.* 2007.

Mrazek, Jan, ed. *Puppet Theater in Contemporary Indonesia: New Approaches to Performance Events.* 2001.

Nicoll, Allardyce. *Masks, Mimes, and Miracles.* 1931.

Oreglia, G. *The Commedia dell'Arte.* 1968.

Schechner, Richard. *Performance Studies: An Introduction.* 2002.

Silverman, Kenneth. *Houdini! The Career of Ehrich Weiss.* 1996.

Wilmeth, Don B. *American and English Popular Entertainment: A Guide to Information Sources.* 1980.

Young, Percy. *The Concert Tradition: From the Middle Ages to the Twentieth Century.* 1965.

## Suggested Films

Paratheatricals: *Ben Hur* (1959), *Spartacus* (1960), *Gladiator* (2000)

Tournaments: *A Knight's Tale* (2001)

Vaudeville: *Gypsy* (1962), *Funny Girl* (1968)

Stand-up comedy: *Punchline* (1988), *The Aristocrats* (2005)

Puppetry: *Being John Malkovich* (1999), *Team America: World Police* (2004)

Magic: *The Illusionist* (2006), *Houdini* (1953)

## Glossary

**Bunraku** Extraordinarily lifelike, classical Japanese puppetry form in which each puppet is manipulated by three puppeteers.

**commedia** A popular form of comedy that developed during the Renaissance in Italy and was based on improvisation and stock characters.

*lazzi* Improvised "comic bits" of commedia.

**mime** Originally a form of variety entertainment begun in ancient Greece that could include brief plays, dance, singing, juggling, acrobatics, and more. Eventually the term came to refer to a stylized form of silent performance, possibly derived from commedia dell'arte, in which the actor often wears white makeup to emphasize facial expressions.

**pantomime** Originally a storytelling form of dance that eventually developed into the "pantos" popular in England, based on the stock characters of commedia.

**paratheatricals** Roman entertainments outside of the "regular" tragedies and comedies, such as gladiator combats, chariot racing, *naumachiae* (re-created sea battles), *venationes* (animal fights), mime, and pantomime.

**stand-up comedy** One-person, partly improvised performance, often utilizing a microphone and involving direct interaction with audience members.

**vaudeville** Variety entertainment enormously popular in the late 19th and early 20th centuries in the United States; a precursor to the American musical.

**ventriloquist** A person who manipulates his or her voice so that it appears that the voice is coming from elsewhere, usually a puppeteered "dummy." The practice originated in ancient Greece and continues today.

*zanni* Masked stock characters in commedia who represent servants.

## Key Concepts

- Popular entertainment attracts large audiences, is often affordable, and does not always rely on a written text; each form says a lot about the culture that creates and embraces it.
- Mime and pantomime were both popular in the ancient Western world, although they both have developed into more modern manifestations.
- The blood sports of the ancient Roman paratheatricals were the most popular forms of entertainment then; today, they have their equivalents in both live and mediatized forms.
- Commedia dell'arte was the most popular form of entertainment in Europe for over 200 years.
- Vaudeville and circus were both popular nineteenth- and twentieth-century forms that have evolved into current entertainments.
- Puppetry, concerts, and stand-up comedy all enjoy popularity as both live and mediatized entertainments today.

# INDEX